THE FINAL STORM

THE DOOR WITHIN TRILOGY CONCLUDES . . .

BOOK  3

THE FINAL STORM

BY
WAYNE THOMAS BATSON

Tommy nelson™
For tweens and teens

A Division of Thomas Nelson Publishers
Since 1798

www.thomasnelson.com

THE FINAL STORM

Copyright © 2006 Wayne Thomas Batson

Third in a series of three novels.

Published in Nashville, Tennessee, by Tommy Nelson®, a Division of Thomas Nelson®, Inc.

Visit us on the Web at www.tommynelson.com.

Tommy Nelson® books may be purchased in bulk for educational, business, fund-raising, or sales promotional use. For information, please email SpecialMarkets@ThomasNelson.com.

Library of Congress Cataloging-in-Publication Data

Batson, Wayne.
    The final storm / by Wayne Thomas Batson.
      p. cm.
    Sequel to: The rise of the Wyrm Lord.
    Summary: Paragor unites with the Wyrm Lord and the Seven Sleepers to launch an assault on the kingdom of Alleble and its allies, who face the coming onslaught believing that they will be victorious with the help of the Three Witnesses.
    ISBN-10: 1-4003-0783-X (hardback)
    ISBN-13: 978-1-4003-0783-8 (hardcover)
    [1. Space and time—Fiction. 2. Christian life—Fiction. 3. Fantasy.] I. Title.
    PZ7.B3238 Fin 2006
    [Fic]—dc22

2006011777

Printed in the United States of America

06 07 08 09 10 QW 9 8 7 6 5 4 3

To the one true King, the battle rages on,
but victory will be yours.

CONTENTS

Principal Cast

AIDAN (AY-DEN) THOMAS

When Aidan's parents move the family to Colorado to take care of his wheelchair-bound grandfather (Grampin), the teenager discovers the Scrolls, which start him on an adventure of a lifetime.

ANTOINETTE (AN-TWA-NET) LYNN REED

A believer in King Eliam and friend of Aidan's in the Mirror Realm.

BALDERGRIM

A warrior from Yewland.

BOLDOAK

A warrior from Yewland.

FALON

The elder of all mortiwraiths, who are enormous, venomous underground serpentine creatures.

FARIX (FAIR-IX)

Glimpse warrior, who does not wear armor.

HALBERAD

Apprentice tracker to Sir Thrivenbard.

KALIAM (KAL-EE-UM)

Glimpse warrior, who is also known as Pathfinder, and is the fourth Sentinel of Alleble.

KING BROWER

Blustery King of the Blue Mountain Provinces.

KING ELIAM (EE-LEE-UM)

The noble and wise monarch of Alleble, who invited Aidan to his Kingdom.

KING RAVELLE

Ruler of Mithegard.

LADY MEREWEN

Once a follower of Paragor, a capable silver-haired swordmaiden in the service of Alleble.

LORD RUCIFEL (ROO-SÍ-FELL)

Paragor's Lieutenant, who wields two swords.

MALLÍK (MAL-ÍCK)

Glimpse warrior, who wields a massive warhammer.

NAYSMÍTHE

Second Sentinel of Alleble; master swordsmith.

NOCK

A highly skilled Glimpse archer and warrior from Yewland.
Twin of Bolt, who died in The Door Within #1.

PARAGOR (PAIR-AH-GORE)

The first Sentinel of Alleble, who now rules over Paragory.
He intends to defeat Alleble, and make himself king of The Realm.

ROBBY PÍERSON (PEER-SON)

Aidan's best friend in Maryland.

THE SEVEN SLEEPERS

Seven powerful ancient enemies of King Eliam, buried in the Blackwood forest.

SÍR OSWYN

Herb-meister, skilled with potions, cures, salves, and unusual battle-potions.

SÍR ROGAN

Tall blond warrior from Mithegard. He carries a broad-bladed battleaxe.

THRÍVENBARD

Alleble's finest woodsman and tracker.

TRENNA SWÍFTFOOT

Yewland Glimpse held in bondage by criminals in Baen-Edge until rescued by Antoinette.

WARRIANT

First vanguard and ruler of forest village of Balesparr.

THE WYRM LORD

The firstborn dragon in all The Realm, the lord of all wyrms.

ZABEDIEL

The scribe for King Eliam when this world was new. Sometimes called Zabed.

PRINCIPAL SETTINGS

ALLEBLE (AL-EH-BULL)

The first Kingdom of The Realm. After The Schism,
Alleble remained the center of The Realm.

BALESPARR

A hidden village, nestled at the roots of the great trees in King's Forest.

THE BLUE MOUNTAIN PROVINCES

Mountainous region inhabited by the stoneworking Glimpses of Mallik's kin.

CANDLEFORGE, FROSTLAND, INFERNESS

Cities across the Cauldron Sea in the far west of The Realm,
and Paragory's three secret allies.

THE GATE OF DESPAIR

A huge pair of black iron doors built into the side of the Dead Mountains.
The entrance to Paragor's castle.

THE GRIMWALK

A sprawling wasteland at the foot of the Dead Mountains.

PARAGORY (PAIR-AH-GOR-EE)

A kingdom built by Paragor and his army.

THE SACRED REALM BEYOND THE SUN

The eternal dwelling place of all servants of King Eliam.

Adventures are
funny things.
Many are merely happy
accidents—
a single spark that ignites
an unexpected chain of events.
But some adventures are meant
for you and you alone.
And whether you want them or not,
they seek you out of a great crowd and
take you somewhere
you never thought you'd go.
Often, these unlooked-for adventures
require a sacrifice too great
to imagine.

Into the Storm

Aidan searched for Gwenne's image in the thunderclouds. But the aircraft banked hard to the right and threw him back into the seat. *No, not into the storm!* Aidan thought urgently. He grabbed the armrest and tried to pull himself back up to the window.

"Aidan!" his dad yelled. "Aidan, sit back!"

The airplane was steering directly for a massive black cloud fortress. Lightning rippled across the cloud, turning it the color of an ugly bruise. And there in the center of the massive thunderhead was a hollow of darkness.

The plane began to shudder and bounce like a speeding boat on rough surf. Lightning lit up the cabin. Passengers shrieked and gasped. The engines screamed, and the plane banked back to the left. Everything shook. It felt as if the cabin would break apart under the strain.

Then, just as suddenly, the plane leveled out. The lights came back on. Hundreds of passengers sighed.

"You okay?" Aidan's dad asked.

Aidan wasn't sure. He wasn't hurt, but he didn't feel okay exactly either. "I saw Gwenne," he whispered.

"What?"

"When the lightning flashed, I saw her in the window. She looked scared, Dad. I think she's in trouble."

"You've been thinking a lot about Antoinette being in The Realm, and Gwenne is her Glimpse. They look alike . . . maybe—"

"Dad, I saw her," Aidan replied. "Something has gone terribly wrong. The clouds outside . . . the storm—it wasn't normal."

"This is your captain speaking," came a tinny voice from the speakers. "Sorry about the bumps back there. The thunderstorm to our south intensified. We've, uh, adjusted our course to keep our distance."

"Well, duh!" someone said in the seat behind Aidan. "That sounds like a plan!" The passengers nearby laughed nervously.

"We will be beginning our initial descent into the Baltimore/ Washington area in about a half-hour," the captain continued. "We don't anticipate any more problems."

"That's a relief," said Aidan's dad. The other passengers buzzed with conversation. A little blond girl in the next row tugged at her mother's sleeve. Aidan nodded and turned to look back out of the window. Intermittent bright flashes of lightning illuminated the dark clouds bubbling in the distance.

Why did I see you, Gwenne? Aidan wondered, closing his eyes and picturing her beautiful pale face. Was it a foretelling as so many of his visions had been? Had something happened to Antoinette in The Realm?

A strange noise from the rear of the plane interrupted Aidan's thoughts. It reminded him of the buzzer for the dryer that lets you know when the cycle was done. He turned, unclasped the seat belt, and looked back over the headrest. A muffled boom followed. Then a sharp cracking sound. The plane shook. Some of the passengers cried out. A businessman's laptop skittered into the aisle.

"Aidan, sit down and put your seat belt back on," said Aidan's father in a quiet but commanding voice.

Aidan sat down hard and clasped his seat belt. He looked up at the flight attendant, who was still buckled into her own seat behind the cabin. An older gentleman had gotten up and peppered her with questions. Finally she ushered him back into his seat. She belted herself in again and grabbed an intercom mic. The last thing Aidan saw, before the curtain hid her from view, was her colorless and terror-stricken face.

"Dad?" Aidan asked. But suddenly, there was another cracking sound from behind. And then the hissing sound of air from all around. Passengers became frantic, looking from face to face for answers. The lights flickered, and the plane lurched forward with such force that Aidan hit his head on the back of the seat in front of him. He fell backward, disoriented and frightened. There were screams and people shouting at one another. Aidan turned and saw his father slumped in his seat, his head flopped down at his chest.

"Dad!" Aidan yelled. He grabbed his father's shoulder. "Dad, wake up!" The airplane began to shake. Aidan gently lifted his father's chin and tilted his head back. A welt was already forming in the center of his dad's forehead. "Dad, oh no! Please be okay! Dad!" But his father did not answer. The plane lurched again. The lights went out and did not come back on. Aidan heard the plane's engines whining, and the plane dipped down.

This can't be happening! Aidan thought. *We're going to crash.* Lightning flickered and lit up the cabin. The other passengers were frantically grasping at their seat belts, their chairs—they too had come to the grim conclusion that the airplane was going down.

CHAINS OF THE ENEMY

Antoinette heard the jangle of keys, followed by a metallic click and the groan from the hinges of the chamber door. "Kearn!" she called out to the darkness.

"Yes, m'lady," Kearn replied, stepping forward into the moonlight. "I have brought you something to eat, but a moment, please. This darkness will never do." Kearn placed a tray on the one chair in the chamber and disappeared into the hallway. He returned bearing a large torch, which he placed in a holder on the wall.

"There, now we can look upon each other." He grinned as he placed the tray on the floor by Antoinette's cell. "Please, eat, m'lady."

"I'm not your lady!" Antoinette growled.

"Be that as it may," he replied, "you must have something. The meat is cured, the bread is fresh—it is all unspoiled. The mug is full of water from snowmelt. You will find it quite refreshing."

Antoinette was starving. *Well, if they wanted me dead, they could've done that long ago,* she thought. She reached through the bars and grabbed a piece of bread. At first she took only a tentative nibble. The bread wasn't just good—it was fantastic. Feathery-light texture, sweet, and still warm! Antoinette tore off a large hunk and jammed it into her mouth. She kept eating until the plate was clear.

"Excellent, Antoinette!" Kearn laughed. "Now it is time for a little exchange of information."

Antoinette eyed Kearn suspiciously.

"Nay, m'lady. I guess your mind," Kearn said. "Fear not. I have not come to pry from your lips King Eliam's secret battle plans, for they matter little to my master."

"Then why are you here?" Antoinette asked pointedly.

Kearn's eyes flickered red. He stood and paced near the cell. "I am . . . troubled," he whispered. "Your actions thwart every reasonable explanation! You hunted me across a hundred leagues, and yet when I was snared, you did not kill. Thrice you placed your life in jeopardy to save mine—even when I made it perfectly clear that I serve Paragor and no other. Tell me, are all the beings from the Mirror Realm so stubborn?"

Antoinette actually laughed. "No, I'm about the most stubborn person I know."

"I doubt it not," Kearn replied. "But there is also courage . . . and strength. The very mention of my name strikes terror into the hearts of my foes, yet you stood up to me . . . *to me!* And while I can dispatch most knights five at a time, I could not defeat you without guile. Even though you are my enemy, I do respect your strength."

"It is not *my* strength, Kearn," Antoinette replied.

"Nonsense!"

She stood as best she could, hindered by the chains around her ankles. "I have strength and skill because King Eliam willed for it to be so. While most other girls in my world were playing with dolls, I was taught to fight with a sword. And I have the advantage. I attack without fear, for I know that if I die, I will go to the Sacred Realm Beyond the Sun."

"There is no such place."

"You said yourself that those who served Paragor well will be remembered in the world to come. You must believe something happens after you die," Antoinette said.

"Yes . . ." Kearn hesitated. "It is as I said. Paragor will ultimately triumph over Alleble and hold dominion over all The Realm. On the rubble of Alleble, Paragor will create a new kingdom where those who served the master well will have riches and be revered by all those beneath us!"

"Paragor promises you power and fortune, if you'll serve only him. It is the same thing he promised the kingdoms of Mithegard, Acacia, and Clarion—right before he destroyed them. It is his way. If I had my *Book of Alleble* I could show you."

"You mean that worn-out leather volume over there?" Kearn asked, pointing to the corner of the chamber far outside her cell. Her book lay open, facedown in the shadows. "The guards no doubt cast it aside."

"My book!" Antoinette replied eagerly. "May I have it . . . please?"

Kearn looked over at the book and back at Antoinette. "Nay, you have your head already too full of Alleble's harvest tales. Let it lie there and mock you."

"Kearn!"

"No, you have said your piece!" Kearn roared. "Now, I will say mine. You came after me, you say, to see me turn from my master and bend the knee to King Eliam. That is your wish?" Kearn turned his back to Antoinette for a moment and continued. "You say to me to leave the riches, adoration, and power I have here to be a common knight in the Kingdom of Alleble? Betray my master simply on your word, and let my eyes reflect back the weak blue of King Eliam's servants . . . that is what you are asking, is it not?"

Antoinette stared at his back.

"Well, m'lady of the Mirror Realm," he said, his voice deep and stalking. "I give you what you ask." Kearn turned around suddenly, and as Antoinette looked into his eyes, she swayed as if she might fall. For Kearn's eyes flickered blue as only the eyes of those who follow King Eliam do.

"How can this be?" Antoinette asked.

Kearn laughed and held up a small corked vial. He took out the cork and sipped from the bottle. He closed his eyes, and when he opened them again, they flickered red in the manner of Paragor's servants.

"Yewland," Antoinette gasped. "That's how you fooled Queen Illaria in Yewland, isn't it?"

Kearn nodded. "Yewland and so many other places! It is remarkably easy to turn King Eliam's allies against him. You would think they would be more . . . devoted."

"Trickery!" Antoinette yelled. "Deceit! Don't you see, Kearn? That's just another example of Paragor's way!"

"Silence! How easily you cast out such accusations. Do you think your own King, the noble King Eliam of Alleble, is without guile? Would it pain thee then to know that he has kept hidden his true purpose for you in The Realm?"

Antoinette stood very still.

"Oh, yes, your *good* King has very interesting plans for you, m'lady . . . for you and the others. But Paragor has plans for you as well—much better plans," Kearn said. "You see . . . *they* are out there. My master knows, and he will find them before King Eliam. And in that moment, Alleble will be utterly destroyed."

"That will never happen! King Eliam defeated Paragor the first time and cast him into exile. He will do it again."

"Pity, no," Kearn replied. "Alleble will fall. Your beloved King knows this."

"Lies!" Antoinette cried. "Stop it! It's all lies!"

"If they are lies, Antoinette," Kearn said with a hideous smile, "then they are King Eliam's lies. For Alleble's destruction is foretold in the Scroll of Prophecy written by King Eliam's own hand!"

Kearn took the torch from the wall, left the chamber, and locked the door behind him. Antoinette was left in utter darkness. Tears ran down her cheeks.

Antoinette awoke with the dawn. She found a new tray of food just outside her cell. She took a bite of the bread and savored it. Surely this was not the kind of food that prisoners in Paragory usually received. She went to take another bite, but then dropped the bread on the floor. Her *Book of Alleble*, which had lain in the corner of her cell just the night before, was gone.

THE STONES OF OMEN

Sir Kaliam, Sentinel of Alleble, stood at the large window in a lofted keep high in the castle and stared out over the kingdom and the moonlit lands beyond. Sir Thrivenbard, Alleble's chief tracker and woodsman, entered the room and stood respectfully behind him.

"Well?" Kaliam demanded.

"My Sentinel," Thrivenbard said, and bowed to the knight. "It is with a sad heart I bring you the news that the body of Sir Gabriel was found among the twisting paths and dark boughs of the Blackwood."

Kaliam was silent.

"Sir, it has been three days since our search parties have discovered a survivor. We are only finding those slain, and Sir Aelic was not among them."

Kaliam did not turn around. "Thrivenbard," Kaliam said quietly, "I do not expect you to find Sir Aelic among the slain."

"But my Sentinel," Thrivenbard said. "So much time has passed since the battle and—"

"Nonetheless!" Kaliam shouted, before mastering himself and turning to face the knight. "Nonetheless, you will not find him among the dead. The Battle of the Blackwood raged from one end of the Forest Road to the other, from the borders of Yewland and into the heart of the Blackwood itself. In such a large area, a lone knight might be missed."

"My men are skilled," said Thrivenbard. "They have searched every thicket and under every bough—"

"Then you go, Thrivenbard," Kaliam exclaimed, "and search every thicket and under every bough again! No one in all The Realm has your skills in tracking and knowledge of the woods—not even the elder scouts of Yewland." He walked over and put a gentle hand on Thrivenbard's shoulder. "Thrivenbard, much depends upon your success."

"I will see to it, my Sentinel," Thrivenbard replied. "With King Eliam as my guide, I will not rest until I find Sir Aelic."

"Thank you, servant of Alleble," Kaliam replied. He knew if anyone could find Sir Aelic, Thrivenbard could.

"Never alone!" the Sentinel said.

"Never alone!" Thrivenbard replied as he bowed. Before taking leave, Thrivenbard stopped. "Sir?"

"Yes?"

"Since we have not found Sir Aelic," Thrivenbard said, choosing his words carefully, "is it possible that he was taken alive as a prisoner of the enemy, as was Lady Antoinette?"

Kaliam turned his back to Thrivenbard and stared out upon the moonlit realm again. "Losing Antoinette to the enemy is already a great blow to our cause. If Paragor has Sir Aelic as well . . ."

Thrivenbard bowed again and walked swiftly from the chamber.

The moon was much lower in the sky when Lady Merewen entered the library and found Kaliam at the window. "How long will you stand there?" she asked in a gentle voice. With great difficulty she lowered her dark hood, and her long silver hair spilled out upon her bandaged shoulders.

"Merewen!" Kaliam turned, and she went to him. Kaliam looked at her and put the back of his hand to her brow. "Your fever has passed! How do you feel?"

"Sir Oswyn says I was fortunate only to have been scratched by one of the Sleepers and not bitten," she replied, her violet eyes gleaming. "Herbs to treat my wounds are readily available, but not so for a bite. I am to be fine, Kaliam. But I am not sure you can say the same. You look in need of rest."

"I cannot rest." He sighed. "I am the Sentinel of this kingdom. I have charges."

"And you will do your charges no good if you kill yourself with anxiety."

Kaliam stared west into the night sky. "Paragor has released the Wyrm Lord and the Sleepers from their tombs. Alleble must prepare. Sir Aelic is still lost, and we cannot abandon Lady Antoinette to torment behind the Gate of Despair!" Kaliam's head fell to his chest. He seemed suddenly aged, burdened with a weight that he could not bear.

Lady Merewen kissed him on his forehead and gently raised his chin. She stared kindly into his dark eyes. "In the midst of my darkest doubt," she said, "you lifted my chin and told me, 'Dwell not in dreary chambers of the past!' You reminded me of the hope that we have as servants of King Eliam. This hope I return to you now. Stare not west where shadows dwell, but upon Alleble and be reminded!"

Kaliam looked down to the Seven Fountains. The moonlight danced in the high plumes of water and mist, and for a moment, his heart was glad. Then he saw the seventh fountain now so long dry, and his hope fled.

"You see," he said, "even in the most glorious places in Alleble, the enemy's black touch can be felt! I see below me a place empty and barren, save for memories of pain, despair, and . . . Paragor's treachery!"

"Nay, m'lord! That is the site of our King's greatest victory!"

"But Paragor remains. He has brought evils out of legend into his service and amassed at least an army to match our own."

"King Eliam defeated death!" Lady Merewen said sternly. "Who shall stand against the one who rose again?"

Kaliam and Lady Merewen searched each other's eyes and in the silence found hope. In the moonlight, they embraced.

Suddenly, a storm of arrows whistled into the nighttime air from the battlements. Alleb Knights scrambled into action below.

"What is there?" Lady Merewen asked.

"A dragon!" Kaliam said. "Ridden by a servant of the enemy."

"But why would he send a single dragon rider?" Lady Merewen asked. "Against our defenses, that is madness."

They watched the creature, black against the moon, streak from the sky. Heedless of the hail of arrows, it dove down over the fountains, and then soared almost straight up. It seemed to climb forever. Until, barely visible, it dropped something jet black from its talons.

The object crashed down upon the wide balcony near the Guard's Keep. Kaliam leaned over the window ledge and gaped down at the balcony. A chill came over him, and he felt his heart falter. "Antoinette," he whispered. "It is what she saw in her vision."

Far below, the pristine white marble altar upon which King Eliam sacrificed his life had been smashed. Lying in the countless fragments of marble was a sinister black stone.

Many voices cried out then from below, and more volleys of arrows whistled into the sky from the battlements. "They come again!" someone roared.

Kaliam and Lady Merewen looked up. The sky was filled with innumerable dragons flying almost wingtip to wingtip! They began to break formation and rapidly descend. Again they dove low before surging up above the tallest turrets of the castle.

As the Alleble archers' arrows found their marks, dragons crashed bodily into the castle walls or slammed to the cobblestone road.

But countless survived, and dark stones fell from the sky like a deadly black hail. They smashed through thatched roofs, cracked walls, and crushed the few Alleb Knights who could not find shelter. When the barrage ended, Alleble's streets filled with frenzied activity as knights raced from door to door, and Glimpses awakened by the commotion sought to find out what had occurred.

An enormous Glimpse warrior dressed in black fur stormed into Kaliam's chamber. He had a tremendous hammer in one hand and a large black stone in the other.

"What devilry is this?!" Mallik demanded.

Kaliam grabbed the huge stone. Red markings were gouged into the diameter of the stone.

"A new weapon of the enemy?" Mallik snorted, brandishing his hammer. "It is so like him to attack without warning while we sleep!"

"No, Mallik," Kaliam replied, looking up from the stone. "It is not a new weapon but rather his oldest and most favored . . . fear. Since his exile, Paragor has chosen his battles, attacking our weaker allies and waylaying our diplomatic missions. But always, he has known his limitations. The attack on Mithegard was different. The armies of King Ravelle were many and skilled, and yet Paragor attacked. Then, with the aid of the ancient evils, he brazenly conquered Clarion and crippled Yewland! These that drop on us now are The Stones of Omen. Paragor has declared his rule over all The Realm. Soon . . . he comes to claim his throne."

CALL TO ARMS

The morning sun glinted off the tips of a thousand spears as a caravan of many Glimpses marched out of the west toward Alleble. It was not an invading army from Paragory, and it was not all soldiers. But even so, the advancing multitude caused Kaliam great dread as he watched from a tower near the main gate. He knew the dark blue and gold livery of the heralds to be that of the realm of Mithegard. And Mithegard's approach could only be another omen of what was brewing.

Kaliam dreaded the arrival of Mithegard's ruler, the brave King Ravelle, because Aelic was his son. As Kaliam descended the stairs from the tower, he wondered how he would break the news that Aelic was still among the missing.

"Hail and well-met, Sentinel of Alleble!" said King Ravelle as he leaped down from his unicorn and clasped Kaliam's shoulders. "It is far too long since I have looked upon the Seven Fountains." And though his words were full of vigor, his face was grim.

"Well-met, indeed!" Kaliam replied, looking out over the line of Glimpses that reached from Alleble's main gate seemingly to the horizon. "But King Ravelle, why has Mithegard emptied? Or am I mistaken and this is not your entire city?"

"Your eyes do not deceive you, Kaliam. We come seeking refuge—and to add our swords to the forces of Alleble. Though the Seven Towers stand again and our walls are rebuilt, we cannot survive alone in the shadow of the enemy. I bring news of a threat the likes of which The Realm has never seen before."

"Then much news will be shared," said Kaliam. "But some news should not wait for the council this evening. As soon as you have marshaled your people within the walls, come to Guard's Keep."

"King Ravelle, I am glad you have come," said Kaliam outside the door to Guard's Keep.

King Ravelle nodded and followed Kaliam to an alcove down the hall. A single torch flickered on the wall and Kaliam's face was half in shadow. "I have news that I would not deliver in front of all," Kaliam said, choosing his words carefully.

"Speak on, Kaliam," King Ravelle replied. "Do you have word of my son?"

"M'lord, Aelic is among the missing," Kaliam said. "Some fear the worst, but I believe your son is yet alive. And I have my best knights joining Yewland's braves in the search."

"There is much talk of the dark things that occurred in the forests of Yewland. Talk of legends and loss. When I did not see Aelic here—" King Ravelle continued but now with a tremor in his deep voice. He swallowed hard and nodded as he spoke. "I feared worse, Kaliam. May the King of all this Realm guide them in their search."

A massive fire crackled in the corner of the chamber within Guard's Keep. Kaliam, King Ravelle, Lady Merewen, Mallik, Farix, Rogan, and many others from Alleble and Mithegard were seated around the huge table inside the chamber, awaiting the start of the council.

At last, Kaliam stood and said, "King Ravelle, trusted friends from Mithegard, welcome to our kingdom—and into the confidence of the Elder Guard! You have no doubt heard much rumor about the events that occurred in the forests of Yewland. It is time you hear the full tale."

For more than an hour, Kaliam chronicled everything that had happened. The Glimpses from Mithegard were horrified to learn about the Wyrm Lord and the Seven Sleepers, about the devastation the ancient creature had caused in Clarion and on the Forest Road. As they listened, the Mithegardian Glimpses slumped back in their chairs, afraid.

Then the King of Mithegard stood and addressed the gathering. "Worthy Knights of Alleble, the news of our enemy bringing ancient horrors to life is grievous indeed. But especially so in light of what I must share: My countrymen have come to seek shelter within your walls. We fled our home because Paragor is now mustering an army, a fraction of which would overwhelm the city of Seven Towers."

"How does he manage such a force?" Mallik spoke his thought aloud.

"Long has the enemy hidden his true strength," Kaliam explained. "In the catacombs beneath his city and in the hollows of the dark mountains, there are captives from Paragor's conquests . . . but there are also descendants from the brood that led the rebellion against King Eliam that fateful night."

"But that is not his only source," said King Ravelle. "You see, after the attack that destroyed my city, I have kept a constant network of spies coming and going into the enemy's dark realm. Paragor's force has more than tripled, due to a steady stream of soldiers from the far west."

The council was stunned into silence.

"Paragor has dared to cross the Cauldron Sea. He has made alliances with Frostland, Inferness, and Candleforge—for my spies have seen their colors enter the dark land."

Sir Rogan slammed a fist on the table. Mallik stood up and growled, "This cannot be! Frostland, Inferness? Those places have been our allies of old!"

"Long before Paragor's rebellion even," said Kaliam. "Merewen, do you know anything of this?"

"Of his armies beneath the ground and in the mountains, yes," she replied. "But I had no knowledge of Paragor's dealings with the far west. I doubt very much that he would have entrusted that part of his plan to any but his closest lieutenants."

Farix paced restlessly. "I do not understand why old allies would turn against us now."

"Perhaps he has sent more false ambassadors," Mallik said. "Like Count Eogan, who for a time was able to embitter Queen Illaria at Yewland against us."

"That may be," said Kaliam. "But I fear we are partially to blame. We have trusted in history for too long, looking to the allegiance of other more volatile kingdoms and taking the far west for granted. Candleforge, Inferness, Frostland . . . perhaps they misinterpret our lack of contact as ambivalence."

"Or perhaps Paragor has helped them to see things in that way," King Ravelle said. "And perhaps there is a stalwart remnant in each of those realms who remain faithful to King Eliam. It may be just a portion of their Glimpses who have renounced the old allegiances." He paused and his voice grew deeper and more grim. "But that is enough to create an unsurpassed army. Kaliam, they are now grown to such an extent that they cannot be housed within the catacombs or mountains of Paragory. They gather openly now upon the plains of the Black Crescent. There are tents, new stables, and fires as far as the eye can see."

"Then our course of action is clear," Kaliam said. "We must answer the challenge by summoning all of our allies to our aid. For the first time since the Cold River Battles, we will send forth riders upon the blue dragons. They will go to the four corners of The Realm, and then we shall more than match Paragor's force."

The knights gathered there banged their fists on the table and cheered. But King Ravelle spoke over them. "That must be done!" he shouted, and the gathering quieted. "Send the blue dragons tonight if it may be, but you will need to do more to prepare."

"What do you mean?" Kaliam asked.

"The walls of Alleble are mighty," he said. "But perhaps it has been too long since an enemy has approached them." The Knights of Alleble stared at one another.

"Many of you witnessed firsthand what Paragor did to my city," King Ravelle went on. "And upon the plains of the Black Crescent he has put his minions to work building more weapons of war: catapults; tall, rolling siege engines; and stout battering rams—many already built as of a fortnight ago but far more being prepared. You must mobilize your engineers . . . dig rings of deep trenches far beyond your walls, so that their rolling machines cannot approach. Bring forth your own catapults. Mount them upon the turrets! And as for the walls themselves, if there is any way to fortify them against Paragory's exploding fire weapon, you should do so."

"Mallik?" Kaliam looked at his hammer-wielding knight.

"Aye!" he replied heartily. "I have a mind of what we can do, but . . . in order to do it we will need more skill than there is in Alleble. Let me travel to my kin in the Blue Mountains. They will come to Alleble's aid to build and to fight!"

Kaliam grinned at his friend's unbridled enthusiasm. "Excellent, but Mallik, instead let us send word to your kin via the dragon couriers. Perhaps you could pen a note to King Brower? We need you here."

Mallik smiled and nodded. "Of course."

"But can they do it in time?" Lady Merewen asked.

"I can answer that," King Ravelle said. "The Glimpses of the Blue Mountains rebuilt my entire city in a month. They will craft new walls in far less time."

"Good," Kaliam said. "Even so, we need to loose the dragons as soon as may be."

"Agreed!" Mallik bellowed. "When my doughty folk arrive, we will build such walls that should the Seven Sleepers try to breach them, they will break their teeth!"

"One more thing, Kaliam," King Ravelle said. "After the Battle of Mithegard, a number of my best archers came to me with an idea for a new weapon." He motioned to a nearby attendant, who handed him a very strangely shaped bundle.

King Ravelle carefully unwrapped an unusual-looking device made of wood with components of iron. It looked like a small bow laid flat and affixed to a stock of wood.

"This," King Ravelle said proudly, "is an *arbalest*. Too often were my bowmen cut down as they struggled to aim and draw back their bows in the same instant. With the arbalest, your arrow—or *quarrel*, as we call the short arrow we have created—can be loaded and drawn back ahead of time. The archer can then aim and fire at will."

A murmur broke out among the Knights of Alleble. "Loaded and drawn ahead of time?" one asked incredulously.

"It is so small!" scoffed another. "It will do no damage."

"Allow me to demonstrate," King Ravelle said. And he began to turn a small iron crank on the arbalest. Slowly, the bowstring, short though it may have been, began to stretch backward. He turned the crank until the string was as far back as it could go. Then, the attendant handed him a short arrow that was painted blue and had a long, sharp golden tip. The King placed the quarrel on top of the arbalest. He pointed it at a large silver shield that hung above the fireplace. Then, he fired.

The small shaft left the arbalest faster than the knights seated there could follow with their eyes. Suddenly, the silver shield split near the top. It fell with a crash, splintered, and bits flew into the fireplace. Sparks and embers flew everywhere, some onto the table where they sat. The knights looked up and saw the blue quarrel half embedded into the mortar of the wall.

"Nock's going to want one of those," Mallik said.

"Then he shall have it!" King Ravelle replied. "Kaliam, the smithies of Mithegard will deliver to you five hundred arbalests. They will be put to good use in the defense of Alleble!"

Guard's Keep had emptied, except for Kaliam. He sat alone by the fire, turning the short arrow from the arbalest round and round in his hands. There came a soft rap at the door, and Farix entered.

"The messengers upon the blue dragons are away," Farix said. Kaliam nodded, but Farix did not leave.

"My Sentinel," he said, his arms crossing and his hands disappearing into the long sleeves of his surcoat. "There are many kingdoms in The Realm who ought to come to our aid. But now we hear of broken alliances—Inferness, Frostland, Candleforge. What of the others? Who will come?"

"Our true allies will come," Kaliam said. He looked up at Farix and then quickly broke eye contact. "They will come, for the enemy brings the firstborn dragon, the Seven Sleepers, and an army of a hundred legions. If our allies do not come, and Alleble falls . . . The Realm falls with it."

CLOSE CALLS

S ure, it was scary," Mr. Thomas continued. "But we're safe now, back on the ground in Maryland. Yes, he's standing right here." He handed the phone to Aidan as they waited in some airport offices for the paramedics, along with other passengers from the flight.

"Hi, Mom!" Aidan said into the phone. "I thought we were done for, but King Eliam had other plans! . . . I know you don't believe any of that, but you should . . . I am totally okay, Mom— but Dad's got a great big knot on his head! They are taking him to the hospital . . . because he passed out."

"Aidan!" His father shot him a look.

"Okay. I love you too, Mom," Aidan said and returned the phone to his father.

Mr. Thomas sighed. "I'm really fine. It's just precautionary, they are going to run a few tests . . . in case I have a concussion. . . . Honey, I'm sure it's nothing." He listened intently for a few minutes. "We'll see you then." He closed the cell phone. "Your mother is taking the next available flight to Baltimore."

After loading their suitcases into the back of the taxi outside of the hospital, Aidan and his father slumped into the backseat and closed their eyes.

"Some trip, huh, Aidan?" Mr. Thomas said.

"Yeah," Aidan replied.

"First, the flight gets delayed . . ."

"Then, we nearly crash, and you end up in the hospital."

"I told them I didn't have a concussion," Mr. Thomas complained.

"So you're an accountant—and a doctor?" Aidan laughed.

Mr. Thomas smiled, but rubbed his head. "This has been the longest day," he said. "What time is it, anyway?"

Aidan sat bolt upright and craned around his seat to see the clock on the taxi's dashboard. "Ten thirty, shoot! I knew I should have called Robby from the terminal. Do you think it's too late to call?"

"Why do you need to call him?"

"I forgot to tell him how early you'd be dropping me off at his house in the morning. Do you think it's too late to call him?"

"On a Friday night?" he replied, delicately rubbing the growing welt on his head. "No, it's probably okay on a Friday night." He handed Aidan the cell phone, and Aidan dialed. It rang once, twice . . . a third time, but no answer. Aidan felt something strange come over him—an urgency to hang up. Fourth ring. *What nerve you have calling so late.* A voice came into his mind. Fifth ring. *You'll make his mom angry!* Sixth ring. *Hang up now!!*

"Hello?" Robby answered on the seventh ring.

"Robby? Hi! It's Aidan."

"Uh, hey, Aidan."

"I called to tell you what time I'm coming to see you tomorrow."

"Uh, righ-ight," Robby replied, a strange detachment in his voice. "About that . . . I don't know if that's really a good—"

"My dad is going to drop me off about eight fifteen in the morning."

"Eight fifteen?" Robby echoed. "Well, I was startin' to say, uh, tomorrow I gotta—"

Aidan interrupted him again. "Good then," Aidan said decidedly. "I'll see you then. I can't wait to see you, Robby. We have a lot of catching up to do. Bye." Without waiting for a reply, Aidan closed the cell phone.

"That was kind of abrupt," Aidan's father said without opening his eyes.

"It was the only way I could keep him from getting out of it," Aidan replied as the taxi came to a stop at the hotel. "I'm telling you, Dad, I don't know what's gotten into Robby."

Robby stared at the phone receiver. Then he looked up at the man sitting across the kitchen table from him. He felt the man's piercing green eyes boring into him. "He hung up on me."

"Well, what did he say before he hung up?" the man asked pointedly.

Robby swallowed. "He said he'll be here a little after eight in the morning."

The man stood suddenly and knocked the phone out of Robby's hand. It clattered to the floor and slid across the linoleum. "I told you he's not welcome here, didn't I?"

Robby cowered. The man stood just a foot away, and his thick, muscled arms dangled at his sides like a gunslinger's. "Didn't I?!"

"Uh, y-yes, sir," Robby whispered. "But, sir, you didn't tell me that until after I'd told him he could come." The big man raised his hand as if to strike, but the strike didn't come. Instead, the man laughed, and he patted Robby on the head as if he were a cocker spaniel.

"On second thought, Robby, let Aidan come," said the big man as he turned to leave the kitchen. "I just may have to stay home from work tomorrow. It's time to find out what Aidan's made of."

The Skill of Thrivenbard

I mean no disrespect, Sir Thrivenbard, but we have followed many trails of this kind already. And each time, promising though they may be, they lead us to fallen braves, or the carcass of a dragon. Could we not renew our search on the Yewland side of the forest?" Halberad asked his mentor.

Thivenbard knelt on the forest floor, but did not look up. "Hal, you are a fine tracker in your own right," he said. "But think not of what you expect to find. Read the signs and allow them to show you what may be found."

"Have I missed something?" Hal asked.

"If we left this path now, you would. Follow me, and be my shadow to the right side of the path. You see, the Braves of Yewland, skilled as they are, followed this track to one end not realizing that there was another."

And, with his eyes locked onto the ground, Thrivenbard moved quickly into the heart of the Blackwood. Halberad marveled at his commander's movements. He was as surefooted as anyone Hal had ever seen, but it was more than that—when he moved, his limbs seemed to stretch and twist into just the right position so that he could pass soundlessly between, under, or over root and tree. He sometimes seemed to disappear behind a large tree trunk only to appear seconds later several yards ahead—and yet, no one had seen him pass between the two points. *Like a wood ghost, he is,* Hal thought.

They traveled forty yards north and came to a large area that had been flattened as if by a great weight. Thrivenbard motioned for Hal to wait and then he skirted the perimeter. "Now, Halberad, if you please, look and tell me what you see."

Halberad circled the area as he had seen his commander do. He studied the ground, seeing the trampling of boot prints and gigantic wolvin paws, the imprint of Glimpse bodies, scratches and notches in the surrounding trees, and many dried bloodstains. Evidently, Thrivenbard saw something more. Inwardly, Hal groaned, for he knew this was a test. Nothing hurt worse than feeling he had disappointed his commander. Wait! A chill of excitement shot up his spine, and he lowered himself slowly to the ground. At the northernmost edge of the scene, not far from where Thrivenbard stood, there was a complicated sign.

"Here the print is multilayered," Hal said, thinking as he spoke. "But I think not from the same wolvin, and . . ." He stepped a few paces into the trees. "Not coming from the same direction!"

"Excellent!" Thrivenbard clapped. "More! Tell me the full story!"

Halberad smiled and followed the trail. "The braves ran from the Forest Road into the Blackwood. They were pursued by one of the Sleepers to this point, but here they stopped, made such a defense as they could, and . . ."

"And?"

"And here . . . another of the Sleepers found them. The poor souls! They were caught between two of the foul beasts. They were slain in seconds."

"Bravo, Hal!" Thrivenbard exclaimed. "You are almost there!"

Almost? Halberad frowned.

Thrivenbard nodded. "You have uncovered more of the tale than the Braves of Yewland were able to see. Though I suspect that many of Queen Illaria's search parties cut short their efforts. For them, the Blackwood is hallowed ground. And to learn that the legends of foul things lurking here are true . . ."

Halberad stood up a little straighter and looked slowly about the Blackwood. It was still an hour before sundown, but already the woods took on a creepy gray half-light. Hal shivered and drew his cloak tightly about him.

"Yes," Thrivenbard continued. "Fear can silence the inner questioning that all trackers must hearken to. It was here that the bodies were found. But . . ." Thrivenbard waited.

"But where did the other wolvin come from?" Hal finished the thought.

"Exactly!" Thrivenbard said. "Let us trace the creature deeper into the woods and see what the others might have missed!"

The two trackers left the small clearing and delved deeper into the Blackwood. Some eighty yards beyond, they began to detect a pungent aroma they knew only too well. It was the sickly sweet smell of decaying flesh. The two men covered their noses.

The trail of wolvin tracks led to the edge of a deep valley in the middle of the Blackwood.

"Over here!" Thrivenbard called, and he led Hal down a strange stairway that seemed to have been pounded recently into the raw earth. When they descended into the valley, they found themselves in awe of what they found. The place was void of trees—except for seven enormous Blackwoods that were uprooted and fallen, leaving a deep pit at the base of each. And near the grasping roots was a pile of gray rubble as if a large stone had been shattered and lay in pieces by each fallen tree.

"Not easily do these stout trees fall," Thrivenbard said. "Look, they were leafless, dead before their time! And see the stones! Halberad, do you know where we are?"

"It is the Sepulcher of the Seven," Halberad whispered. "To hear that they are real is one thing, but to step into such a place and see for yourself . . . it is like living a cruel dream."

Thrivenbard, in his usual painstaking way, began to search the valley, and Halberad carefully went behind him. They stopped at each fallen tree, looked upon the exposed roots, and found they were gnawed thin in many places. Then, Thrivenbard searched the ground around the deep pits. He began to look into the pits one by one, but there wasn't enough light to see to the bottom.

"Thrivenbard!" Hal called. "I have found the source of that sickly smell. Come over here." In a shaded corner of the valley lay a dead dragon. Its body was gouged cruelly as if by deep claws, and its neck was severed. Thrivenbard and Hal came closer to the beast. "This is a dragon steed from Alleble!" Halberad exclaimed.

"Yes," Thrivenbard muttered, deep in thought. "Here we find answers to many riddles, but new riddles take their place." He crouched and began to walk like a spider around the dragon's corpse.

"I have seen this dragon before," Thrivenbard said quietly. "Unless I am mistaken, it was Lady Gwenne's proud steed."

"Gabrielle, one of the silver line," Halberad agreed. "Sir Aelic rode her into the battle, did not Kaliam tell us this?"

"He did," Thrivenbard replied. "But where then is his body?" Thrivenbard strode carefully around the dead dragon, making increasingly larger concentric circles. "Here then is the tale these signs tell. Sir Aelic was cornered here by one of the Sleepers. His dragon came to his aid and fought valiantly. For there is more than dragon blood spilled upon this earth. At last, the Sleeper took the dragon's neck within its jaws and slew it. But where the Sleeper dispatched Sir Aelic, I cannot tell. The creature's track leads out of the valley, presumably to the ambush of the braves. Ah, we need to continue to search this place, and we must hurry, for we do not have much light left."

Thrivenbard and Halberad spread outward, scanning the ground for missed signs, but then they heard the faintest sound. "What is that?" Halberad asked.

Thrivenbard shushed his apprentice and waited. At last, a faint call of help rose up from one of the pits, and the two trackers raced to the dark hole.

"Speak to us, if you can! Make a sound!" Thrivenbard called down into the inky darkness. "Are you there?"

They heard a wet cough, and then a weak, "I am here."

"Hal, go back up the trail," Thrivenbard commanded. "Find the others, especially Sitric, for he is skilled with herbs. Seek the braves as well. We will have need of a rope ladder among other things."

Halberad ran out of the valley, disappearing into the forest.

Thrivenbard looked down into the pit. "Take heart. Help is coming," he said. Then, hardly daring to hope, he asked, "What is your name?"

"I am Aelic."

"Aelic, son of King Ravelle, ruler of Mithegard?" Thrivenbard asked.

"Yes. . . . Please hurry . . . I am hurt." And the voice fell silent.

PRINCIPLES OF POWER

Aidan and his father stared at the sleek black sports car parked out in front of Robby's house. It had a sharklike profile and sat very low to the ground. Even in the early morning sun, it looked menacing. Menacing, fast, and expensive—all the more so compared to the humorous little orange compact car Mr. Thomas had rented at the hotel.

"Wow!" Aidan exclaimed. "Whose car is that?"

"I don't know," said Aidan's dad. "That car's probably worth sixty grand."

"It can't be Robby's mom's," Aidan said. "I mean, I guess it could be if she got a big raise or something, but when we lived here, the Piersons were just barely scraping by."

Aidan opened the door, grabbed his backpack, and climbed out of the little orange roadster. "So, you're coming to get me around five or six?"

"Yes," Mr. Thomas replied.

Aidan frowned and shifted his backpack onto his shoulder.

"Things are going to be fine," Mr. Thomas said. "Never alone!"

"Never alone," Aidan answered back, and smiled. "Thanks, Dad."

Aidan watched his father drive off, took a deep breath, then walked up the steps to Robby's front door. He looked at the old-fashioned black mailbox next to the door, the diagonal house numbers—7012—and faded welcome mat. How many times had he waited at this door for his best friend? *Why does it feel so weird now?* Aidan wondered. *I feel like a stranger here.*

Aidan gently rapped on the door. He hefted the backpack and waited. The door swung open, and a very tall man stood just inside the door staring down at Aidan. The man wore a black turtleneck under a brown tweed jacket. His face was tanned and rugged-looking. His green eyes looked somewhat sunken behind smallish wire-framed glasses. His hair was pale blond, close cropped around the ears with a wavy fold gelled on top.

"You must be Aidan," he said with a slight Southern accent. "I'm Kurt Pierson, Robby's father."

Father!? The word crashed into Aidan's mind like a brick through a window. That just couldn't be. Aidan knew that Robby's father had run out on Robby's family when Robby was little.

"I've heard an awful lot about you," Mr. Pierson said. He reached out his hand to Aidan and smiled. Aidan shook his hand, but something about that smile didn't seem right. It was a sickly smile like the ghastly grin of a skull.

"Is Robby here?" Aidan found himself asking.

"He'll be down in a minute," Mr. Pierson said. "Why don't you join me at the dining room table." The request sounded more like a command, and the man turned his back to Aidan and walked up the hall. There was something familiar about the way the man walked. He took long, confident strides with a slightly delayed turn of the shoulders. It reminded Aidan of the way disciplined soldiers march.

Aidan followed him into the dining room. Mr. Pierson took a seat at the head of the long, dark table. He gave Aidan another one of those skull-grins and motioned for him to sit. "So you and Robby used to be good friends."

Aidan didn't much like the sound of "used to be," but he replied, "Yes, sir. I lived down the street until July. We were best friends, but then I had to move."

"That's a real pity," Mr. Pierson replied. "Colorado, is it?"

Aidan nodded.

"That's a long way from Maryland, Aidan. A long way." Mr. Pierson whistled. "I guess by now you've probably made quite a few more friends like Robby has."

Aidan didn't like the direction Mr. Pierson was leading things. "Is Robby coming down soon?"

"Oh, he'll be along," said Mr. Pierson, and he cracked his knuckles. "As a matter of fact, Robby did have plans today with one of his buddies from school, but I told him he ought to stick around for an old friend." The way he spoke—gesturing grandly and raising his voice far louder than necessary—it reminded Aidan of someone. An old teacher? Maybe. A relative? Aidan wasn't sure.

"So, Robby tells me you like to write stories, Aidan," Mr. Pierson said, and he waited for Aidan to answer. Aidan just stared back. "I'm a writer too. Did you know that?"

Aidan shook his head no. Mr. Pierson smiled. "Oh, yes! I write self-help books, a couple of bestsellers. Maybe you've heard of my latest. It's called *Principles of Power*. No? Maybe I'll get you a copy from my car. I'd be happy to sign it for you. Yes, I bet you could really get into my book. You look like you could use some power. My principles could help you."

"What do you mean?" Aidan asked.

"Well, I certainly don't mean any offense, but look at you. You live now over a thousand miles away, and here you are trying to keep alive an old friendship. When what you really ought to be doing . . ." Robby's dad snatched off his glasses and leaned forward till his eyes seemed to triple in size, "is getting on with life—find yourself new friends. That's one of the secrets to real power, Aidan—never look back."

Aidan remained silent. He felt extremely threatened by this man who claimed to be Robby's father. And on top of that, Aidan had the strangest feeling of alarm as if there were invisible enemies all around and they were beginning to close in.

"Everyone needs personal power, Aidan," Mr. Pierson continued. He slid his glasses back on and tilted his head slightly. "It's the only way to feel totally secure in a very *dangerous* world." He put a sinister emphasis on the word *dangerous*, and Aidan felt a chill.

"Wouldn't you like to feel powerful, Aidan?" Mr. Pierson asked. "I could show you how . . ."

Aidan knew now where true power could be found, and it wasn't in the pages of Mr. Pierson's book.

"No thank you, sir," Aidan replied, trying to avoid the man's eyes. It wasn't that Aidan was afraid to look at him eye to eye, but he had a feeling this man was very shrewd, that he might be able to guess his thoughts. Aidan didn't want to give him the chance. "I appreciate the offer. But really, I just came here to catch up on things with Robby. My dad had to visit his home office in the city, so I just tagged along." Aidan glanced slightly at his backpack. He felt suddenly very conscious of his bundle of scrolls inside. "My dad will be back to pick me up between five and six."

"Will he?" Mr. Pierson leaned back a little and smiled. He put his thick arms behind his head like a chess grandmaster whose move had been countered but still had a secret play left. "Well, that should give you and my son a nice long day together, now, shouldn't it? Yes, I expect it will. Normally, I spend a day like today writing over at the local coffee shop, but I think today I'll just stick around the house. So let me know if there's anything I can do for you."

"Thank you, Mr. Pierson," Aidan replied, and he grabbed his backpack and started to get up from the table.

"Oh, Aidan, one more thing," Mr. Pierson said. "What have you got in that backpack of yours?"

Just then, Robby came bounding into the dining room. "Hey, Aidan!" he said, and for the first time since Aidan moved, Robby sounded like the old Robby again. Aidan slung his backpack over his shoulder and walked toward his old friend.

"I was thinkin' Aidan and I could ride bikes up to the park and throw the football around." Robby turned to Aidan. "That is, if you don't mind ridin' Jill's hunk of junk." Aidan shrugged. He didn't mind.

"That all right with you, Dad?"

"That'll be fine, son," Mr. Pierson replied, but the smile was gone. "Just remember what I told you."

"I will, Dad. I will."

❧

"Why didn't you tell me about your dad?" Aidan finally blurted out as they pedaled up Mazzoni Hill on their way to the park.

"I dunno," Robby replied. "I guess I'm still getting used to the idea myself."

"Well, is he . . ." Aidan chose his words carefully. "Is he like he used to be?"

Robby pulled ahead a little. "Some," he replied. "But he's changed in a lot of ways. He's rich."

"I noticed the car in front of the house!" Aidan replied. "And he told me about his book."

"Yeah, he called and said he was sorry. Mama and Jill just welcomed him back with open arms."

"What about you?" Aidan asked.

Robby pedaled in silence a few moments. "Yeah," he said finally. "I mean, it's great to have my dad back. He's real smart—helps me sort out my problems. C'mon, Aidan! Almost to the top, and then we coast!"

Robby poured it on. He rode a sleek racing bike and had little trouble getting up the hill. Aidan zipped along as best he could on Jill's no-name bike, with the little plastic streamers coming out of the grips and a banana seat. They crested the hill and coasted side by side.

"Where were your mom and Jill? I didn't see them at your house."

"Shopping," Robby replied as they reached the bottom of the hill. "If it's a Saturday, then they're shopping. They like spending Dad's money." Aidan and Robby sped through the park entrance toward the game area.

They secured their bikes, and Aidan dug into his backpack and reached for the football. As he did, his hand brushed against the Scrolls. There was so much he wanted to say, and he had rehearsed it in his mind a hundred times. But still he couldn't quite get himself to bring it up. Aidan zipped up his backpack, and Robby went long. *Maybe I'll tell him after lunch*, Aidan thought as he threw the football. It was a perfect spiral, but it sailed well past Robby's outstretched arms.

Robby came huffing back. "That was a launch, Aidan! You been practicing?"

Aidan smiled and shrugged. "Not really." *There's a lot about me that's changed*, Aidan thought.

They played catch while the morning sun climbed, until Robby yelled, "Punt the ball to me and then try and catch me! I've got a move for ya!" Aidan kicked the ball high in the air. Robby caught it and rumbled toward Aidan. Robby was fast, and he juked to the left to get by his friend. But Aidan paid no attention to the move. He watched Robby's waist and slammed into his buddy like a freight train. Robby sprawled backward on the turf, and the football came loose and tumbled away.

Aidan held out a hand and helped Robby to his feet. "Nice hit," Robby muttered, followed by a cough. "I was fixin' to fake you out, but you nailed me."

Robby shook his head as he walked over to pick up the football he had dropped.

"Mmm." Aidan smiled, his mouth full of pizza. "Bambinos!"

"Thanks for getting us pizza, Dad," Robby said.

"I figured two strong boys like yourselves could use a big lunch," said Mr. Pierson. He patted Robby on the shoulder as if he had always been dear old Dad, but Aidan noticed that Robby flinched ever so slightly.

"So what are you boys going to do now?"

Robby shrugged. "Maybe play some video games. What do you want to do, Aidan?"

Aidan felt Mr. Pierson's gaze falling steadily upon him. "That'd be good," Aidan replied. "What games do you have?"

"Name it," Robby replied. He got up and took his plate to the sink. "Dad got me all the systems. And a bucket of games for each."

"Cool!" Aidan said as he stood.

"C'mon," Robby said, and he made his way to the door to the basement. "I've got a really nice setup down here . . ." Robby hesitated. "Oh yeah, I forgot. You don't like basements very much, do you?"

"Really not a problem anymore," Aidan said, grabbing his backpack and heading down the stairs.

Robby's basement was divided into two areas joined by a door at the bottom of the stairs. One side was comfortable, furnished, and cheery. That was where Robby and Aidan used to hang out. The other side, the work side, was exactly the opposite. It was a cold, shadowy place filled with rotting scrap wood and all manner of tools.

Cobwebs adorned every corner, and the cinderblock walls had been stained long ago by some dark substance. The one light on the work side rarely worked. It hung from the ceiling like a hangman's noose.

"So basements don't bother you anymore?" Robby said, and he too glanced at the work-side door.

"We used to work ourselves up pretty good," Aidan replied. Inwardly he struggled. He knew that Robby had presented him with a perfect opportunity to talk to him about the Scrolls. But that strange feeling he'd had earlier—like there were invisible enemies all around—was back and stronger.

"You want to play *NHL Hockey Supreme?*" Robby asked. "Or wait, I've got this cool two-player adventure game called *Oswald's Quest*. I bet you'd like that."

Three hours later, the boys were still playing *Oswald's Quest*. And while Aidan seemed on the outside totally engrossed in hunting huge, hairy goblins, collecting piles of gold, and buying weapons and armor, he was really just playing on autopilot. Inside, his mind whirled. *Get the Scrolls and tell him!* he kept urging himself. But other thoughts kept complicating it. Why was Robby's dad here? Why was he so interested in Aidan's backpack? Why did he want Aidan to leave Robby alone?

"Score!" Robby exclaimed. "We did it! We got to the final level! I could never do it by myself. I wonder what the monster's gonna be."

Aidan snapped out of his trance and looked at the screen. Robby moved his sword-wielding character near the opening to a massive cave where he could ambush whatever came out. Aidan directed his bowman character into a covering position in the boughs of a tree. Aidan and Robby watched as a three-headed dragon slowly emerged from the cave. Robby attacked immediately, unleashing huge chopping strokes on the creature's scaled belly. Most swordstrikes did no damage, but the ones that struck the dragon's chest did. Each time Robby slashed there, all three of the dragon's heads roared, and the creature's eyes flashed bright red.

Suddenly, one of the dragon's heads plucked Aidan's archer from the tree and began to gobble him up in a very colorful way. But Aidan was not concerned any longer about the game. Seeing the red eyes flash cut through Aidan's indecision at last. He put down his controller and went to his backpack and fished out the Scrolls.

"Aidan, you're gettin' walloped!" Robby said, peppering the buttons on his controller.

"Robby, could you put it on pause for a minute?" Aidan asked as he sat down next to Robby on the floor and began to untie the Scrolls.

"Okay. What is that?" Robby asked. The basement became eerily silent.

"Robby, this is what I've been trying to tell you about ever since I left Maryland," Aidan said, taking a deep breath. "These are The Scrolls of Alleble." Robby stiffened. His eyes darted just for a second to the stairs.

Aidan went on. "Do you remember before I moved, you told me that life seemed like a cruel joke?" Robby sat very still.

"I didn't know what to say," Aidan continued. "I felt the same way at the time. It just didn't make sense that I had to move so far away right after I finally found a good friend. But there was a reason."

Aidan went on to tell Robby about finding The Scrolls of Alleble and how Grampin helped him understand how to answer the invitation and enter The Realm. Aidan spoke of The Schism that divided The Realm from earth. He described the beings known as the Glimpses and told of their connection to their twins on earth. Aidan told of his training to be a knight in the service of King Eliam and of the great victory Aidan had played a role in, saving many lives.

"If I hadn't moved," Aidan explained, "I might never have figured out that the Scrolls were more than just a story. I needed to be near Grampin—he knew all about it, Robby. Grampin showed me the path to the other world."

Robby looked at Aidan as if he had just told him the blue sky he'd been living under his entire life was actually purple. But Aidan was undaunted.

"Robby, you told me you hated how tragic and unpredictable life is. You said you always wanted something you could count on." He flipped through the Scrolls and found the account of the Great Betrayal. "Robby, there is someone you can count on. He is the ruler of Alleble, and his name is King Eliam the Everlasting. I want you to read this and see what the King did for his people."

Robby said nothing, but began to read the account. Aidan would have given his right arm to know what Robby was thinking at this point. But soon, Robby's facial expressions began to tell a story. First there were subtle shakes of the head as if Robby disagreed with what he was reading. Next came the scrunching of his eyebrows and the squinting, and then he took a sharp breath. Just as he was about to speak, the basement door opened.

"It's getting kind of quiet down here, boys," said Mr. Pierson as he hastily descended the stairs. When he reached the bottom of the steps he was smiling. But when he saw Robby with the Scrolls in his lap, his face contorted. His tanned skin, which to Aidan already looked stretched and unnatural, became so taut with rage that it seemed his skull would burst right through. His sunken eyes bulged behind the wire-rimmed glasses, and he directed his stare, heavy with accusation, at Aidan. Then he turned to his son.

"Whatcha got there, Robby?" Mr. Pierson asked, his voice as taut as his skin.

Robby glanced at Aidan miserably. "Scrolls," he muttered at last.

"Scrolls, huh?"

"Th-they're Aidan's," Robby said.

"I think you ought to give them back to Aidan, right about now," Mr. Pierson said in an emotionless voice that was somehow worse than anger. "Don't you?"

"Yes, sir," Robby replied, and he practically threw the Scrolls at

Aidan. Aidan swiftly rolled them up and shoved them into his back-pack. He turned and looked up at the massive figure of Robby's father.

In that moment, Aidan saw in the face of Robby's father a different identity. The skull-like grimace, the barely concealed rage, the arrogant confidence—Aidan remembered. "Rucifel," he whispered.

Mr. Pierson's expression changed. His eyes narrowed, and one corner of his thin-lipped mouth turned up into a clever smile. "Robby, I think your friend Aidan has just about worn out his welcome here." He reached slowly underneath his jacket.

Aidan involuntarily stepped back a pace. Then, to Aidan's relief, Mr. Pierson pulled out a cell phone. "Call your father," Mr. Pierson said. "Tell him to come get you . . . right now."

Aidan punched in the number, spoke for a few moments, and then handed the phone back to Robby's father. "He said he'd be here in about twenty-five minutes."

"Good," Mr. Pierson replied. He led Robby and Aidan up the stairs. When they entered the hallway at the top of the steps, Mr. Pierson directed Aidan to the front door.

"You are no longer welcome in this house, Aidan Thomas. So you'd best make other plans for tomorrow."

And with that, Mr. Pierson ushered Aidan out the front door into the yard. But not before Aidan spied Robby gesturing to get his attention. Aidan stared, and Mr. Pierson turned.

"Son, we need to have a talk," Mr. Pierson said, adjusting his glasses. "Go to your room."

But it was too late. Aidan had gotten the message. Robby had mouthed the word "fort."

THE DEPARTURE
OF SIR ÆELIC

Elspeth banged on Kaliam's door. "M'lord Kaliam! Are you in there? It is Elspeth! M'lord?"

There came a muffled voice from inside. "Elspeth? You had better have a good reason for waking me!" The door swung open, and there was Kaliam, his ebony hair wild and hanging half over his face.

"Beggin' your pardon, m'lord," she said. "Sir Aelic is alive!"

At the mention of Aelic, Kaliam became fully awake. "Alive! Where did you get such news?"

"Thrivenbard sent a messenger from Yewland. He flew all night," Elspeth said. "He said, 'Tell Kaliam that Sir Aelic has been found, and he is alive!'"

Kaliam grabbed Elspeth by the shoulders and kissed her abruptly on the cheek. "Elspeth, this is spectacular news!" he said. "Praise to the King!"

Elspeth seemed a bit taken aback by the kiss and the sudden emotion. "Sir, there is more to the message. Thrivenbard asks that you come at once to Yewland, for Aelic is very ill. Too weak to move, he said."

Kaliam's smile faded a bit, and he slowly stepped backward into his chamber. "Have the dragon master saddle his four swiftest steeds," he commanded. "Get word of this to Mallik, Oswyn, and King Ravelle. Tell them we leave for Yewland within the hour."

They flew through the morning hours in silence, and as the sun rose high into the afternoon sky, the dragons from Alleble descended into the glade known as the Hall of Sun and Moon—the threshold of Yewland.

"Hail, Sentinel of Alleble!" called Baldergrim. He and a squad of braves came forth from the trees. "Welcome to all of you, but do not leave your steeds. Sir Aelic is under care in Her Majesty's castle. It will be faster if we fly above the treetops."

Kaliam nodded. "How is he?" he asked. "How is Aelic?"

"He is awake," Baldergrim replied, but he seemed reluctant. "He has been asking for you, but . . . uh, Kaliam, Sir Aelic has taken grievous wounds. We have tended to him with such medicine as Yewland has to offer, but I do not know if it will be enough."

"Then let us cease this chatter!" Sir Oswyn bellowed. "For I bring salves and remedies like no other in The Realm."

Baldergrim nodded. He turned and whistled a soft, melodic trill. And from the trees, a white dragon spiraled down and landed next to him. Without a word, Baldergrim leaped into the saddle, and his steed swooped into the sky.

The others followed, and from the air, the Knights of Alleble saw that the Battle on the Forest Road had penetrated far deeper into the heart of Yewland than they had imagined. When Kaliam peered down into the woods, he saw open areas with blackened glades and scorched, leafless patches of trees.

The green Castle of Yewland itself did not escape entirely

unscathed. Once a thing of wild beauty, like a solitary flowering plant burgeoning upon its hill with bud and bloom, the castle now seemed more like a rosebush after a storm. Turrets leaned or were roofless—one had even crashed to the hill and lay there in a pile. Several of the elaborate wooden stairways and balustrades were burned. But the main gate was still intact.

Baldergrim's white dragon steed hurriedly descended and landed lightly on the wide balcony of the castle's east side. The others landed, and Baldergrim led them up several curving halls, up one flight of stairs, and to a large arched chamber. The room radiated green light, though from whence it came, none could say. There were no windows and no torches. Still, they could see the room was a house of healing, and the gentle green light was welcome.

There were numerous beds, mats, and cots, and upon them lay many of Yewland's wounded braves. Nock appeared and warmly greeted his old friends. "This way, my Sentinel," he said, and they followed him.

They found Queen Illaria, Trenna Swiftfoot, and Thrivenbard at Aelic's bedside. Aelic lay there, eyes closed, his porcelain white skin now a dull ashen gray. When Kaliam saw the blood-soaked bandages on Aelic's head, arm, chest, and stomach, he wanted to cry out, but he bit his tongue and smiled bravely.

"My son!" King Ravelle cried, and though he wanted to swoop to Aelic's side, he made way for Oswyn, who knelt by Aelic and opened a huge satchel. Oswyn fished around for a while and removed several cloth pouches and a half-dozen small, corked bottles. He went to work at once, examining wounds, crushing herbs from the packets, and daubing Aelic with salves.

"We found him just before sundown last night," Thrivenbard said. "It is no wonder that he was not found before. Kaliam, he was in the Sepulcher."

"The Sepulcher!" Kaliam exclaimed.

"Aelic fell into one of the pits where the Seven were buried," Nock explained. "When Aelic was last awake, he told us that one of the Sleepers chased him there. His dragon rescued him then."

"We found Gabby in that cursed valley," Thrivenbard explained. "She had been mauled. We can only guess that the Sleeper left Aelic for dead."

Oswyn lifted the bandage on Aelic's stomach, and they all heard his sudden intake of air.

"Oswyn, what?" King Ravelle asked, and his voice pleaded. Oswyn turned to the king, started to speak but didn't.

Finally, he looked at King Ravelle and then Kaliam. "He is gravely ill. That is all I can say for now."

"Is there not anything I can do?" Queen Illaria asked. And Sir Oswyn looked at her and was reminded of her kindness to them . . . and their feast the night before the Twelve left for Acacia.

"Maybe . . . ," Oswyn said, half to himself. "Your Highness, would you bring me a flask of Golden Tear?"

The queen did not question. She didn't even command an underling to go and get it. She sprinted herself from the healing chamber and returned in moments carrying a tall green urn.

"Will this be enough?" she asked.

"I am not sure," Oswyn replied. He opened a large leather satchel. Long gray, feathery weeds spilled out. He snapped them again and again until they fit in his mortar. Then he ground them rapidly with a pestle. The air around him filled with a sharp odor. Sir Oswyn took all the contents of the mortar and poured them into the urn with the Golden Tear. He covered the urn with his hands and shook it.

"King Ravelle, Nock, lift Aelic so that I can make him drink this."

The King and Mallik carefully sat Aelic up, and Oswyn slowly poured sips of the mixture into Aelic's mouth. Aelic groaned a little, and he coughed the first mouthful back out, but Oswyn kept pouring. Then Aelic began to swallow.

Suddenly, Aelic's eyes popped open. "Os?" he whispered.

"Shhh," Oswyn said. "Drink this. All of it if you can." Aelic did as he was told, and he drank until the urn was empty. Then they laid him back down.

Aelic's eyelids fluttered, but they remained open. He looked around. "Father!" he cried. And King Ravelle took his hand. "Father, I am sorry . . . I—"

"You have nothing to be sorry for, my son," Ravelle said, brushing the damp hair from Aelic's forehead. "I have heard the tale of how you fought. Valiant, I call you, one who seeks glory for King Eliam the Everlasting." Aelic smiled.

"Enough talk for now," Oswyn said, then gently added, "Leave me with my patient."

There was a spring in Oswyn's step as he walked into the chamber where King Ravelle, Kaliam, and the others awaited word on Aelic's condition.

"You may all see him now, but only briefly. He needs his rest," Oswyn said.

Quietly, they followed Oswyn to Aelic's bedside.

"Look, his skin is better, nearly restored!" Mallik exclaimed. And behold, Aelic's skin had lost the gray cast, though it still lacked the vitality of a healthy Glimpse.

"What was that you gave him?" Trenna asked.

"It is an herb called yarrow, or staunchweed in the common tongue," Oswyn said. "Then I remembered how quickly the Golden Tear restores a knight's energy, and I thought perhaps it would speed this healing herb to unknown wounds within Aelic."

"You are brilliant!" Thrivenbard exclaimed.

"We have great need of such wisdom in this room," Queen Illaria said, and she looked kindly upon Oswyn.

"Do not lavish accolades upon me," Oswyn replied. "Aelic is improving, and for that we have King Eliam to thank."

Oswyn went to Kaliam, leaned toward him, and whispered, "The next few hours will tell us much, but I still do not know if I caught it in time."

"Aelic, lad, you are made of sterner stuff than those trees in Nock's forest!" Mallik laughed. "To tangle with a Sleeper, and then last for days at the bottom of a pit? I agree with your pa, that was valiant!"

Aelic smiled at Mallik, but then he coughed and winced in pain. "The wolvin was far beyond my skill," Aelic said. "It brushed me aside like an insect."

"And if I ever find that wolvin," Mallik said, "he will pay ten-fold what he did to you, and I will collect with my hammer!"

"Well, it should be easy to recognize it," Aelic said, closing his eyes. "Before I fell, I saw Gabby take a chunk out of the back of the Sleeper's neck."

"I will remember that," Mallik said.

"Kaliam," Aelic called. His voice sounded weaker than before. "Kearn took her. He took Antoinette. He said he would take her beyond the Gate of Despair—that she would be tortured."

Kaliam knelt by Aelic. "Aelic, do not fear," he said.

"Kaliam, I know she wrongfully left our company, but we cannot abandon her to that dark place and—"

"We will not abandon her, Sir Aelic," Kaliam assured him. "King Eliam has a plan for her rescue, of this I am certain. And even in that place, she is not alone."

Aelic turned to look at his father. "What about Mother?" he asked.

"She was in Acacia for a time," King Ravelle said. And in his voice there dwelled an ancient sorrow. "I have searched there many times, but in vain. I dispatched messengers there before we left Alleble to come here."

"You were in Alleble?"

"Yes, all of Mithegard dwells there now—safer than being a close neighbor to the enemy!"

"It makes me glad," Aelic said with a soft chuckle, ". . . even in such a time as this. For the Glimpses who serve the everlasting King should be together. Does it not seem so?"

"Yes, it does, my son. It is now as it always should have been." King Ravelle looked up at Queen Illaria and shook his head slowly. "How so many, including myself, distanced ourselves from Alleble . . . abandoned Alleble . . . it was folly."

Aelic nodded, coughed again, and then suddenly clutched at his stomach. He yelled and fell backward. Oswyn was there in a flash. He delicately pressed his fingers at various places on Aelic's stomach. At one place he paused, felt again, and then he looked up grimly.

"Oswyn?" King Ravelle cried. "What is happening?"

"Mallik, Kaliam, please take King Ravelle outside," Oswyn said gently, but urgency ran through his words like a current. Kaliam and Mallik firmly escorted King Ravelle from the room.

Some time later, Sir Oswyn and Queen Illaria emerged from the chamber and found Kaliam, Mallik, and King Ravelle sitting along a wide hearth.

"Oswyn!" King Ravelle exclaimed, and they all stood. "How is my son?"

"He is resting," Os replied. "Aelic had worked himself up, and jostled his wounds before they were healed. A little more yarrow and Golden Tear I gave him, and now he rests."

"Will he survive this?" King Ravelle asked plaintively.

"I cannot say," Os replied. "But I suspect that those wounds which remain will—" A shrill scream followed by the breaking of glass cut Oswyn's words, and they all raced into the house of healing. They found one of the nursemaids standing over Aelic's empty cot. She wore a horrified expression and turned to Oswyn.

"My lords!" she cried. "Sir Aelic sat up and asked me for a flask of water. I was away just a moment. When I returned . . . he was gone!"

They gazed down at the cot, empty except for *Fury* in its sheath and the bloodstains on the sheets. Aelic was gone.

THE FIRST MOVE

Antoinette woke to the eerie sounds of war horns echoing off the dark mountains of the Prince's Crown. Startled, she rose to look out her cell's single window. It was just barely dawn, and a sickly red haze enveloped the Grimwalk far below. Antoinette saw a dark line of knights snake slowly out from the Prince's fortress. Antoinette had never seen so many soldiers—some on foot, some mounted—row upon row upon row. And now visible flying above them were huge black dragons. They were thick-limbed and had impossibly wide wings. Each dragon carried beneath it, dangling from a web of cables, what looked like a carriage filled with yet more troops.

There were waves of these dragon-transports, and they soon outpaced the soldiers on horseback and on foot below. But they all went to the northeast.

"Behold the power of Paragor's hand!" Kearn said from behind her.

Antoinette jumped and spun around. "Kearn!" She sighed forcefully. "How long have you been here?"

"Oh, for some time," he replied, walking casually to the bars of her cell. He ran a long, pale finger up one of the bars. "You seemed so anxious for news, and that, among other reasons, is why I am here."

"And what news do you have?" Antoinette asked, suspicious of Kearn's motives.

"Why, good news, m'lady," Kearn said. "Today is a momentous occasion, for Paragor has unleashed the first wave of his final campaign. A force four times that of the one we spent on Mithegard and double that of the army we used to lay waste to Yewland. In a day's time, the stubborn Glimpses of the Blue Mountain Provinces will be dealt such a blow that they will be unable to supply the help that your precious Alleble requires!"

Mallik's folk, Antoinette thought. "This is not good news."

"Did you think I meant good news for you?" Kearn laughed.

Antoinette ignored the slight and asked, "Why the Blue Mountains?"

"I would not expect you to understand my master's strategy," Kearn said. "Your Sentinel, Kaliam, saw firsthand the devastation at Clarion. And he knows full well that even now the Wyrm Lord is being nursed back to the strength he wielded of old. He knows the walls that surround Alleble will fail under the withering heat of the Wyrm Lord's breath. So to whom would your mighty King turn to have the walls of his city rebuilt? The Blue Mountains, of course. Should they be allowed to fortify King Eliam's walls, our conquest of Alleble would be . . . delayed. Paragor will strike first, and the Blue Mountain Provinces will go the way of Clarion!"

"King Eliam will go to their aid!" Antoinette said defiantly.

"He may," Kearn replied. "This too works to our advantage. You see, King Eliam will know nothing of our attack until it is too late. Alleble's forces will not arrive in time to stay the damage we will do to King Brower's stoneworking equipment. They will have no way to transport their precious blue granite, and Alleble's walls will remain vulnerable. Then the true strength of Paragory will be unleashed, and Alleble will fall!"

"Kern, you seem so confident," Antoinette said skeptically. She twisted at the silver ring on her finger. "Do you really think it will be that easy to defeat King Eliam and his allies?"

"War is never easy," Kearn said. "King Eliam has daunted Paragor at every turn. But the advantage is ours now . . . in numbers, strength, and strategy. We will win."

Kearn and Antoinette stared at each other in silence as if the war between Paragory and Alleble were being waged in their gaze. With a flourish of his cloak, Kearn turned to leave the chamber.

"Wait!" Antoinette called to him.

"What is it, Lady Antoinette? I have duties."

"Tell me something before you go," she said, seeking his eyes with her own. "Why did you take my *Book of Alleble*?"

Kearn immediately looked away. "I did no such thing."

Antoinette ignored his response. "You've been reading it, haven't you?"

"Do not be absurd," Kearn replied. He opened the chamber door and was halfway through. "What in The Realm would lead you to believe that?"

LEGEND OF
THE THREE

Praise to the King that you have returned!" Farix exclaimed as he helped Kaliam with his dragon steed in the pens behind the Castle of Alleble. Farix looked among the other riders: Mallik, Nock, Oswyn, King Ravelle, Thrivenbard, Trenna Swiftfoot, and a few braves from Yewland he did not recognize. "Where . . . where is Sir Aelic?"

"I wish I knew," Kaliam replied. "He was grievously wounded and seemed near to death, but Oswyn's skills may have delivered him from that dark door. Yet, Farix, in the midst of treatment, Aelic vanished!"

"You mean, he has gone to the Mirror Realm?"

"I do not know. I need to seek our King's wisdom on what this might mean."

"Go, then, to the King's chambers," Farix said. "For he is looking for you also. Much has transpired in your absence. More of our allies have come, seeking refuge within our walls. Acacia and the other small realms closest to us."

"Any word from the Blue Mountains?" Mallik asked.

"Nay. But that is not unexpected. They will be bearing slabs of blue granite and an array of equipment. It will take some time for them to transport such things."

"True, but please bring word when we hear from them." Kaliam turned to leave, but Farix stopped him.

"There is one other thing. Our citizens have begun to speak in whispers about the war. They are asking about the Three."

Kaliam stared. "The Three Witnesses of Legend?"

"Yes," Farix replied. "Naysmithe and others have been gathering. They are convinced that the Three are abroad."

"I really need to see King Eliam," the puzzled Sentinel said, and quickly took his leave.

Several anxious hours later, King Eliam's throne room doors opened. Brilliant white light spilled into the hallway and Kaliam emerged. He seemed to be staring into a distant place that only he could see. He walked right by Lady Merewen, who had been waiting for him.

"Kaliam!" she called, and hurried to catch up. "Were you going to simply pass me by?"

He stared at her for many long moments before recognition dawned on him. "M'lady Merewen! Prithee, forgive my lack of courtesy. I . . . my mind was in another world."

"What?"

"The Mirror Realm," he said to her. "And perhaps, in coming days, all of us will be looking there as well."

"You speak in riddles," Lady Merewen said.

"I only echo the riddles spoken to me by our King."

Lady Merewen took Kaliam's hand. "Come, my Sentinel. Dark

halls lit only by torches are no place to discuss such mysteries. Allow me to bring you to a brighter place where light may be shed on all that is unknown."

Kaliam mumbled an agreement and Lady Merewen led him past the throne room doors on the right and then left at the next hall. A moment later, she stepped over a threshold and into a passage. From a distance it looked like a solid wall, for the stone inside blended wholly with the stone on the outside wall. At last, they passed through a pair of tall, arched doors that groaned of many years with little use as they moved them.

They entered into a glad green courtyard bathed in the golden light of the late afternoon sun. Tall white statues of fair maidens and strong warriors stood at the openings of flagstone paths that wound their way through a maze of blossoming hedges. Vines with tiny pink, purple, and blue flowers clung to the stonework, benches, statues, and walls, filling the courtyard with sweet smells and a feeling of safety.

"I'd forgotten about this place," Kaliam said. "This courtyard brings peace to a troubled mind! I do not recognize the shrubs or the flowers that grow here now, but I would wager they have some curative potency. We best not let Sir Oswyn know of this place, or he may dig up all the plants to discover their secrets!"

Lady Merewen laughed. She led Kaliam along one of the green avenues until they came to a small fountain where many of the paths met. The water trickled happily down its three tiers, and its music joined that of the songbirds and the whispering wind.

For a long while, they sat on a stone bench near the fountain. "Now, tell me what troubles you."

Kaliam inhaled deeply and began. "I brought Fury to the King . . . and the news of Aelic's strange disappearance."

"Mallik told me what happened," Lady Merewen said. "Do you think Aelic still lives? Could he have gone to the Mirror Realm?"

"I do not know. But if he has, his twin, Sir Aidan, will come back to The Realm! If this is so, I would like to know when and where he will appear." Kaliam sighed and rubbed his temples.

They sat and listened to the trickle from the fountain for a long time. At last, Kaliam said, "We are living in a time when legends come to life. First, the Wyrm Lord is freed. Then, the Seven Sleepers are called from their long slumber. And now, I learn that the three ancient heroes are real as well!"

"Who are they?" Merewen asked. "How will we know them?"

"My very questions to King Eliam," the Sentinel explained, again rubbing his temples. "The King put his mighty hand on my shoulder, looked me in the eye, and said, 'Kaliam, a time will come when all in The Realm will know the identity of the Three Witnesses, for a Herald will proclaim their arrival. So it is written in the Scroll of Prophecy.'"

"The Scroll of Prophecy?"

"Yes." Kaliam smiled. "At last we gain the answer to one riddle. We know now that the Scroll of Prophecy is what was hidden at the core of the Ancient One. That is why Paragor destroyed that great tree. And now, he has the Scroll in his possession."

"But why would he want it?"

"The Scroll of Prophecy is an ancient document. It came into existence at the beginning of all things when King Eliam saw the future of The Realm roll out like a blanket before him. He saw events that might later come to pass—if the beings of this world were noble and chose to keep peace. But it also showed what could come to pass if evil arose and The Realm became divided. The prophecy spells out two destinies for us all. With such knowledge, Paragor could bring about the destruction of Alleble."

The sun slipped below the roofline, and the golden light was gone. Now gray shadow hung over the courtyard.

"Can we not stop him?" Lady Merewen asked.

"The Three Witnesses can," Kaliam said. "But until they arrive, there is much we must do."

"I do not understand."

"King Eliam revealed to me that he has called another young champion from the Mirror Realm. He is to be the Twelfth Knight on a journey into King's Forest."

"King's Forest?" Lady Merewen echoed. "Why?"

"This was another riddle, but not the last," said Kaliam. "In the heart of King's Forest, there lives an ancient scribe who served the King long before Alleble came to be."

"But that would make him—"

"Ancient beyond count," Kaliam said, finishing her sentence. "He is the only remaining Glimpse who can properly translate the Scroll of Prophecy. If Paragor knows of the scribe, and I fear that he does, he will seek him. The future of all things depends on who gets to the scribe first."

"Alas, I have delayed you with my questions!" Lady Merewen cried, rising to her feet. "You must prepare the team!"

"Nay, m'lady," Kaliam said. He took her hands in his and brought her to sit again at his side. "We cannot depart for King's Forest until the warrior from the Mirror Realm arrives. Your questions have helped to clear my muddled mind. In the days to come, I will have much need of your sage advice."

"What do you mean, my lord?" she asked.

"The final riddle," Kaliam replied. "But by King Eliam's request, I cannot share it with anyone."

Lady Merewen looked up. Her teary eyes flashed blue. Kaliam put a hand gently under her chin.

They were interrupted by the slamming of the doors, heavy, frantic footfalls, and then a voice. "Lord Kaliam, Lady Merewen, are you here?!"

And suddenly, Elspeth appeared from one of the paths. She was out of breath, but that did not stop her from talking. "I thought I might find you here," she began. "You must come to Guard's Keep right away! Our messenger brings distressing word from the Blue Mountain Provinces: Paragor has Ludgeon under siege!"

A Visitor from The Thread

Wide awake, Aidan tossed and turned in his hotel room bed. He stared at the soft glow underneath the curtain from the outside lights and listened to the hum of the air conditioner. *I'm never going to get to sleep!* he thought. He turned onto his other side and lifted his head a little. *Mom and Dad don't seem to be having any trouble sleeping.*

Aidan tried to see the little alarm clock radio on the bedside table, but it faced his parents' bed. It cast a red light upon his mother's face. Aidan felt a chill and looked away.

He shimmied down under the sheets and pulled the bedspread over his head. The day sure hadn't turned out the way he had hoped. He had wasted most of his time with Robby. And Robby's father had ruined the rest. *Lord Rucifel.* Aidan sighed. *My best friend's father is Paragor's chief warlord—or at least, his Glimpse is. How am I supposed to fight that?*

Things hadn't gone very well with his mother either. When the airport shuttle dropped her off at the motel, she'd practically smothered them both in kisses. That was okay. But later that evening, when

Aidan's father had brought up the subject of King Eliam and the reality of another world, well . . . that was when things had gone sour.

"Everyone grieves in different ways," Aidan's mom had said as she slammed shut her suitcase. "And I know losing your father has been hard on you. But, the truth is, you were right to dismiss Grampin's crazy ideas in the first place. The Realm, Alleble, King Eliam—it's all the creation of some writer somewhere. You said it yourself . . . it's a fairy tale."

Aidan winced. His father gritted his teeth. "I was wrong," he said sullenly.

"No, you weren't. You were thinking clearly. You saw that Grampin's mind was starting to go, and—"

"You think my dad was senile?" he asked. Aidan's father pulled an old book from his suitcase and held it up like evidence. "He started writing about King Eliam and The Realm in this diary when he was in his thirties!"

That was when they had sent Aidan to fill the ice bucket and get some sodas from the machine at the end of the hall. By the time he returned, the discussion had ended, and an icy quiet had descended on the hotel room.

Aidan shuffled around in bed, trying to get comfortable. But it was no good. He got out of bed and went over to the ice bucket. The sodas were gone. Aidan frowned and stood deep in thought in the darkness. Then, he tiptoed over to his father's side of the bed.

"Dad?" he whispered. "Dad, can I walk down to the machine and get a soda?"

"Huh?" his father mumbled. He rose slowly on an elbow and glanced across the sleeping form of his wife to the clock. "A soda? It's eleven thirty."

"I know, but I can't sleep, and I'm thirsty."

"I guess," Mr. Thomas replied. "Take the room key, and hurry back. And don't get anything with caffeine in it. Then you really won't be able to sleep."

⟨❧~

The night air was cool. Maryland was like that in September—hot like summer during the day, but cool like fall at night. Except for the occasional whoosh of cars on the interstate, it was very quiet. Aidan trotted along the walkway. He passed hotel room doors on his left and caught luminous, wavering glimpses of the hotel's pool on his right.

He stepped up to the soda machine and fumbled through the change in his pocket for five quarters. One at a time, he dropped them in and then scanned for a caffeine-free selection. *Looks like ginger ale for me,* Aidan thought, and pushed the button. As he reached for his drink he heard behind him a sound like a heavy curtain flapping in the wind. Aidan spun around, glancing toward the blue-green glow of the pool. There was no one there. No breeze either.

Aidan shrugged, uncapped his drink, and took a long sip. A warm breeze washed over him that made chills tiptoe up and down his spine. Then from the pool area came what sounded like a whip cracking. Aidan jumped, dropped his soda, and turned toward the sound. A pale figure stood very still but shimmered as the pool's undulating surface reflected waves of light over its body. Aidan stepped barefoot into the grass, making his way toward the pale figure. It was a tall girl with long, golden hair. She was dressed in silver armor. Her skin was pale like ivory, and her eyes were luminous blue like the pool.

"Gwenne!" Aidan shouted, and he ran to her. "Gwenne! What are you—how are you . . . I can't believe it!" They embraced for a moment and each had tears in their eyes when they parted.

"Sir Aidan," Gwenne said at last with that crooked smile of hers. "It seems you were right."

Aidan looked at her strangely. "What do you mean?"

"Before you left The Realm that night, you said to me, 'See you soon!' And by the favor of our King, here we are."

"Gwenne," Aidan said. "I've had visions, dreams about you. You looked frightened. And Antoinette—your twin—I fear she is in trouble!"

"And so we both are," Gwenne replied, "in very grave danger. I have been in your world for just a short time, but I have been constantly assailed by the enemy."

"Here?" Aidan exclaimed.

"Yes, Aidan," Gwenne replied. "Did you think that only servants of Alleble could travel to the Mirror Realm? I've come by what is called The Thread. It is the last remaining link between your world and mine, and the path the visions travel. But it is traveled by all Glimpse-kind, and within it I was waylaid by those not true to the King. Aidan, it is the way you will return to The Realm."

Aidan was stunned. "I'm going back?"

"Yes. I was sent to tell you it is the King's will that you return to The Realm. But I also bring warning: Be wary of all you meet— in this world and in mine. Not everyone is who they appear to be."

Aidan frowned. He felt strangely like he did the first time he met Gwenne—like everything she said was a riddle.

"What task does the King have for me?"

"I do not know, Aidan," she said. "But the King has told me you will return on The Thread, and that The Thread has grown unstable—stretched near to its breaking point. Traveling The Thread has become a dangerous journey."

There came a sudden, alarming sound like the crackle of electricity, and a strange warm breeze blew from somewhere behind Gwenne. And as if a bright light was slowly losing power, Gwenne began to fade.

"Gwenne, what's happening to you?" Aidan cried. He reached for her, touched her skin, and a shock went up his arm. He immediately jerked his hand back.

"I am being drawn back to The Thread!" Gwenne cried.

"What?" Aidan blurted out. The breeze vanished, and suddenly Gwenne was completely there again. Her hands were trembling.

"Aidan," she whispered. "Take my hands." Aidan reached for Gwenne. This time her skin did not shock him. She felt warm.

"Gwenne," Aidan asked, "what was that?"

"The Thread," she replied, glancing nervously over her shoulder as if something might be creeping up behind her. "I thought for a moment that the enemy had found me and was pulling me back. I do not understand how The Thread works, so I do not know how much longer I can remain."

At that moment three things happened simultaneously: someone called Aidan from behind, the warm wind kicked up even stronger than before, and there was a loud snapping sound like a large branch had been broken.

Aidan felt a painful quiver in his hands. It began to burn. Gwenne's pale skin dimmed and she began to fade. "Aidan!" she shouted. "You must let me go!"

Aidan felt as if he held a white-hot piece of iron, and all the muscles in his arms began to convulse. Still he held on. He felt if he let go, he would lose his friend forever.

"Aidan!" Gwenne's voice echoed as if she were in another place. "Aidan, let go!"

There was a bright flash, a sound like thunder, and Aidan flew backward up into the air. He landed unconscious in the pool and sank like a stone.

"Aidan! Aidan!" He heard a female voice, but it was not Gwenne's. Aidan opened his eyes, saw a blurry night sky and then a face.

"Mom?" Aidan whispered. He stared at her. She was soaking wet. Then Aidan realized he too was drenched. "Mom?"

"Oh, Aidan!" His mother hugged him. She began to sob, and her whole body shook. "I thought I lost you. You went under so fast."

There was a warm hand suddenly on his shoulder. "When Mom pulled you out," Aidan's father said, "you weren't breathing."

Aidan sat up abruptly, and his mother slowly released him. He was in the grass about ten feet from the pool. But for the life of him, he couldn't remember how he got there, or how he got wet for that matter.

"Who was that?" Mr. Thomas asked. And then, it all came flooding back. Gwenne . . . The Thread.

Aidan grabbed his mother's shoulders. "Mom! Did you see her? Did you see Gwenne?!"

Mrs. Thomas shook her head and burst into fresh tears. "I don't know what I saw, Aidan! I . . . it can't be real." Her voice became a choked whisper.

❦

By the time Aidan got out of the warm shower and dressed, his father was already fast asleep. His mom was still awake, her back toward him, apparently reading. Aidan shimmied down into his bed once again. He looked across the room at his mom, and she turned away. But she hadn't turned fast enough to keep Aidan from seeing she was reading *The Story*, and open in her lap was Grampin's diary.

THE KEEPER OF POWER

Aidan and his father sat in the car outside the woods near Robby's house.

"I should be getting to the office, Aidan," said Mr. Thomas. "I called the Martins, and they said they'd be happy to have you come over if Robby doesn't show, or . . . if something goes wrong."

"The Martins?" Aidan objected. "My old babysitters? Dad, I don't need a babysitter—"

"But you might need somewhere to go," Mr. Thomas argued. ". . . Maybe I should just stay."

"Dad, I'll be all right. It's just Robby."

"I know, but what if his father shows up? If he's directly in the service of Paragor like his Glimpse, Rucifel . . ."

"Then I'll call you on the cell," Aidan said as he grabbed his backpack and got out of the little orange car. He leaned in the window and smiled bravely at his father. "Besides, if Mr. Pierson showed up and got dangerous, I'd lose him on the trails. I know the woods around our fort like the back of my hand."

"Son, I'm worried about you," he said. "The more I've read of Grampin's diary, the more I understand the evil we are up against.

I don't trust Robby's father—not by a long shot. It's too much of a coincidence that he shows up now. And if Robby's Glimpse already serves Paragor, how can you be sure you can even trust Robby?"

"I can't be sure," Aidan said. "But I'm not alone."

Aidan's father had never seen his fourteen-year-old in this light before.

"Never alone," Mr. Thomas said. Aidan smiled as he turned and walked away. "Never alone," he repeated as he watched his son hike up the gravel road and disappear into the dark, whispering trees.

Aidan easily found the fort. He and Robby had built it between four towering pine trees in the heart of the woods. Assembled from an odd assortment of planks, two-by-fours, and sheets of plywood, the fort was as ugly as it could be, but to Aidan and Robby it had been *Castle Courage*, the home of truth, justice, bravery—and the largest assortment of comic books and hand-held video games known to mankind!

Aidan stood there for a few moments, letting the memories wash over him. Then he stepped over a few fallen trees, ducked under a low bough, and slid a small square of plywood away from the entrance. *No sign of Robby.* Aidan carefully laid his backpack on the fort floor and then walked around to the backside. There a shaky ladder stood, leading to the roof of the fort. Aidan climbed to the roof and tested his weight on the old boards. They held. *It's ugly, but it's strong.*

He brushed away some leaves, stretched out on his back, and stared at the treetops. Aidan watched a single leaf sail on a breeze and then spiral down. He began to feel drowsy.

"You fall asleep, Aidan?" Robby asked as he climbed onto the fort's roof.

Startled, Aidan sat bolt upright. "Yeah," Aidan said. "I wasn't sure if you would make it. How'd you get away from your dad?"

"Aw, he doesn't much care what I do," Robby replied, looking into the woods. He gestured into the fort. Aidan followed his friend inside.

Sitting opposite Aidan, Robby fished out a lantern and flicked it on.

"The fort feels smaller than I remembered it," Aidan said.

"Maybe because you're bigger," Robby said. He laughed nervously. "You takin' vitamins or somethin'? I'd swear you've grown since the beginning of the summer."

"My mom says the same thing," Aidan replied.

An uncomfortable silence settled upon them. Robby began to rock a little, and the lantern cast strange shadows on the fort wall behind him.

Aidan couldn't stand the waiting. He was alone with his best friend at last, and he wasn't about to waste the opportunity. "I brought the Scrolls with me if you want to look at them again."

Robby sighed. "No, Aidan. I don't think I want to look at those again. I know that story very well already."

It seemed to Aidan that the air inside the fort became chill. The shadows behind Robby seemed to grow. At last Robby said, "Aidan, there's something I've been meaning to tell you."

There was, in the way that he said it, a tone that made Aidan wish he had sat closer to the fort's door. Aidan turned to his friend, and there was suddenly an eerie confidence about Robby that hadn't been there just moments ago. "What is it, Robby?"

Robby took a deep breath. "The night you left for Colorado," he began, "I waited until Mama and Jill went to sleep, and I took off."

"You what?"

"I left—ran away, or at least I meant to. Kinda stupid, really. I didn't even pack anything. I walked outta my house with a jean jacket on my back and about fifteen dollars in my wallet. But I didn't care what happened. I just wanted to get away, so I left."

"Why'd you do that?" Aidan asked.

"I don't know," Robby replied. "I was mad, I guess. Mad that you had to move. Mad that my life never felt good for long. Mad at everything." He laughed. "I ran all the way up that old path near the school. You remember the one where we found all those bottles that one time? Well, I stood there in the middle of the night and just went off on the bottles. I smashed 'em with rocks, hurled them at tree trunks—all the while, screaming like some kind of loony!"

Aidan stared.

"And you know what, Aidan?" Robby asked, an eerie gleam in his eyes. "It felt good to bust up the bottles. Like I was getting back at every bad thing that ever happened to me. I got so charged up, I ran up to the bleachers behind the middle school and just lay there staring up at the stars. And for once, I felt like I was in control of things. That's when I heard the voice."

Voice? Aidan thought.

Robby explained. "I was thinking about you, about my dad, about all those things I wished would have never happened. And then this voice was just kinda there all of a sudden. *'You do not have to be afraid, ever again,'* it said. And I sat up on the bleachers fast. 'Who's there?!' I yelled, but no one answered. There wasn't anyone around.

"I was about ready to bolt, but then I heard it again. It was like bein' broadcast into my head. *'I will teach you to control your fears,'* it said. *'I will teach you many things.'*

"I said, 'Who are you?'

"*'In time. For now, you need know only this . . . I am the Keeper of Power. In my hand I hold your future. If you choose, I will make you a champion, a leader, a conqueror. So that you may know that what I say is true, I will provide you three guarantees. The first in one week's time.'*

"And then, Aidan, the voice was gone. I sprinted back home like my heels were on fire. But one week later, my soccer team won the regional championship. We beat the team from Ashburn, the one that hadn't lost in three years. And I scored the winning goal! Aidan, it was like the voice promised—the first guarantee." Aidan frowned.

"I know, I was skeptical at first. But the second guarantee came right after that . . . my dad came back home. It was not luck. It was not coincidence. Dad knew all about the voice. He knew all about the Keeper of Power. You see, Aidan, I know about The Realm. My dad taught me all about it. And now, I've seen it, in my dreams. I know why you wanted me to read those scrolls of yours. But the thing is, Aidan, you're on the wrong side."

When Light and Dark Collide

Robby's comment blindsided Aidan. "What?" he blurted out.

"It's what you said in some of your emails," Robby explained. "You said you side with Alleble and serve King Eliam. But King Eliam betrayed his people—even his most trusted friends, Aidan."

Aidan couldn't believe what he had just heard. "No, Robby, that's not true. King Eliam is noble and good. Paragor is The Betrayer!"

"That's the story you've been told, is it, Aidan?" Robby asked. "There are two sides to every story. See, the voice promised me a third guarantee. C'mon outside. There's someone I'd like you to meet." Robby rose to a crouch and exited the fort.

Aidan emerged from the fort and found it strangely dark outside. Turbulent clouds raced overhead and the towering pines swayed in an unusually cold breeze. From the shadows of nearby trees strode a tall warrior. He was Glimpse-kind and wore the dark blue cape and bright silver armor of Alleble. He had no beard but had long gray hair laced with strands of black and a mustache that curled straight down to his jaw line.

The warrior presented Robby with a long broadsword. "A gift from the master," he said. His voice was rich, almost musical. "Better, would you not say, than the one you have been training with?"

To Aidan's amazement, Robby took the broadsword with both hands and carved a figure eight in the air. "Dad told me I'd be getting my own sword soon," Robby said. "I just didn't think it would be today."

"Do you like it?" the warrior asked.

"It's not as heavy as the trainer," Robby answered. "But tell the master I love it!"

"You shall tell him yourself soon enough," said the warrior, and then he turned and bowed to Aidan.

"Aidan, I'd like you to meet Count Eogan. He is a former ambassador from the Kingdom of Alleble. He's going to tell you the real story about Paragor."

The Glimpse knight extended a pale hand. Aidan looked him in the eye, saw a glint of blue, and warily shook his hand. "Well-met, Sir Aidan," the count said. "Ah, yes . . . I know your name well. Robby has told me all about you. But even had he not, I would have known you for your exploits in Mithegard and upon the Black Crescent."

Aidan stiffened. Couched within the compliment, Aidan felt a veiled accusation.

"This must all be rather startling to you—learning that what you thought was truth . . . was not the whole story—very troubling, I'm sure," said Count Eogan.

Aidan was troubled, but not in the way that the count thought. He glanced at Robby and then back at Count Eogan. "You *used* to be an ambassador from Alleble?" Aidan asked.

Count Eogan tilted his head, smiled, and nodded yes.

Aidan squinted at the count. He wore the armor and colors of Alleble, and his eyes glinted blue, proving his devotion to King

Eliam, but something seemed wrong. Gwenne's warning came back to Aidan, and he asked, "Do you serve Paragor now?"

"Nay, lad," the count replied without hesitation. "I am true to Alleble and to King Eliam—only Alleble as it was intended to be and King Eliam as he once was. For that, even Paragor himself yearns."

"Count Eogan, you don't know what you're talking about," Aidan said abruptly.

"Well, that is for you to decide," Count Eogan said. "But think on this, lad. You read The Scrolls of Alleble, the account of the Great Betrayal, did you not?"

Aidan nodded yes.

"When you entered The Realm, the Glimpses who befriended you did seem to corroborate the tale? Of course they did. But did you ever consider the possibility that they have all been deceived? What if they only believe those stories because that is all they have been fed since the day of their births?" Aidan was silent.

"Come, lads," Count Eogan said, holding out both arms. "Come and sit with me a moment and hear the story in full."

They sat upon two fallen trees spaced a few feet apart. Count Eogan and Robby on one tree, Aidan on the other. The Glimpse adjusted his sword and took in a deep breath. "The tale you have no doubt heard," he began, "is that King Eliam was a noble ruler, fair in all his ways. Paragor was a trusted knight, the Sentinel even, who became corrupted by lust for gold and power and sought to overthrow his kindly sovereign. Was that not what you have been taught?"

Aidan nodded slowly. The count smiled. "I tell you today that things went much differently. You see, it was King Eliam who became corrupt—not Paragor. Paragor was Sentinel of Alleble. And he was wise, powerful, and fair to behold. Soon, dignitaries, ambassadors, even the famed Elder Guard began to seek Paragor's advice instead of the King's. All of this, the King simply could not bear.

"One night, King Eliam gathered those whom he felt he could

still trust. He inflamed them with talk of mutiny and treason. He sent twelve soldiers to slay Paragor while he slept. Then he had the Elder Guard and their families rounded up in the middle of the night and made ready to execute them. But Paragor was far too skilled to be caught in that kind of ambush. He slew his attackers and fled to Guard's Keep. That was when Paragor made the hardest decision of his life. He loved King Eliam but could not bear to watch the innocent die. Paragor fought King Eliam along the parapets. Their duel was the fiercest in the history of The Realm. But in the end, Paragor was the better swordsman. He slew the King.

"In a rage, the treasonous soldiers who served King Eliam set fire to the fountain, which was filled with oil, and watched all of the Elder Guard and their families die. To Paragor's dismay, no one survived," the count said, leaning closer to Aidan.

Aidan looked puzzled, but the count continued: "That very night, Paragor discovered that King Eliam had taken to Black Arts, a sorcery so powerful that it could even bring back the dead. By those Black Arts, King Eliam returned and banished Paragor and those in Alleble who would not blindly follow the King's rule." Count Eogan leaned even closer to Aidan and spoke softly, like a mortiwraith charming its prey. "You see, Aidan, from that time on, the Glimpses of Alleble learned only the King's version of the story. They believe that King Eliam is noble while Paragor is the traitor. Their faith is genuine, but . . . it is genuinely wrong."

The wind picked up and made strange whispering sounds in the pine needles above. Aidan looked up into the sky, and his eyes were glistening. Then he shut his eyes tight and bowed his head. *This could not be true. King Eliam would not deceive his people. But still, if he had . . . I would never know. And Count Eogan's eyes, they . . . THE EYES!* Then he remembered. *Acsriot.*

Slowly Aidan rose to his feet, glaring at the count. "No one survived?" Aidan said.

The count stood and faced Aidan.

"Give it up, lad," Count Eogan said, all humor gone from his voice. "That is the true story of the Betrayal. You may not like it, but do not throw your life away for a lie."

Aidan's eyes were determined. "Your story would be hard to refute, if, as you say, King Eliam made sure there was no one left in Alleble who witnessed the events of that night. But there was someone else who was there. Your master did not tell you of the 'little runt' who got away, did he?"

"That . . . that is preposterous. All of the Elder Guard and their families died in the fire," the count said.

"Valithor escaped," Aidan said. "He saw Paragor's soldiers round up his mother and father and lead them to the fountain filled with oil. He saw Paragor execute King Eliam in cold blood. And he saw the Elder Guard and their families burned alive by Paragor's command."

Robby's mouth hung agape and he moved ever so slightly away from Count Eogan. "Do not believe this rubbish, Robby," Count Eogan said. "This is more of King Eliam's sorcery at work. Aidan, you do not know of what you speak. Valithor was the King's closest ally. Why would you even consider trusting his story?"

"Captain Valithor was the Glimpse of my grandfather," Aidan said, advancing another step. "But even if I did not have a trusted firsthand account of the events of that evening, even then I could expose you for the liar you are."

"I will not stand for this insolence," Count Eogan barked, and he drew a jagged blade from his sheath. "Aidan, you have clearly chosen your path in life. For this, I pity you!"

Aidan eyed the count's sword and took a step back, but he would not be silent. "You have called King Eliam, his greatest servants, and my grandfather evil. And you have put Paragor upon a white pedestal and made him into some noble hero. Robby, listen to me, and Count Eogan, refute me if you can: If your master is so good and noble, his deeds would match, wouldn't they?

"I saw Paragor's armies unleash a deadly attack on Mithegard, a kingdom that had done nothing to provoke warfare. I watched his forces rain poison-tipped arrows down on innocent Glimpse men, women, and children as they sought shelter from the skies. I watched as Lord Rucifel ordered his knights to plunder that city and then burn it to the ground."

"Robby, this upstart is more bewitched than I feared. There will be no turning him. Aidan is the enemy, and he must be . . . dealt with."

Count Eogan let his cape fall to the ground and strode forward. He raised his blade and whispered something in a language Aidan had never heard. Suddenly, the count's sword burst into flame and he slashed it at Aidan's right side. Aidan dodged it easily and maintained his distance from his foe.

Robby stood near the fort. His eyes were restless and he seemed to debate within himself. "Stop," he said quietly, but then yelled, "Stop! Don't hurt him!"

"Nonsense, Robby," the count replied, continuing to stalk Aidan. "You know the first *Principle of Power*: You have to take what you want! Your so-called friend stands in your way."

The count slashed again, a short, measured attack at Aidan's feet. Aidan leaped and then fell backward. Fire lingered briefly on his shoe and pant leg. Aidan stomped at it until it went out.

"Oh yes, young knight," the count said, sneering. "The flames are hungry! Beware of them." Count Eogan pushed the fiery tip of his sword into the boughs of a nearby pine. Instantly, gray smoke sifted out from the center of the tree. A few licks of fire poked out and began to climb. Fire quickly engulfed the trunk—spreading to the fort's roof. Aidan scrambled backward and leaped to his feet, barely ducking a vicious swipe meant for his head.

"Stop now!" Robby yelled. He raised the sword Count Eogan had given him. But the count did not stop. He slashed the flaming sword blade at Aidan's neck, missed, and sheared off a huge bough from one of the pines. Fire leaped to that tree as well. The clearing began to fill with smoke and the smell of burning pine.

Aidan ducked and dodged, always keeping the trees between himself and his attacker, but he was tiring. And the count's sword-craft was strong. There was no way he could elude his strokes for much longer. The flaming blade swept again overhead and then crushed a stump near Aidan's shoulder. Aidan stumbled, turned to run, but then found himself backed up against the burning fort. Count Eogan's thin lips turned upward in a ghoulish smile. "Now," he said, sneering, "you will burn for the offenses that you have brought against the master."

From behind Aidan there came a strange sound. Several loud snaps as if from a bullwhip. A gust of wind washed over Aidan, and the flames on the count's sword went out.

Aidan felt a strange pulling sensation envelop his body, like a strong undertow in the ocean. And then, Aidan's skin began to tingle. It felt like something prickly was crawling down his forearms. Aidan stood very still, feeling the pulling and prickling all over his body. And when Aidan looked down at his arms and hands, they began to fade. *It's happening! I'm being pulled to The Thread!*

Count Eogan knew what was happening to Aidan, and he knew that he had just moments before Aidan would be gone. He drove his long blade straight for Aidan's chest. But Robby swept through with his own broadsword and smashed Count Eogan's blade with such force, and from such an unexpected angle, it wrenched free from his hands and slammed to the ground. The count looked at Robby with utter malice. He drew two daggers from his belt and came at Robby.

But Robby was too fast and too strong. He dropped to one knee and carved a two-handed stroke across Count Eogan's midsection.

The count stopped suddenly, dropped the daggers, and clutched his ruined stomach. Blood poured out between his pale fingers, and he fell to the dirt.

Robby cast his blade down and turned to Aidan. But Aidan was barely there. A strange, wavering version of Aidan's voice said, "Robby, I knew you'd come through!"

Robby reached for his friend.

"Wait! Don't touch me!" Aidan yelled urgently. "You'll get shocked."

Robby pulled back his hand. "Aidan, what's happening to you?"

Aidan smiled. "I'm going back!"

"To The Realm?" Robby asked. "Now?" Aidan nodded yes.

"But Aidan, you can't leave now!" Robby looked back at the prone form of Count Eogan and then down at his own hands. "Aidan, don't go. I'm afraid."

"I'm being drawn in!" Aidan said. "I . . . it's not the same as the first time. I don't think I could stop if I tried. But Robby, do you understand what I've been trying to tell you? Seek King Eliam! Seek him now, Robby!"

"I don't know, Aidan," Robby said miserably. "I . . . I can't. The master promised me so many things. He brought my dad back. I don't know!"

Aidan faded out almost entirely for a moment, and Robby could see the fire continuing to spread. It burned in several places, climbing up the pines, crawling hungrily from tree to tree. The smell of smoke was thick and hot in the air. The fires crackled and hissed. Then Aidan was there again. His lips moved, but at first Robby couldn't tell what he was saying. ". . . your father," Aidan said. "Rucifel. Robby!"

And suddenly, there was a blinding flash and a sharp crack of thunder. Robby fell backward and covered his eyes. When he looked up, Aidan was gone.

Hot air surged over Robby. He stood up. Robby knew if he didn't go soon, he would never leave. "Where are you?!" Robby screamed, watching the flames dance among the pine trees. How had everything, once again, gone wrong? Tears streamed down his face as he whispered, "You said I'd never have to be afraid. You said you'd make me powerful."

From somewhere overhead there came a tremendous crack, and a huge burning limb fell on top of the fort's roof. Robby jolted, spun around, and finally recognized the danger. He started to run, but something made him look back. The plywood square that covered the fort's entrance had fallen off. There, just barely visible, was Aidan's backpack.

Robby ran to the fort, grabbed the backpack, and charged through the pines to safety.

THE THREAD

Aidan found himself standing upon a gray stone path that stretched away into forever in a vast sea of black. It was the connection between earth and The Realm, what Glimpses called The Thread. *Grampin was right,* Aidan thought, and he smiled. *I am going back to Alleble!*

Even as he walked along the path, however, he was haunted by Gwenne's voice: *"Be wary of all you meet—in this world and in mine. Not everyone is who they appear to be."*

Aidan quickened his pace as the black all around him began to flicker and images came into focus. An enormous castle appeared. Among its many turrets, keeps, and balconies rose a nine-tiered tower. There were two enormous twin mountains behind the castle. Aidan knew it well. It was the Castle of Alleble. But the view changed and zoomed in on the side of one of the mountains. From a dizzying height, a great shelf of stone had come loose. It began to slide down the mountainside toward the city. There was a great cloud of snow and debris. When it cleared, the vision had changed.

As if from above, Aidan saw two figures walking across a white wasteland. One of the figures began to run. The vision zoomed in on the other. And though there was a strange haze over all things, Aidan could see that the figure was a young woman with flaming red hair. *Antoinette!* She looked up as if in answer, but then a monstrous shadow rose behind her. She turned to face it, but then the vision changed.

Aidan saw a vast canopy of beautiful wide crimson leaves. Beneath the adorning leaves were huge black limbs and long trunks. And at the foot of the trees there traveled a band of knights in dark armor. The vision sped ahead to a new location. It was a clearing where a tree of surpassing greatness had been felled. The bulk of the tree lay charred, stretching out of sight. At the end of it was a vast stump. In the center of the stump there was a small hollow. And from this hollow a sapling grew. Speared by the limbs of the sapling was a scrap of parchment.

Aidan had seen this vision before. It seemed important, and the vision did not fade. It lingered so close to Aidan that he felt he could venture just a few steps from the path and touch it. But Aidan remembered what happened the first time he left the path. He had entered The Realm, but far from his intended destination. That mistake had caused him to endure a very dark adventure.

But something about this felt different. Aidan felt a strange gravity drawing him toward the scene. It was not the feeling of dread that had driven him from the path the first time. No, this felt more like the gentle urgings of an unseen father.

A rush of noise flooded to Aidan's consciousness. It was like the conversations of great crowds of people, buzzing, loud, unintelligible. But then one voice rose out of the chaos, and the others were silenced. This voice was calm, assured, peaceful. A brightness like the light from a tunnel appeared on the path ahead. Aidan shielded his eyes. It was a being in brilliant white clothing, his countenance too intense to behold.

"Seek what is lost."

"My King?" Aidan asked.

King Eliam nodded and reached out. Something lay in his outstretched arms.

"Fury!" Aidan smiled and took his sword from the King.

"My servant, the time draws near. Seek what is lost. Go, now."

Aidan looked at the scrap of parchment hanging on the end of the sapling. He looked down at The Thread. Aidan swallowed, tightened his grip on Fury, and then leaped from the path.

The vision parted like a curtain and Aidan fell into darkness.

KALIAM'S CHARGE

Wahat size is the force that assails the Blue Mountains?" Kaliam asked Sir Brannock.

The young scout, turned and looked at all the somber faces of those seated at the table in Guard's Keep: King Ravelle of Mithegard, Lord Sternhilt of Acacia, Queen Illaria of Yewland, as well as the heroes of Alleble: Farix, Nock, Lady Merewen, Thrivenbard, Rogan, and Mallik. And they all waited anxiously for Brannock's answer, especially Mallik.

Sir Brannock swallowed and said, "Two legions were brought through the air, transported in great carriages dangling from the largest dragons I have ever seen. They arrived first. By the time I had to flee or perish, there were easily a full six legions more on the ground."

"Eight legions?!" Mallik exclaimed. "That is twice what we faced in Yewland!"

"What of the Seven Sleepers and the Wyrm Lord?" Queen Illaria asked.

"They were not abroad," Sir Brannock replied. "At least they were not when I fled."

"Nay, they would not be unleashed this soon," Kaliam replied. "This attack is a feint of the enemy. He wishes to measure our strength, to draw us out early."

"A feint?" Mallik blurted out. "Eight legions is a feint?"

"Perhaps it is more," King Ravelle said, and all eyes turned to him. "Certainly, the enemy wishes to know how we will respond, both in numbers and in tactics. But could it be that he has guessed our plans to fortify Alleble's battlements with the hard blue granite from Ludgeon?"

"Then he goes to war in the Blue Mountains, not to cripple King Brower . . . ," Mallik began.

". . . but to cripple us," Farix whispered.

"Even were this thrust of Paragor's not aimed at weakening our defenses here," Kaliam began, "we would go to King Brower's aid. They are our allies of old. But how should we respond?"

Mallik pounded his fist on the table. "Swiftly!" he grunted. "With numbers far greater than the enemy's!"

"But what if Kaliam is right?" Queen Illaria asked. "What if Paragor means only to draw us out away from Alleble, so that he can bring his full forces against a depleted city?"

"That may well be his plan," said King Ravelle. "Paragory, now swollen with troops from Frostland, Inferness, and Candleforge, hordes a fighting force of at least ten times what he spends now in the Blue Mountains. If he brought that group, the Wyrm Lord, and the Sleepers to bear upon Alleble in our absence, it could go ill."

"What of our scouts at the Cold River?" Farix asked.

"There has been no report of Paragor moving beyond that border," Kaliam explained. "It would seem that his grand attack is yet many days away. Still, can we take such a chance?"

"Every choice made in war is a chance, Kaliam!" thundered the deep voice of Sir Rogan. Then he bowed and lowered his voice. "Forgive me, my Sentinel, it is just that King Brower and the

Glimpses of Ludgeon wait for help. And yet, here we sit. We must act, or the fate that befell Mithegard will happen again."

Kaliam turned to his right. "Farix, how many dragon riders have we gathered in Alleble to date?"

Farix calculated a moment while staring into one of the chamber's torches. "Counting those brought today by Queen Illaria and the Braves of Yewland, we could muster ten legions airborne."

"Good!" Sir Rogan nodded heartily. "Then I say we set forth to King Brower's aid at once! Empty Alleble of every dragon rider ready for battle!"

"And leave Alleble with no winged defense? Rogan, that is taking a huge risk," Kaliam said.

"He's right," Queen Illaria said. "To allow Paragor's dragons to roam the skies over Alleble unchecked is madness."

"I do not see that we have a choice," Sir Rogan replied. "Paragor's attack on the Blue Mountains continues as we speak. The longer we delay, the greater Paragor's chances of cutting off our ability to fortify the walls. We must go by air! Let us swoop down upon his forces and sweep them away like a storm!" Mallik roared in agreement.

"But what if that is what Paragor wants?" Nock asked. "What if Alleble's scouts at the Cold River fail, and the enemy launches a full-scale attack?"

"Then let him come!" Rogan said. "Alleble is not some tiny village made of thatch! And even with the dragon riders gone, this city is not defenseless! Look who will be waiting. The archers of Yewland, the mounted cavalry of Mithegard, the swordsmen of Acacia—the walls will be manned by such an alliance of hearty warriors that even with the Wyrm Lord, Paragor will find an assault upon Alleble very costly."

Sir Rogan paused and glared at everyone in the chamber. His eyes were afire with pride, and his confidence began to spread.

Seeing the nods and smiles of his comrades, Sir Rogan went on. "If we bring such a lightning attack upon Paragor's troops in the Blue Mountains, we will win quickly. And then, with King Brower's doughty folk as reinforcements, we will return swiftly to Alleble. If Paragor is here, then . . . we will come upon his flank and smash him against the walls of the city like a hammer to an anvil!"

Many of those assembled cheered and slammed fists upon the table. But Queen Illaria said, "Kaliam, I agree with Sir Rogan in one aspect, at least. We must take action now."

"This decision is fraught with peril. Whatever course I choose, lives will be lost," Kaliam said. "But after hearing such prudent counsel, I agree that we must act swiftly and with overwhelming force. I say we saddle every last dragon and leave for the Blue Mountains before the sun sets! If this be a test to measure our strength and our resolve, then let us pass it mightily!"

THE BATTLE OF THE
BLUE MOUNTAINS

What about this one, Mallik?" asked Nock from the post of a nearby dragon pen.

Mallik looked at the dragon and raised his eyebrows. "That is Splinter—a nasty one, she is. I tried to saddle her, but she knocked me aside like swatting a fly. I say we leave her."

Nock took a closer look. The dragon sleeping within the pen appeared black or dark gray in the moonlight. She was large and muscular; her wings stretched lazily at her side. Nock noticed the four ivory-white spikes protruding from her tail, and six more from the bony ridge on the back of her head. *So that is why you are called Splinter.*

"Kaliam said every dragon in Alleble was to be saddled," Nock called to his friend.

"Then you do it!" Mallik yelled. "I will be content with this dragon here. Butterwing, yes, now that sounds like a dragon for me!"

"You see, my rigid friend . . . ," Nock said, opening the pen. The dragon stirred slightly, but did not open its eyes. "There is an art to saddling a raw dragon. You cannot break them in with the same method you use to break rocks with your hammer!"

Nock laughed and put the saddle down inside the pen. He walked slowly up to the creature, and still it did not seem to awaken. "You must show them respect," Nock continued as he slowly approached the creature. "Show them tenderness." Nock brushed his hand along the creature's neck. This earned Nock an ominous low growl.

"Easy, Splinter," Nock said, slowly letting his fingers tickle close to her folded ears. "You see, Mallik, all you have to do—"

Suddenly, Splinter's right foreleg unfolded, and the dragon backhanded Nock so hard that he flew out of the pen and landed with a crash ten feet away. The saddle, torn in two pieces, landed with a *WHUMP* beside the fallen archer. Splinter snorted and went back to sleep.

"Nock!" Mallik yelled, racing to his friend's side. "Are you all right?"

"Uh . . . ," Nock said, steadying himself. "Nothing is broken, if that is what you mean."

"Well, I would not say that nothing is broken!" Mallik laughed, holding up the two jagged pieces of the saddle.

"You were right," Nock said, finally getting to his feet. "We need to leave Splinter behind."

"I will seek another steed!" Mallik said, patting his friend lightly on the back. "I think maybe you should take Butterwing."

Although the glow of dawn already shimmered in the east, the stars still peeked out. Swarming about were the combined dragon riders from Alleble, Yewland, Acacia, and Mithegard. The ten legions of winged beasts swept low to the ground across the hilly terrain just south of their destination.

Queen Illaria led their airborne attack, for there was no one who better understood battle tactics in the air. With her flew Baldergrim, Trenna Swiftfoot, Nock, Farix, Mallik, Sir Oswyn, Sir Rogan, King Ravelle, and Lord Sternhilt. The others remained in Alleble with Kaliam to plan the defense of the city should the enemy attack while the riders were away.

The Blue Mountains, nestled in great climbing forests, loomed ahead. Nock readied his bow and rehearsed their battle plan in his mind. It was time.

The riders split into two teams at the base of Pennath Rugar, the first of the Blue Mountains. Queen Illaria led half the riders around the base to the left. Nock led his team around the base to the right. They continued to stay as low as they could, and the treetops swayed as so many creatures whooshed by overhead.

Nock gasped as he rounded the base and caught sight of Ludgeon, the capital city of the Blue Mountain Provinces. The walls, great angled panels of stone, were not broken, but within those walls, the city burned.

Paragor's forces had placed dozens of catapults outside the many sections of the city walls. The fiery enemy projectiles arced through the night sky and fell unchecked among the inns and cottages.

And worse still, huge, broad-winged dragons brought immense carriages full of Paragor Knights and dropped them on the other side of the city's walls. Mallik had told Nock that in the event of an attack, most of the women and children of Ludgeon would have found refuge in the great caverns of Pennath Hastor, the stony mount behind the city. But still, Nock wondered how many might not have gotten to safety in time. He urged his steed forward and she responded.

Great waves of dragons glided in on both sides of the enemy's ranks. Paragor's forces had no warning.

Led by Nock, the first wave of dragons dove down into the masses of troops nearest the city walls. They grabbed enemy knights, plucking them off the ground or right out of their saddles. And then the dragons rose to great heights and let their cargo fall, screaming back to the ground where they smashed into their comrades.

The large, broad-winged dragons of the enemy were groomed to carry heavy burdens over great distances, but being weighed down with troop-filled carriages made them terribly slow. When Queen Illaria's team of smaller, swifter dragons came after them, they could not escape. Her long black hair trailing behind her like a scarf, Trenna drove her steed beneath one of the huge transport dragons. She kicked her legs against her dragon's flanks, and it responded with a burst of flaming breath. The fire streaked out and melted the cable beneath the transport dragon, and its cargo—a carriage full of fifty knights—plummeted to the ground far below. It practically exploded on impact, sending pieces of debris scattering in all directions.

Farix flew high above the transport beasts and then dove down. He pressed his heel against his dragon's left side, telling it to extend one leg. His dragon responded and trailed its razor-sharp talons across the leathery membrane of the enemy dragon's wings. The shredded flesh could not maintain lift, and the great beast spiraled out of control, slamming into the ground.

Nock put Blackwood shafts into the eyes of several other massive dragons and sent them to their destruction far below. Again and again, Paragor's troop transports fell from the sky until there were none. The enemy's ground forces scattered when the onslaught began, but most rallied around the catapults. They seemed intent on burning Ludgeon to the ground at all costs. Mallik, who preferred to fight on foot, brought his dragon to a hilltop above the catapult nearest the city walls.

"Watch my back!" Mallik yelled to his dragon steed as he leaped out of the saddle. He raced over the crest of the hill and gathered speed down the slope toward the catapult. His hammer crashed into the enemy, sending them flying backward. One of them landed in the basket of a catapult just as it was released. The Paragor Knight flew high into the night sky and disappeared over the city walls.

Other enemy soldiers raised their swords and charged at Mallik. Usually, strength in numbers can overwhelm an opponent, but not Mallik. Mallik's blunt weapon shattered their swords to splinters, crumpled and imploded their plate armor, and smashed their bones. In great bunches the enemy fell until Mallik was left all alone with the catapult. He spun around, looking for opponents, but they had all been slain. Then Mallik noticed a tarped wagon parked near the catapult. Beneath the tarp were dozens of barrels. *I know what those are!* Mallik thought. And then he had an idea.

Mallik pushed with all his might on the back wheels of the catapult until it turned away from the city and out toward the legions of the enemy. Then he grabbed one of the barrels from the wagon, and with the flammable oil sloshing inside, he waddled over and dropped the barrel in the basket of the catapult. He grabbed a torch, lit the fuse on the barrel, and released the catapult's trigger.

The flaming projectile soared into the sky and came down in the center of one of the enemy's legions. It exploded with a blinding flash. Hundreds of Paragor's soldiers fell immediately. Still more were mowed down by the heat wave from the explosion.

Mallik roared, "This is my city! Go back to your dark hole while you can!"

But in his clever designs to use the catapult against the enemy, Mallik had laid down his hammer. He turned to get it, and found it in the hands of one of the biggest Paragor Knights he had ever seen. This giant towered over Mallik and wore black plate armor on his chest, but none on his huge shoulders or arms. He wore no helmet either, and his big eyes flashed red and widened with delight. He looked down at the hammer as if he had just found a new toy. Then he stared at Mallik and grinned.

A full squad of enemy knights, no less than twenty-five, came up behind the gigantic captain. They quickly spread out and encircled their weaponless prey.

Mallik found himself alone at the base of the hill, surrounded by the enemy. He berated himself for leaving his hammer unattended, and he wondered what his dragon had been doing while the enemy sneaked up behind him. "Never trust a wyrm," Mallik grumbled, and then he felt a sudden, urgent need to duck. He dropped to the ground and covered his head with his hands. Not a second later, he heard the swoosh of dragon wings, followed by many wet-snapping sounds. It almost sounded like someone sloshing through a puddle of mud, all the while snapping branches as he went—the only difference was that the sound came from above.

"Try not to lose your weapon next time, hammer-meister!" came the deep voice of Sir Rogan.

Mallik stood just in time to see his axe-wielding friend fly off. Mallik then watched as one by one the enemy soldiers who had surrounded him swayed and fell headless to the ground like toppled dominoes.

"That is most unsavory!" Mallik exclaimed. He grabbed up his hammer and turned to leave. But from the other side of the hill came the calls of angry voices and the pounding of iron-shod feet—the sound of a great charge. He turned and saw Paragor Knights racing over the hill like a swarm of ants.

Mallik glanced at the wagon, then back at the enemy. Then he grinned. "Come on!" he yelled, swinging his hammer in wide arcs. "Come and have a taste of the hard stone of the Blue Mountains!"

But Mallik did not use his hammer against this onslaught. With the Paragor Knights just fifty yards away, Mallik grabbed a torch and lit the fuse of one of the barrels in the wagon. Then he ran with all the speed he could muster.

He sprinted along the bank of a small stream, glancing back just in time to see the enemy reach the base of the mountain where he had stood only moments ago. Then, he tripped and fell into a drainage culvert.

Seconds later, a sound like thunder shook the valley. Harsh orange light flashed, and a searing wave of heat overcame every living thing within a hundred yards of the wagon.

The dragon force from Alleble that had been diving into the enemy ranks below relented their attack at the sound of the explosion. Sir Oswyn saw the flash from across the battlefield, and raced off to see what had occurred. He found a burned-out hollow and, within, the charred frame of a catapult and the blackened remains of numerous soldiers. Sir Oswyn hadn't seen destruction like this since witnessing the aftermath of the Wyrm Lord's attack on Clarion. He looked up at Ludgeon's walls, wondering what weapon the Glimpses of the Blue Mountains might have that could cause such devastation.

He brought his dragon steed to land and began to search for answers. Most of his findings were burned beyond recognition, but at last he found a half ring of charred wooden slats connected loosely to a thin iron band.

Of course! Sir Oswyn thought. *This is not a weapon of the Blue Mountain folk!* He leaped upon his dragon and went for a closer look at one of the other catapults. It was just as he suspected. The Paragor Knights kept their barrels of oil very close to their catapults. And that gave Oswyn an idea. An idea, he thought, that might end the battle far quicker than they might ever have hoped.

He wheeled his dragon steed about and searched the skies for the leaders of their teams of dragons. He found Queen Illaria and many of the Yewland Braves first because their white dragons were easy to spot. He flew close to each of them and told them of his plans. And in turn, they each responded, "Clear the skies? Are you mad, Sir Oswyn?"

"Trust me," was all he could say in reply.

Oswyn drove his dragon till he thought it might simply fall out of the sky from exhaustion. Back and forth across the sky he went until he was convinced that he had connected with enough of the leaders to get their forces out of the air.

He flew to a hilltop to watch, and behold, it did seem that the skies were clearing. The Paragor Knights cheered and created an intolerable clamor. They thought their ferocity had driven Alleble's forces away. They had no idea what was about to occur.

Finally, Oswyn spotted Nock, so he drove his dragon steed to intercept him.

"Hail, archer extraordinaire!" Oswyn sang out as he steered his dragon as close as he could to Nock's. "I see that Butterwing has put up with you so far!"

"You laugh in ignorance!" Nock yelled back. "She has bore me well into more victories than I can count!"

"Make haste then and follow me," Oswyn yelled. "And you shall triple your victories!" Oswyn pointed to the enemy catapults, many of which were still bombarding the interior of Ludgeon with fiery projectiles. Then he explained his plan to Nock.

Oswyn reined his dragon steed and was about to take flight. He turned to Nock and warned, "You will have to be swift and your shot sure, for I do not have enough for a second try."

"I will not miss," Nock said with one eyebrow raised.

Oswyn took off and raced his dragon steed toward one of the catapults. The Paragor Knights saw his approach and unleashed a barrage of arrows. One bounced off his shoulder armor. Another stuck in his saddlebag. Ducking and dodging, Os steered his dragon through the storm, for he had to get close for his plan to succeed.

At last he was within range of one of the catapults and their supply wagons. Oswyn reached down to one of the saddlebags and removed a long corked tube. He yanked the cork out with his teeth and began to pour out a fine white powder. It drifted down on the air like a fine mist as Oswyn encircled the barrel-filled wagon below several times. The enemy archers finally chased Os away, but he kept pouring the white powder out as he flew from one catapult to the next.

"Fly, beast!" he yelled, and he spurred his dragon. He needed the creature's top speed. He had used up five tubes of the powder when he came finally to the last catapult. He looked back at his work; the white powder hung in the air, crisscrossing the battlefield like a spider's web. He just hoped that Nock was able to get in range and fire quickly enough.

Nock had gummed an arrow with a substance that would burn and not go out, even when fired with the great force of a Blackwood bow. He saw the target, a white cloud floating down toward one of the tarped wagons. "Go, Butterwing!" he cried, and then Nock was aloft. He drove his dragon toward a fire burning in the midst of the battlefield. Then he leaned over precariously in the saddle and thrust the point of the arrow into the fire as they flew just above it. "Please, King Eliam, let it light!"

The arrow came out of the fire smoldering, but not alight. Frantically, Nock pulled it up to examine it. It smoked and sputtered. Nock wasn't sure why it didn't kindle to a flame. But he was out of time. He fitted the arrow to the string, aimed at the falling white cloud of powder, and let the smoldering arrow fly. Then he wheeled his dragon about and raced away.

The arrow sliced through the air, and the air fed the arrow, which ignited in full flame just before entering the white cloud of falling powder.

Sir Oswyn's fire powder erupted in a swirling inferno around the tarped wagon. The barrels of volatile oil exploded immediately, incinerating the enemy knights who stood near. Instantly the catapult became a charred black skeleton of what it once was. And so began what the Glimpses of the Blue Mountains described as the greatest fireworks display in the history of The Realm.

Fire streaked overhead this way and that, punctuated every few seconds by deafening blasts as the wagons full of oil barrels ignited and went off. Heat washed over the dragon forces of Alleble as they watched from a safe distance upon the foothills of Pennath Rugar.

"I would say we passed Paragor's test!" Sir Rogan said, slapping Oswyn on the back. Cheers erupted, but one voice was not among them.

"Where is Mallik?" Nock asked.

TO SEEK WHAT
IS LOST

Aidan lay on his back in a huge pile of crimson leaves. He opened his eyes and looked up drowsily at the towering black trunks surrounding him. Aidan blinked and sat up as if waking from a dream. *I'm back in The Realm!* he thought.

Adrenaline surging, he grabbed Fury and leaped to his feet.

Aidan remembered King Eliam's command: *"Seek what is lost."*

He turned in a circle, trying to get his bearings. He knew he was in the forest he had seen in his vision—for never had he seen such a forest before. But where the monumental fallen tree was, he had no idea.

A light breeze stirred the leaves and brought with it the faint scent of smoke. *Fire!* Aidan thought. *The great tree was burned!*

Aidan wet his fingers, felt for the wind, and sprinted off in the direction he thought he should go. It was uneven ground. Huge twisted roots snaked in and out of his path, and leaves guarded hidden pits. Aidan discovered right away that sneakers were not the best footgear for this terrain!

Still, he trudged on, the smell of smoke growing as he went. At last he came to an opening that appeared to be a tunnel made of living trees. Long, smooth black trunks and massive boughs reached overhead on both sides of the passage.

Aidan plunged into the passage, unafraid of the darkness but still wary. He kept Fury high and his other hand out to the side, feeling from trunk to trunk as he blindly made his way. The smell of fire was almost overpowering, but moments later he emerged on the other side of the passage into a vast clearing where a grand tree lay sadly in the center. It was the tree in the vision.

Aidan ran to the wide stump. Growing up from the hollow center was a sapling with tiny oval leaves of red. Pierced through by the top limbs of the sapling curled a small scrap of parchment. He clambered up on top of the stump and grabbed the parchment. He was about to jump down from the stump when he heard deep voices, and not far off! *Soldiers!* Aidan had to leave immediately, but then he spotted the sapling.

Aidan had the sudden urge to take the sapling, even though he was quite sure its roots went far down into the stump. He pulled the sapling, and to his surprise it came free as if it had leaped into Aidan's hand. Aidan smiled and climbed back down from the stump. With Fury in one hand, the parchment and the sapling in the other, he turned to run for the tunnel. Too late. The soldiers were entering the other side of the clearing. They would see him if Aidan went for the tunnel. Instead, Aidan raced into the woods and ducked behind a wide trunk. Peeking around it, he could just see the soldiers.

"Here it is," said the soldiers' leader, who bore a crooked sword.

"About time," said another. "I do not much like being so close to those bowhawkers!"

"Nor do I, Galdoth!" said the first. "They'd fill us full of shafts, like as not, for what we have done. But the master says go back to the Blackwood, so we go."

"Right, Drang! Obedient to a fault, we are!" Galdoth replied.

"Never thought I would see the day when Knights of the First Rank would be turned into errand boys. First Kearn and then Paragor himself."

"Yes," said a third enemy knight, a short, stout soldier who stepped away from the rest. He carried a long, barbed spear and looked warily into the woods. "But we do not even know what we are supposed to get this time." Aidan ducked down, feeling like this knight was looking straight at him.

"Just between us, Blarrak," said Drang, "I do not think even the master knows. 'Go and find the great tree,' he says. 'We may have missed something.' So here we are."

Blarrak laughed, and it sounded like he coughed up something in the process. "You could have at least asked him what we should look for!"

"And have my head knocked off my shoulders, like poor Miggot?" Drang replied. "Now look alive. Search the clearing, especially around the big tree. If you find anything, come tell me right away!"

Aidan watched as the soldiers spread out. He counted eighteen knights—all wearing full armor and bearing weapons. They kept their eyes down, scouring the ground. The one with the spear, called Blarrak, tromped over close to the edge of the clearing where Aidan was hiding. He stood there scanning the quiet woods. Aidan's heart raced. He felt sure he could handle this enemy, but if he let out a yelp, the rest would come. Eighteen against one, and Aidan with no armor . . . not very good odds.

Aidan shifted a tiny bit, and a twig snapped. He froze. Blarrak looked immediately into the woods.

"Here now! I found something!" called one of the knights who stood near the stump. To Aidan's great relief, Blarrak turned and ran over to join the others. Aidan watched intently as they all surrounded the base of the fallen tree.

"Footprints?!" said one.

"Yeah, but what kind?" asked another.

"Certainly not shod in boots," said Drang. "Probably one of the archers." The knights looked warily up into the trees surrounding the clearing as if enemies might be perched all around.

"Print looks recent," Galdoth said. "We had better get to the dragons."

"But we have not found anything!" Drang exclaimed. "Look here. The prints are on the stump. Plainly he was looking in that hole in the center there. Get up and take a look yourself."

Galdoth hoisted himself up onto the stump. He edged closer to the hollow in the center and looked nervously as if he feared a snake might spring out. "I cannot see anything in there."

"Well, reach in and see!" said Drang.

"Not with my hand," Galdoth argued. And he pulled his sword from his sheath and slowly pushed it into the hole in the center of the stump. "There!" he said. "Nothing down there. My blade goes smoothly all the way to the bottom."

"Fine!" Drang said. "Get yourself down."

But Galdoth couldn't get his sword out of the stump. "It is stuck!" he said, yanking at the hilt. "Makes no sense at all!"

"Oh, you weakling!" Blarrak said. He leaped up with ease and walked over to the sword. He grinned as if he might pull the sword free with one hand. But he couldn't. He tried again to no avail. He tossed his spear to Drang and yanked at the sword with both hands. It didn't budge. Aidan thought this was uproariously funny, and it was all he could do to keep from bursting out laughing.

In turn and in groups, they all tried to dislodge the sword, but it would not come free. "Come on then, you slugs!" Drang said at last. "No use. Leave it! Galdoth, I guess you are glad you used your blade instead of your hand! We might just have to leave you here stuck in this cursed stump!" There was coarse laughter from everyone . . . except Galdoth.

"We have been here long enough," one of the knights said.

"But we have nothing to show for it," Blarrak said. "We must continue the search."

"No," Drang replied. "Can you not see? Whatever 'it' is was taken by another. A bowhawker more than likely. We cannot afford the time. Thanks to Kearn, we might already be too late."

"The big push?" Galdoth asked.

"What else?" Drang shook his head. "I shudder to think how it will look if the Black Breath has started already and we show up late and empty-handed."

"At least Kearn will not be disappointed," Galdoth said. "Now that we fetched that pretty sword for his flame-haired pet!" Aidan heard this and went stock-still.

"More like a guest, she is!" Blarrak laughed. "The way he put her up in the top chamber like that. Feeds her better victuals than what we get! I have no idea what he sees in her. Strange skin." He paused and made a face that would curdle milk. "So dark and . . . pink!"

"She bested him with the sword," Drang said. "I know. I was in Baen-Edge when it happened. I think Kearn finds that . . . attractive."

Antoinette! Aidan thought. *A flame-haired swordmaiden with pink skin? It has to be!*

"Maybe you are right, Galdoth!" Drang said wickedly. "Maybe Kearn will put in a good word to the master for us. Might save our heads too. Come on, men!" And with that, the eighteen Paragor Knights surged into the woods a little to Aidan's right.

Aidan watched them go. He stood up, his mind whirling. "What do I do? They have Antoinette locked away somewhere in Paragory!"

"Much has been lost," came the voice of King Eliam. *"Much must be found. I will be with you."*

Aidan tucked the parchment into one jacket pocket and the sapling carefully into the other. Then he tore off after the Paragor Knights without a clue as to what he would do when he caught up to them.

The Paragor Knights moved surprisingly fast on foot through the forest. Apparently they were used to the uneven terrain. Aidan tripped and staggered along behind the knights as best he could. Eventually, Aidan got the hang of it, and he began to gain on them. But his mind raced faster than his feet.

He needed to do something . . . and fast. If they left the forest and got to their dragons, they'd go airborne. He would never catch them then. There was really only one thing to do. After all, Galdoth was unarmed. All Aidan had to do was wait for the right opportunity.

He didn't have to wait long. Aidan saw the Paragor Knights round a bend in the forest path, and Galdoth—without a weapon— was last. Not far ahead of him was Blarrak. Aidan quietly sprinted up behind Galdoth, grabbed the collar of his armor, and rammed him headfirst into the nearest tree. Galdoth fell away limp.

Aidan turned just as Blarrak's barbed spear came stabbing for Aidan's midsection. Aidan rounded his back, and the spear stuck into the nearby tree, leaving Blarrak with little to defend himself . . . except the war horn that hung from his neck. As he reached for it, Aidan used both hands to thrust Fury at Blarrak's chest. Blarrak fell forward.

The battle had been brief, but it had cost Aidan precious minutes. If he couldn't catch them in time, all his efforts would be for nothing. Aidan looked at the two fallen warriors. Between the two of them, he thought, there ought to be enough armor that fit.

In King
Brower's Palace

Mist and smoke from burned-out fires drifted over the eerie quiet of the now still battlefield. Paragor's attack had been repelled, his forces overwhelmed by Alleble's response. It seemed at first to be a total victory against the enemy.

Nock flew low to the ground, searching the blackened wreckage. It was a grim task, looking for a friend among the dead. Still, Nock searched on. He had never known another Glimpse with as tough a hide as Sir Mallik. If anyone could survive such carnage, Mallik could.

So lost in thought was Nock as he flew over a thin veil of mist that he almost missed it. He pulled on his dragon steed's reins and circled back to the hilltop. The haze parted as the winged beast lighted on the ground. Nock leaped off and ran to the charred remains of another dragon . . . Mallik's.

The stench was overpowering, but Nock knelt down, staring at his friend's steed and thinking. The dragon had died in the fire— that much was clear. No shaft or spear had forced Mallik out of the sky. *Mallik always did prefer fighting on foot,* Nock reasoned. *But why did he come to this place?*

Nock found the answer at the bottom of the hill. There, blasted and burned, was the skeleton of a catapult. Scattered all around it were dozens of bodies, and, to Nock's disgust, not one of the bodies had a head.

This was a great puzzle indeed. For surely the dragon was the one Mallik rode from Alleble. And no doubt Mallik would wreck a catapult and take on its crew, but the dead there had not been smashed by Mallik's great hammer. *This is blade work,* Nock thought. *Or axe.*

A shadow glided across the ground, and a large green dragon landed next to the wrecked catapult. "This is the very spot where I last saw Mallik!" said Sir Rogan as he clambered out of his saddle. "Your eyes are sharp, archer!"

"Not as sharp as your axe," Nock replied. "Unless my eyes deceive me, this was your work."

"It was." Sir Rogan bowed and his long blond hair draped over his face for a moment. "Mallik was surrounded by the squad you see here—Paragor's finest, but I, uh . . . removed the threat."

Nock swallowed and adjusted the collar of his tunic on his neck. "Did you see where Mallik went after that?"

"Nay, I flew off and busied myself among the enemy," Sir Rogan replied. "But it was not long afterward, I heard the explosion that engulfed this place in fire."

Nock nodded. "Oswyn's fire powder."

"Again, nay," Sir Rogan said. "Our healer's lethal powder might have taken out the rest of the catapults, but not this one. The blast here was well before the others."

Nock looked again at the siege weapon's twisted frame. "So Mallik found a way to destroy the first," he said, thinking aloud. "Perhaps he threw a torch into one of their wagons. To linger here would have ended his life, so he must have fled. But then where did he go?"

Nock walked around the perimeter of the scene. His eyes came to rest on a little stream that carved a narrow way through the battlefield. He shook his head.

"We will find him," Sir Rogan said. "If Mallik's hide was thick enough to endure a strike from the Wyrm Lord, he would certainly survive this little blast. And besides, this is Mallik's country. I would not be the least bit surprised if he knew some secret passage. For all we know, he could already be in King Brower's hall toasting our victory!"

Nock smiled. "Your words hearten me," he said. "Maybe we should—" Without finishing his sentence, Nock was off and running.

"Wait! Where are you going?" Sir Rogan called after him.

Nock did not answer; he was headed for the stream. If Mallik was trying to escape a fiery blast, he might just seek refuge in the water. He ran along the edge, staring down into the stream. There were bodies—all enemy soldiers—but Nock saw no sign of his friend. Then he stumbled and almost fell into a ditch.

"Sir Rogan, come quickly!" Nock called. "I have found him!"

There in the bottom of the ditch lay Mallik. His beard and hair were singed and he was completely covered in black grime. Blood had trickled and dried on his forehead, and he lay very still.

Sir Rogan ran up, saw the hammer in the muddy water, and then, next to it, the massive body. "Oh, no," he whispered. "So he was caught in the blast." Sir Rogan yelled and slammed his axe to the ground.

Nock leaped down and went to Mallik. "Alas, my friend," Nock said, collapsing upon Mallik's chest. "I did not think we would part ways like this. We should have stood together upon the walls of Alleble, defying Paragor and his minions."

"We might yet," came a quiet voice. "If you would just get off of my chest so I can breathe!"

"Mallik?" Nock fell away.

Mallik's face contorted into a grin.

"Mallik! Praise to King Eliam! You live!"

Mallik coughed harshly and tried to sit up.

Rogan leaped down into the ditch. "You big ugly ogre!" he said, laughing and wiping his eyes. "How long were you going to let us believe you were dead?"

"Not long," Mallik said with a wink. "I must say it is comforting to know that you both care!"

The three of them howled with laughter.

Several hours later, after Mallik had been tended to, the leaders from Alleble met in the cavernous throne room of King Brower, the ruler of the Blue Mountain Provinces. Dark purple banners hung from the arched ceiling, and golden light rained in from a row of diamond-shaped windows on the east side of the room. Dozens of doughty Glimpse warriors stood like statues in perfect rows on either side. Each soldier's hands folded atop the haft of a hammer, mace, or axe. But if the Great Horns of Ludgeon sounded, the Stone Sentries—as they were called—would spring to life and defend the Blue Mountains with the ferocity of a sudden storm.

King Brower sat upon an uncomfortable-looking gray throne roughly hewn from a massive block of granite. He wore an assembly of plain leather and plate armor. He had no royal scepter, but a fearsome warhammer was slung on his back.

"I do not understand," whispered Nock to Mallik. "Why does a great king sit upon such an unremarkable throne?"

"King Brower could have a magnificent seat, it is true," Mallik replied quietly. "Hammer and chisel would sing at his command, but King Brower wishes to remember his place before the one true

King of this Realm. And so he chose not to have his throne made of blue granite."

"Which one of you is called Oswyn?" King Brower asked. His voice was deep and resonated in the cavern.

Sir Oswyn bowed and said, "I am he."

"Come nearer, Sir Oswyn," the king commanded, peeking out from underneath his thick white brows. His pale blue eyes were kindly but possessed the tranquillity of a snowcapped volcano.

Sir Oswyn stepped forward. "I am at your service, sire."

"Nay, Sir Oswyn," said the king. "It is I and the whole of the Blue Mountain Provinces who are at your service. We deem ourselves the friends of fire, for by it we forge and make metals do our bidding. But never have we seen fire do what you made it do."

King Brower stood and inclined his head. His mane of white hair flowed over his broad shoulders. His beard, forked into two simple braids, dangled for a moment and came to rest again upon his chest. Sir Oswyn noted that the only ornament upon the king was a large purple gem set in a silver necklace that rested on his chest.

King Brower smiled, noting Oswyn's gaze. "It is an amethyst," the king explained. "Mined by my own hand from the caverns at the bottom of Falon's Stair. I will see to it, clever knight, that you have such a stone before you depart this place."

Sir Oswyn bowed low again. "Thank you, Your Majesty."

King Brower nodded and then spoke to all of his visitors. "I see represented here many of our most dependable allies: Alleble, Yewland, Acacia, and the surviving remnant of Mithegard—our trading partner from the west. You came to us in our time of great need. Our walls might well have held against Paragor's thrust. But I fear the enemy would have been patient . . . content to burn us out. But tell me, how did you know to come? And how did you coordinate your forces so quickly in response?"

King Ravelle stepped forward. "The answer to both questions is the same," he said. "King Eliam the Everlasting has sent forth his messengers to the four corners of The Realm. All of the friends of Alleble were summoned to form a common army against Paragor's new threat. The messenger who traveled here returned to us with an account of your siege. It was Kaliam's decision to send this combined force to swiftly counter Paragor's strike."

Queen Illaria came forward and bowed. "Master of the Blue Mountains, Paragor's army has swelled beyond reckoning. Armies from the far west—Candleforge, Frostland, and Inferness—have taken on the black harness. King Eliam calls for your aid. Will you and your people come?"

"Even had you not rescued us today, bringing a net of fire to snare our common enemy . . . even then, we would come," declared King Brower, and his eyes glinted blue. "I will not forget the kindness Alleble has shown the Glimpses of the Blue Mountains through the long years. By King Eliam's hand the trade routes have stayed open and Ludgeon has prospered. By King Eliam's wisdom we were able to see that the enemy's offers of might and wealth were control and decay in disguise. And by King Eliam's promises we all have a hope beyond this life. In two days, every hammer, blade, and axe will come before the walls of Alleble and offer our service to the one true King!"

The Stone Sentries pounded the hafts of their weapons upon the room's floor. Others followed suit with their weapons. When the ruckus died down, Mallik approached the throne. "King Brower, the thunder of your hammer still booms!" he said, garnering instant approval from the other Blue Mountain Glimpses. "But Alleble needs more than just our hammers for this scrap. Paragor has new weapons at his disposal, perilous creatures, and a beast whose flame can melt stone!"

Anxious murmurs swept through the hall. Mallik went on. "Alleble's walls are stout, a match for most any attack. But for this foe, and for this battle, King Brower, Alleble needs new walls crafted by our hands. Walls built from the matchless blue granite of this land! King Eliam will need every hammer, yes, but before that, he needs our craft and our skill to rebuild the walls of Alleble to a might never before seen in The Realm!"

Mallik expected cheers and patriotic clamor, for he knew his people took great pride in their stonecraft. But instead, pained looks were exchanged and troubled expressions appeared. King Brower sat down hard on his throne.

At last, King Brower broke the brooding silence. "Alas, Mallik, kindred of this land, had you asked for anything else, I would have given it freely. But while Paragor's attack took away relatively few lives, he has yet robbed us. Now it becomes clear that was his plan all along. He had no intent to invade, capture, or conquer. No, Paragor knew that Alleble would need our help to fortify their defenses. Paragor's attack destroyed all of our wind-carriages and most of our stone-cutting tools. Mallik, we will come to fight for King Eliam, but it will be a year or more before we are able to build new walls."

BEYOND THE GATE
OF DESPAIR

Wearing the armor of Galdoth and the helmet of Blarrak, Aidan raced through the Blackwood after the other Paragor Knights. They were already mounting their dragon steeds when Aidan burst out of the forest. He stumbled and went over a sudden down slope and crashed with a yelp into the midst of the enemy. Blarrak's barbed spear clattered at the feet of Drang, the leader of the enemy expedition. Aidan quickly got to his feet and stood up, feeling as if every enemy knight could see right through his disguise.

"It is about time, Blarrak, you sloth!" Drang said, shoving the spear into Aidan's hand. "We were about to take flight without you! Aye, where is that slowcoach Galdoth?"

Aidan made his throat as rough as he could and spoke deeply. "The bowhawkers!" he yelled. "They shot Galdoth from behind!"

A murmur swept through the Paragor Knights. "Lads," said Drang as he leaped into his dragon's saddle, "I think it is time we bid Yewland a less-than-fond farewell. Blarrak, tether Galdoth's steed to your own. Make haste!"

Aidan waited a few nervous heartbeats as the other knights mounted up, for he didn't want to accidentally sit in the saddle of a dragon that wasn't his own. Even so, there were two dragons without riders: a long, narrow dragon the color of red clay, and an ugly, thick-limbed beast with a scarred gray hide. Aidan guessed. He figured Blarrak had been about as ugly as they came, so Aidan took the ugly dragon. He quickly lashed the reddish dragon's reins to his dragon's saddle harness.

Drang and the others spurred their dragons and took to the air. Aidan leaned forward in the saddle and pressed his knees into the creature's flanks. Blarrak's dragon sniffed at Aidan a few times, but Aidan gave the reins a swift snap, and the winged beast lifted off as well.

Aidan was relieved that he didn't have to steer his dragon very much. It simply followed the others. They climbed high into the evening sky. The sun soon was swallowed in the cold murk on the western horizon, and Aidan spent the long flight to Paragory in the dark . . . thinking.

He thought about his mother and Robby. They had both shown encouraging signs before Aidan left for The Realm. *But would they take the next step?* Aidan wondered. *Mom might because Dad'll get after her. But Robby, who would get after him? He had killed Count Eogan, a servant of Paragor. What would come of that?* Aidan shuddered.

Then Aidan's thoughts turned to Antoinette. *How had the enemy captured such a skilled swordmaiden? Antoinette would have fought her way out of—oh, no!* he thought. *What if she got caught trying to get to Robby's Glimpse? Then her capture would be . . . my fault.*

Aidan shook his head. Maybe it wasn't Antoinette who had been captured at all. But that didn't make sense. This Kearn, whoever he was, had someone from the Mirror Realm imprisoned. Drang's description made it almost a certainty that it was Antoinette. And King Eliam had directed him to attempt this rescue. As the hours sailed restlessly by, Aidan pondered these things.

Suddenly, the air whooshing around Aidan went icy cold. The great desolate expanse known as the Grimwalk lay below in bleak gray shadows. And the jagged mountains of Paragory came into view. But something was very different. The Prince's Crown was dotted and streaked with orange like a large piece of firewood, blackened but lit with smoldering embers. *Torches!* Aidan realized. *And they're moving.*

Aidan knew that meant an army, an army of unbelievable size. "Never alone," Aidan whispered. He reached behind his breastplate and touched the sapling hidden there. *What am I to do with you?* he wondered. But as Aidan removed his hand, the sapling caught on the rough Paragor armor. The newborn tree tumbled out. A rush of wind tossed it about in the air. Aidan tried to catch it, but all he could do was watch the sapling fall into the murky gray of the Grimwalk.

The dragon riders led by Drang spiraled downward and landed in half-frozen muck outside of two tall arched doors made of some ancient black metal. *The Gate of Despair!* Aidan shuddered, for he remembered the first time he had encountered that gate.

Drang sounded a large horn. Another horn answered from within, followed by a muffled boom, and the slow rumble of grinding metal. The two massive doors began to open, and from the thin fissure between the doors, harsh red light spilled out. Black smoke began to snake out near the tops of the doors. The knights around him covered their mouths and noses. Aidan followed their lead to avoid drawing attention, then steadied himself and issued a silent plea to King Eliam for strength.

As the opening widened, a wave of horror and revulsion washed over Aidan. He constricted his grip on the reins and fought off the violent churning heaves in his stomach. For an odor came forth from the gate. There was the sickly sweet smell of rot, the acrid stench of burning flesh, and something else—foulness beyond the smell of death and decay! It was as if someone had unearthed the bowels of The Realm where many dead things had been buried, and in so doing had released a river of sewage and gore.

Aidan gagged, but somehow managed to keep his stomach. He had to avoid drawing any unnecessary attention to himself.

"Come on, lads!" bellowed Drang. "Lord Kearn will be most anxious for our return!" The opening widened more, and the dragons ambled forward. As Aidan's dragon drew closer, Aidan shifted uncomfortably in his saddle.

Within the cavern there were hundreds of knights marching purposefully between uncountable racks of swords, barbed spears, wide double-bladed axes, wickedly serrated swords—and scythelike weapons Aidan had not seen before. These had a long wooden staff and at the end bore a long, curved, sicklelike blade.

Dozens of wooden towers stood dormant like silent giants along the sides of the cavern. Each one had wheels at its base, six armored compartments, and an adjustable platform at the top. Next to these Aidan saw row upon row of catapults and tarped wagons full of barrels—*These are the siege weapons used against Mithegard!*

The ceiling was smoky and filled with jagged stalactites. Hung among them were great chains of iron and odd-looking long cages filled with black dangling moss.

Paragor's Knights nodded or saluted as the soldiers passed. Drang stopped the caravan and leaned from his saddle to talk with a sentry. This knight raced off into one of the yawning tunnels that ran around all sides of the cavern. The dragon riders began to dismount, and the massive doors shut behind them with a thunderous boom.

Aidan released the reins and slowly looked up to one of the long cages hanging directly overhead, and for several agonizing moments, he could not focus on what he saw. Still staring at the basket, Aidan reeled and nearly fell out of his saddle. For dangling from the basket, with black rotting flesh barely clinging to it, was a skeletal arm.

Aidan staggered down from his saddle and landed with a sickening splatter. He refused to look down at his boots.

"Line up, you louts!" Drang hissed. "Lord Kearn is coming!"

The dragon riders quickly formed two rows of rigidly straight lines. Aidan joined them, barely breathing. From across the cavern, marching with confidence and purpose, strode a tall caped warrior. His hair was long and blond. He carried a massive wide sword in one hand, and in the other what looked like a book.

Aidan knew this warrior. "Robby's Glimpse," he whispered. The red glint in Kearn's eyes made Aidan cringe.

His menacing sword at his side, Kearn strode up to Drang. "What in The Realm took you so long?" he demanded in a very deep, commanding voice with no hint of Robby's tone or accent. "The Black Breath begins in an hour. We march in three!"

"Lord Kearn," Drang said with a bow. "We took the time as was necessary. Nothing more. Our errand, as you know, was for Paragor first."

Kearn closed in and held the blade of his weapon to Drang's neck. "Trifle me not with your priorities. I know them well enough. Paragor, no doubt, will wonder why you took so long as well. I am certain that he will have less patience for your excuses than I."

"B-but, Master Kearn," Drang said. "We have brought back what you asked for. That Baen-Edge miser Ebenezer drove a hard bargain, but ours was harder." Drang and the others laughed. Kearn sheathed his sword.

"Let me see it," Kearn commanded. "And you had better hope that you brought back the right one."

Drang turned to one of the other dragon riders, who handed him a bundle. Drang unwrapped it and handed a beautiful sword to Kearn. "You see, Lord Kearn," Drang said, pandering to his superior. "The seabird wings on the crossguard, just like you said. The runes, the spiraling banners on the ivory grip. It is the very blade!"

"I misjudged you, Drang. Yes, this is the one!" Kearn exulted. "You have done well, Drang. Very well."

"You going to taunt her with it, eh, Kearn?" Drang asked slyly.

"What else?" Kearn replied curtly. Drang's smile disappeared.

Aidan stared at the blade. *The Daughter of Light, Gwenne's sword. Would Antoinette have been given it to use in The Realm?* he wondered.

"You will no doubt be wanting your gold," Kearn said.

Drang shifted and looked back at the other knights. "If it is all the same to you, Lord Kearn, we would like half of the gold we agreed on."

"Half?" Kearn raised an eyebrow.

Drang swallowed. "Well, sir, we went to the old tree like Paragor commanded, but there was nothing else there. So, uh . . . we had hoped that you might put in a word on our behalf . . . to the master, that is."

Kearn laughed. "You mean you want me to excuse you from Paragor's rage for your failure to complete his mission?"

"Well, sir, it is in both our best interests," Drang replied. "Our side errand to fetch the sword might have been the reason we missed whatever was at the old tree."

"Why, you conniving little wretch!" Kearn hissed. "Dare you threaten to blame your incompetence on me? I ought to feed you all to the firstborn!" Kearn pointed his sword to the dark hollow in the back of the cavern.

"No, please!" Drang pleaded. "I did not mean it as a threat! We would not tell Paragor at first that you sent us on an errand without his leave. It is just that, well . . . the master is very wise—and persuasive! Sooner or later he would dig the truth from us—unless someone he trusts gives him a reason he will believe."

Kearn lowered the sword. "Very well," he said. "I will clear your name before Paragor, and you will get one quarter of the promised gold!"

"One quarter?" Drang exclaimed.

"Silence!" Kearn commanded. "Be content that I give you any gold at all."

And with that, Kearn turned to leave. Aidan frowned. He had wanted to follow Kearn, hoping that if Antoinette was nearby Kearn would lead him to her. Now Kearn was headed to see Paragor. Aidan had no desire to sneak into the lair of Alleble's most powerful enemy.

"Oh, one more thing, Drang," Kearn called out, turning and walking back. "You took a team of eighteen. And yet I count only seventeen who return."

"It is Galdoth you miss, sir," Drang replied. "Great lummox lost his weapon—got it stuck in the stump of the old tree, he did. He and Blarrak fell behind after a turn, and then the bowhawkers came upon them! Slew Galdoth with their cursed shafts! Blarrak just barely escaped. Hearing the news, we mounted up and flew home at all speed."

Kearn strolled over and stood in front of Aidan. "Is this so, Blarrak?" Kearn asked, his voice clipped and tight. "You were nearly slain by the Yewland Braves?"

Aidan nodded. He was thankful for the close-fitting helmet, for it hid his face. Kearn might not recognize Aidan personally, but they all would certainly recognize that Aidan was not Glimpse-kind.

"They missed you?" Kearn said, nodding in an exaggerated fashion. "I find that very interesting. The Braves of Yewland do not often miss."

Aidan knew he had to say something. Once again, he lowered his voice and tried to speak in the manner of the enemy. "Galdoth fell behind me, black shaft buried deep in his back. I escaped around a bend and tumbled down the hill before they could hit me!"

"I suppose that is possible," Kearn said. "The archers would have been on the run, firing at a running target. Perhaps when you fell, their fire went awry. But there is something more troubling to me."

Aidan swallowed.

"You see, our scouts reported that Queen Illaria and her kin had sought refuge within the walls of Alleble. There should not be even a single brave left in that part of The Realm."

Aidan felt like his blood had turned to ice water. He had no idea what to say.

"No, you were not pursued by Yewland's Braves, were you, Blarrak?" Kearn said, his eyes glinting red. "A convenient story—but not especially intelligent. I know what you did."

TWISTED PATHS

Aidan gripped Blarrak's barbed spear so tightly that his knuckles cracked. His other hand drifted slowly to the hilt of Fury. His stomach was tied in knots.

"I guess your game all too easily," Kearn continued. "You never liked Galdoth much, did you? And this was a perfect opportunity to do something about it. You had Galdoth unarmed, at your mercy. With him out of the way, more gold for all of you. Greedy scoundrels!"

"We did no such thing," Drang said. "Though it is true none of us liked Galdoth very much . . . we did not do him in. We found many prints near the old tree. The bowhawkers left a company of braves behind . . . or maybe more. Perhaps Queen Illaria sent back a company to search the old tree."

Kearn stared at Aidan, and then backed slowly away. "Say what you wish," Kearn said at last. "But with a few creative twists of my own, I can use your lame excuse for a story to persuade Paragor to spare your miserable hides." And with that, Kearn turned and walked swiftly out of the main cavern.

Aidan sighed. Kearn had been far too close for comfort. But in those moments while Kearn had been so close, Aidan had seen the book he carried. He was almost certain it was Antoinette's *Book of Alleble. She must be here,* he thought.

Drang and the other dragon riders headed to a dining hall through a descending tunnel on the left of the cavern. Aidan hung back. At the first bend in the tunnel, he left them and ran back to the horrific cavern just inside the Gate of Despair.

The activity level in the cavern had increased markedly: Dragons were being saddled; the catapults and wagons were being wheeled out; and soldiers were arming themselves at the racks of weapons.

Drang had said that Kearn kept his pet in one of the towers. Trying not to be conspicuous, Aidan began making his way around the perimeter to the back of the cavern, searching for an opening that led upward. The first two clearly went down. The next one had a very tall arched entrance. The path beyond went neither up nor down, but rather straight in.

While he pondered where to go next, a strange warm breeze wafted out from the depths of the passage. *Could the tunnel open up somewhere else, perhaps even outside?* Aidan placed his hand on his sword's handle, and warily made his way into the tunnel.

The passage was lit with torches, but the light was weak and flickered with the breeze. The terrain continued to be flat, though here and there Aidan's boots crunched down on something brittle that snapped or splattered in small dark pools. "Oh, man!" Aidan exclaimed when he turned a corner. The odor was far stronger here. "If I survive this, I won't be able to smell anything for a month!" he said as he made a feeble attempt to bury his nose and mouth in the crook of his elbow.

Aidan pressed on, until at last he came to a place where the path widened into a large room. Though the light from the torches was almost useless here, he could see about a half-dozen barred cells on either side of the passage. Beyond the cells, Aidan noted that the path split. The fork to the left was very narrow and looked to slope upward. The fork to the right had an enormous jagged appearance, but Aidan could not see well enough to tell what direction the other path took.

Aidan approached the first cell cautiously. It turned out to be empty. Just a small stool and an old tunic, tattered and stained. The next two cells were empty as well.

"Please, no!" came a raspy voice from behind. Aidan spun around and saw a pale withered arm flailing from a cell across the room. "Leave us be!"

"What?" Aidan exclaimed. "What did you say?"

Suddenly, a pale face appeared between the bars. It was a Glimpse with a long white beard and sunken eyes. "Please do not take me!" he said, and his eyes glinted green.

"I'm not taking you anywhere!" Aidan explained, realizing there were other cells nearby and all were filled with prisoners.

"Let us starve!" said the prisoner. "But please do not take us to—" He never finished the sentence, for there was a sudden noise from the other side of the room. Soldiers were coming. Their torches lit the way ahead of them, and they appeared from one branch of the path that Aidan hadn't realized was forked. Aidan barely made it to a pocket of shadows near where he had come in.

"How many?" asked one of the Paragor Knights, gesturing to the cells.

"All of them," replied another.

"All of them?" asked the first. "Are you sure?"

"There is no mistake," replied the other. "By order of the master: The firstborn must be given all, for he has much work to do."

The first knight turned to his men. "Open the cells. Get the lot of them!"

Aidan watched as systematically the Paragor Knights went from cell to cell, dragging out the frail Glimpses from each one. The prisoners shrieked and scratched, but they were far too weak to offer much resistance. Soon all the cells were empty, and the Paragor Knights rushed off with their captives down the fork.

Though he knew he probably shouldn't, Aidan left his hiding place and followed them.

MEMENTO

Antoinette sat in the center of her shadowy cell. The gray light from her small window wasn't much, but it gave her enough light to fiddle with her ring. *He called this a riddle ring,* she remembered, thinking of the craftsman in Edge who had given it to her. *More than meets the eye, he said.* She could see the dozens of interlocking gold and silver bands, but she couldn't find the point where they unwound.

She looked again at the keyhole on the shackles that held her ankle chains to the cell floor. More determined than ever, she went back to tugging at the ring. *If I could just get this . . .* she gritted her teeth and twisted the blue onyx. Suddenly there was an audible click. The onyx came loose, and a silver band of metal sprang free.

"Yes!" she exclaimed, but before she could unravel the rest of the ring, she heard footsteps in the hall. The chamber door swung inward and Kearn appeared. Antoinette hid the ring behind her.

He entered the chamber without a word and placed a long bundle upon the stool near the corner. Then he turned and looked at Antoinette. There was something strange about his demeanor. He did not bear his usual confident sneer. He stood with his head slightly downcast and his shoulders hunched. His hair was unkempt and his cloak was draped unevenly on his shoulders. Kearn looked worn out, withered, defeated.

"Kearn?" Antoinette whispered gently.

"I have just come from speaking with my master," Kearn said almost inaudibly. "The attack in Ludgeon is under way. We begin the march to Alleble in two hours' time. In a few days our forces will be arrayed before the walls of your city . . ."

"But?" Keeping the ring behind her, Antoinette stood to see Kearn's eyes. Kearn looked past her to the window.

"You will be left here under heavy guard until after King Eliam has fallen and Alleble is secure. Then you will be summoned." Kearn's voice trailed off again, and he turned away.

"He plans to kill me, doesn't he?" Antoinette asked him.

Kearn did not turn around. "Turn you or kill you. Yes, that is his plan."

"I will never turn to him," Antoinette said. "I follow King Eliam and none other."

Kearn spun around and, with anger burning in his eyes, flew to the bars of Antoinette's cell. "Then you will die, you willful, stubborn wretch! Do you not see how futile your allegiance is? The power is ours now!"

"I already told you." Antoinette stretched her chains to their limit and stood face-to-face with Kearn at the bars. "Power is not all there is!"

Kearn grumbled and flung his hands in the air. "Wake up, Antoinette! Power is the way of things. It is mirrored in nature—predators and prey. The strong devour the weak. The strong take from the weak! And I for one would rather be doing the taking!"

"That is because . . . ," Antoinette whispered, talking more to herself than to Kearn as her ideas crystallized. "Of course. You covet power because . . . because you're afraid."

"Me? Afraid?" Kearn laughed scornfully. "Pray tell then, what does Kearn, the left hand of Paragor, fear?"

"You said it yourself, just now," Antoinette said. "You're afraid if you don't have the power, if you don't do the taking, that someone else will take everything that matters away from you!"

"Ridiculous!"

Antoinette threw aside all caution and said, "If it's so ridiculous, then why do you care if I die?"

"What do you mean? I do not care—" Kearn's mouth snapped shut. He crouched low and clutched his head with both hands as if to keep his mind from exploding. At last, he looked up and quietly said, "When I first saw you, I wanted nothing more than to drive my sword through your heart and rid The Realm of yet another weak enemy. In Baen-Edge I tried to kill you, but you defied me and lived on. You challenged my swordcraft, and for that I grew to respect your skill, but there was something else. There is something inside of you . . . something that I long for, but for the life of me, I do not know what it is. I only know that now I cannot bear the thought of losing you."

Kearn buried his head in his hands and seemed to shake. "I feel . . . I feel like I plummeted in my sleep to the bottom of a black lake," came his voice, thin and half choked. "I awakened but could not tell the direction to swim for the surface. But suddenly, there was a glimmer of light, and I knew where to go. But the light wavers now and threatens to go out. I am left alone, in the depths . . ."

"Look at me, Kearn," Antoinette said. He lifted his head a little. "What if I told you that I know a power beyond the sword? Beyond conquering armies? Beyond crowns and thrones?" She had his full attention now.

"With this power," she continued, "you can step forward when others shrink back. You can face obstacles, knowing that if you fall you will be caught. You can let go of the fears that race around in your mind . . . and simply rest in the knowledge that you will be taken care of. But most of all, Kearn, with this power . . . you will never be alone."

Kearn stood and looked at her. "All of my life I have been taught to take what I want. To force my will upon others. To mold things in the image I would have them be. Lord Rucifel, my father, showed me!"

Rucifel? Antoinette's mind raced.

"And I have succeeded!" he exclaimed. "And not because of my father's position. He gave me nothing but bruises if I dared prevail upon his name. By the sweat of my brow and the blood of others, I have clawed to a magnificent peak! I have riches—more than I could ever spend in ten lifetimes. I have power—great physical strength and the ability to command legions! And next to the Prince and my father, there is no one in Paragory who is so well known as I. But now that I have these things, I find it maddeningly not enough! The peak I have reached is actually a precipice, and I stand at the edge."

"But you don't have to go over that edge," Antoinette said, her voice pleading. "There is another way. Will you see it?"

Kearn's familiar sneer appeared again. He put both his hands high on the bars of Antoinette's cell and leaned forward. "This other way you speak of . . . by that you mean renounce my allegiance to Paragor? You mean bend the knee to King Eliam on the very eve of his defeat? Antoinette, you must know that I cannot. I would lose everything."

"Maybe that's just what you need to do."

"What?"

"Maybe," Antoinette repeated, "maybe you need to abandon all those things that you thought would satisfy you—the gold, the respect, the power. Cast them aside. They have not fulfilled you the way you thought they would, right?"

Kearn's hands fell to his sides. His eyes glinted red, but weakly.

Antoinette continued. "When you throw yourself on the mercy of King Eliam, you will finally let go of the fear you have only managed by your own power. You will finally see that power is not in controlling . . . but in letting go."

Kearn's face was a mess of emotions. He walked over to the stool and picked up the bundle he had laid there when he entered the cell. When he again stood before Antoinette, he looked utterly defeated and hopeless.

"There will be no mercy for me," Kearn said. "If I brought myself before King Eliam's throne he would know my crimes against Alleble, and he would have me executed. And he should! For I have ever been his mortal enemy, and I have slain with my own hands hundreds of his followers. And I have led many, many more into the places of torment within this fortress. No, there will be no mercy for me."

"Now you're being the stubborn one," Antoinette accused. "Yes, King Eliam knows of your deeds, but as to the consequence, you leave that to him."

"I marvel at your faith in your King," Kearn said, and his hopeless demeanor hardened into grim resolve. "But I cannot do what you ask."

"Kearn—"

He raised his hand to silence her. "No, our conversation has reached its due end. There is but one more thing—the very deed I came here to do." He began to unwrap the bundle. Antoinette stared. Her lips parted, but no words came forth. Kearn held in his hand the Daughter of Light, the sword Antoinette had traded for Trenna's freedom.

"The sword," Antoinette mumbled. "How?"

"That Ebenezer is a miserly old fool." Kearn smiled. "But in the end, my knights were able to persuade him to accept my generous offer of gold. They returned from Baen-Edge with it. I was going to keep it mounted on my chamber wall, a memento to remind me of a worthy opponent. But when the master revealed his plans for you . . . well, then I had a different thought."

Antoinette wasn't sure she liked the sound of that.

"I am going to give you your sword," he said. "It will not cut your chains, nor will it open the locks that bind you. But no warrior should be killed by an executioner's axe, dying like some common criminal. No, you keep your sword. Hide it under this cloth in the corner of your cell. And when at last the walls of Alleble have fallen and Paragor sends his guards for you . . . unleash your blade. Fight like you never have before, and take out as many of them as you can. Die well in battle. A true warrior deserves as much."

Kearn bowed to Antoinette and went to hand the sword to her. But suddenly a blast from a war horn rang out, and Antoinette turned to the window of her cell. In that moment, she heard the clatter of metal hitting stone and she jumped. Antoinette turned and whispered, "Kearn?" But he did not answer. He was gone from the cell, vanished as if he had never been there at all. Only her sword remained. Antoinette thought she knew where he had gone, but she wondered what that could mean.

Antoinette lunged toward the sword that lay beyond the bars. She stretched and pulled at the chains, but she could not reach the sword. Remembering the ring, she sat down in the center of the cell and began to twist it. The one loose metal band slithered out several inches. Antoinette slid it into the keyhole of the lock that held her ankle chains. She fished it around for a long time, until she felt something inside give a little. She threaded another inch of the metal band in, and then twisted it. *Click!* The lock opened!

Antoinette yanked the chains loose from the floor and dragged them to the bar. This time she had easily enough reach. She grabbed the Daughter of Light and drew it into her cell. It felt like meeting an old friend, and she hefted the blade in each hand. She placed it nearby and went to work on the locks at her wrists and ankles. With some effort, they each came free. The only lock left was the one on the cell door. Antoinette didn't think the riddle ring's metal band was strong enough for that.

But before she could make an attempt, a wailing howl rose up from outside. Antoinette covered her ears and fell to her knees. The sound rose in pitch and at last trailed off. She had heard that mournful cry before on the Forest Road.

Antoinette stepped to the window and looked out. She squinted and rubbed at her eyes, for she wasn't sure what she was seeing. Far down on the Grimwalk, near the base of the Prince's Crown, something dark began to creep. It was like shadowy tentacles at first, but then it began to gush forth from within the mountains. It spread and became like a dark fog bank, slowly advancing across the Grimwalk.

Then Antoinette heard other sounds. She looked to the left. What she saw made her blood run cold. Below, filling every path and marching along every bridge and rampart, was an endless army of soldiers. Thousands upon thousands they marched forward, eventually disappearing into the mists upon the Grimwalk. The flow of soldiers did not slow. This army was ten times those she'd seen before, and there was nothing but greater numbers behind them as far as she could see.

Antoinette knew where they were going. These soldiers were bound for Alleble. Paragor's attack was about to begin.

A Father to
the Fatherless

Robby hoisted Aidan's backpack behind him and made his way home, his mind spinning. He sighed with relief when he saw that his father's sleek black sports car was gone. Robby crept into his house. There was no sign of anyone, so he ran upstairs to his room, shut and locked the door, and lay down on the bed.

Is it possible that everything Dad taught me about The Realm, about Paragor, is a lie? Robby turned onto his back and looked up at his shelves crammed with trophies. He saw the tall state championship trophy, delivered by his game-winning goal. He thought of his father returning after so many years. He thought of Count Eogan coming to earth. Paragor's three guarantees had all come true! *That's got to mean something.*

Then he thought of Aidan. Robby had never had a friend like Aidan before. Not in all the years in Florida, not on any of his sports teams. Never. All those other kids that called themselves friends—Robby knew they just hung around because he was good-looking and very good at every sport he ever tried. Fashion friends. That's all they were.

Aidan, on the other hand, took the time to get to know Robby. He listened when Robby was feeling down. Robby grinned. *Aidan wouldn't care if I looked like a catfish on a bad hair day or I couldn't hit the broad side of a barn with a baseball. He'd still be there for me.*

But Aidan hadn't been there when Robby needed him. He had moved. Once again, Robby had been hurt by someone he trusted. Paragor had promised to give Robby power enough so that no one would ever hurt him again. And Paragor had brought his father back. Robby could not ignore that.

But as much as Robby wanted to be powerful—invulnerable even—he could not dismiss what he had just seen. Aidan had shown Count Eogan's stories for what they were: lies. Aidan really had been to The Realm. Robby could tell by the changes in Aidan's personality—his confidence, his attitude, his actions. And Aidan had seen things that Count Eogan could not refute. Robby just couldn't make his mind stop spinning.

Then, as if painted in large letters on the side of a building, came an answer: the Scrolls. Robby grabbed up Aidan's backpack, started to open it, but stopped and looked at his bedroom door. He knew the consequences would be severe if his father caught him reading Aidan's Scrolls. *No,* he thought. *I'll hear Dad's car pull up. I'll just stash the Scrolls if he comes home.*

Robby took out the Scrolls and untied the leather lace that bound them. He stared down at the first line:

**Outside of time and place,
there is a realm of
great nobility and renown.**

As Robby began to read, he felt a peculiar sense of nostalgia, like after being away on a long trip he had finally come back home. Line after line, page after page, his excitement grew. But then he came to the story of a brave young knight, rising through the ranks to become one of King Eliam's elite Elder Guard. It was the story of Paragal, the King's most favored.

Something came over Robby as he began to read the account. He found that he couldn't focus. His vision blurred. And then Robby's eyelids fell, and his mind's eye wandered far away. A picture began to emerge. There was a handsome young knight seated at a table in a very small chamber. Behind him were shelves piled high with innumerable rolls of parchment. As Robby stared, the picture became remarkably clear, more like a window.

Robby's door flew open so hard that it slammed into the wall. Robby jumped up, scattering pages of parchment.

"What are you doin', son?" Robby's father asked, his jaws so firmly set they appeared to bulge. "And why was your door locked?"

Robby shook his head and retreated until his back hit the wall on the other side of the bed. "I . . . I have Aidan's Scrolls," he whispered, trying desperately to summon more courage. "I was reading them."

"I thought I made it clear you were not to see Aidan again." Robby grabbed up all the loose pages and clutched them to his chest.

Mr. Pierson glared at his son. "Give those to me right now, Robby!"

Robby swallowed and stood to face the man in his room. "I know what happened in Alleble that night," Robby said quietly. "Aidan saw it. And now, I've seen it. I know that Paragor plotted behind King Eliam's back and murdered him and his Elder Guard. And at last, I know that everything you ever told me about The Realm is a lie!"

Mr. Pierson raised a fist, but Robby was too fast. He ducked the blow, slipped out of his room, and swiftly pulled the door shut behind him. Then, Scrolls in hand, he bounded down the stairs and out the front door. Mr. Pierson slammed open the bedroom door and leaped down after him. But by the time Mr. Pierson strode out into the front yard, Robby was on his bike and a hundred yards down the street.

"You won't get away, Robby!" Mr. Pierson screamed. "Paragor will find you!"

Robby pedaled with all his might. At the turn in the road, Robby tried to jump the curb. But he didn't make it. His shins and elbows burning from new scrapes, he stood up and saw that the bike chain was broken.

Not knowing what else to do, Robby grabbed up the Scrolls and sprinted into the woods.

The sun was just about gone, so when Robby disappeared under the canopy of trees, he found himself in a landscape of shadows. Gnarled trees with grasping branches rose up on both sides of the narrow path. Unseen briers ripped at his pant legs. Invisible spiderwebs caught in his face and mouth. Still, Robby ran on! Not knowing where he was going—just running . . . escaping. Then a voice inside his head said . . .

"There is nowhere for you to hide. You cannot escape me. You are mine."

Robby's heart hammered against his rib cage as he sprinted up the path recklessly. His gait, normally graceful and athletic, was now awkward, frantic, even crazed.

"I will never let go of you. I am always waiting, even in death."

"No, stop it! Get out of my head! Stop!" Robby tripped over a root and flew headfirst into a thicket of briers. His face stung from a dozen fresh scratches and his body ached. He clutched the Scrolls and curled up at the base of a tree, staring out into the dark woods.

A great winged shadow rose up among the trees, and Robby heard the cracking of branches. This thing was getting closer.

Robby shook uncontrollably. From the shadows came a long hissing intake of breath and then a deep, angry growl.

"Please, King Eliam . . . ," Robby cried. "I . . . I don't know if you're out there! I don't know if it's too late, but please help me."

No sooner were those pleading words spoken than there was a blinding flash of blue light up ahead. The creature roared, but the roar was cut short by a crack of thunder. And then, all was still.

Robby's mind raced, and he wondered what had happened. Had King Eliam rescued him? Robby tried to remember everything Aidan ever told him about the King of Alleble. But the thought that kept coming to his mind was to look at the Scrolls.

Robby stared at the Scrolls. It was impossible. Too dark to see anything. But then Robby felt a tingle in his right hand. And suddenly that page of parchment began to shimmer. Words began to appear written in bright golden light, as if an invisible hand was writing upon the Scroll.

Line after line appeared until, at last, there was a glowing block of text right there in front of Robby. He gasped and began to read:

There are passages and doors
And realms that lie unseen.
There are roads both wide and narrow
And no avenue between.
Doors remain closed for those
Who in sad vanity yet hide.
Yet when belief is chosen,
The key appears inside.
What is lived now will soon pass,
And what is not, will come to be.
The Door Within must open,
For one to truly see.

A poem! Robby thought. Aidan had said something about a poem. *But it's like a riddle. What is "The Door Within"?*

Then, as before, in glistening golden light, two new lines of text appeared.

Do you see?
Believe and enter.

Yes! Robby thought. *I want to enter! I want to go where Aidan went. I want to get out of here right now!*

He waited a few heartbeats, wondering if King Eliam would just suddenly appear and whisk him off to The Realm. Nothing happened, and that, Robby thought, meant there was more to figure out.

Robby had never been very good at riddles. Still, he felt passion stirring inside, and he wanted desperately to understand. *Realms that lie unseen—that's got to be The Realm,* he thought. *Doors remain closed for those who in sad vanity yet hide.* Robby knew that *vanity* was kind of like being conceited or prideful. His sister Jill and her constant primping came suddenly to mind.

"But no," he voiced his thoughts aloud to the Scrolls. "I'm the one who's been hiding, aren't I, King Eliam? Aidan tried to tell me about you, but I didn't listen. My dad came home, and I bought every one of his lies just because I wanted a father again. I figured I was finally getting life to go my way. Now look at me. I feel more powerless now than I ever have in my whole life, and I still don't have a father!"

"My power can work through your weakness." A voice spoke to Robby. Not the raspy, condemning voice he'd heard before. No, this voice felt warm and somehow wholesome. There was safety in this voice—and understanding. *"No servant of Alleble will remain fatherless."*

Tears streaked down Robby's face, and he stood up. The terrors of the woods were gone—vanished like storm clouds driven by strong wind. *When belief is chosen, the key appears inside.* It was all starting to make sense. One by one, the answers to the riddle began to appear.

"I choose to believe in you!" Robby cried aloud. "I want the key!"

A warm breeze flowed over him, and he stared down again at the golden text upon the Scroll. *What is lived now will soon pass, and what is not, will come to be.* Robby felt a yearning, an aching of his heart to let everything go—to leave all the frustrations, fear, and loneliness behind. To throw himself on the mercy of King Eliam and be a servant of Alleble.

The Door Within must open, for one to truly see. The final piece of the puzzle became as clear to Robby as the dazzling golden text upon the Scroll. *I need to enter a door inside me!* he thought excitedly, and he closed his eyes.

At first, Robby tried to imagine a picture of a door, but soon he simply relaxed and let his mind wander. The darkness lifted and before him was a cliff. A narrow, rickety-looking plank and rope bridge extended out over a chasm of unknowable depth and disappeared into the white haze far away.

Robby pictured himself approaching the bridge, and somehow it was clearer in his mind's eye than anything he had ever imagined before. He looked warily down at the foundation of the bridge, staked down to the cliff. It seemed secure, as if it had been there for many ages past and would be there for many ages to come. Robby took a step closer, and peered over the edge. The distance fell away so quickly that Robby caught his breath and hurriedly stepped backward.

It was silly, Robby thought, to be afraid of something that he had just conjured up in his imagination. But there was little comfort in that thought, for the bridge—and the potential to fall—began to feel more real than the woods on the edge of his neighborhood. Tentatively, Robby reached back with his free hand to feel the large tree that should be behind him. But there was nothing behind him.

The bridge beckoned, and Robby knew he must cross.

THE DOOR WITHIN

A gentle breeze played with Robby's long blond hair as he stepped out on the bridge. With the Scrolls clutched in one hand, he used the other hand to grip the rope guides and bring his other foot out as well. Slowly, one tentative foot after another, being sure not to look down, he made his way across. But the whole time, his legs were shaking and unsteady. *C'mon, Robby!* he berated himself. *Get a grip. You're a star athlete. This should be easy!*

But it was anything but easy. Sweat poured down his face, his throat dried up, and he felt his stomach twisting in knots. And even though the planks beneath his feet had not even so much as creaked, Robby had a constant, nagging fear that his next step might break a board, and he would fall through . . . fall into nothingness.

He quickened his pace—all the while staring ahead into the haze for some sign of where the bridge might end. It seemed to go on and on, and Robby certainly wasn't going to try to look back over his shoulder to see how far he'd come.

The wind picked up, and the bridge began to sway. Robby shook so hard he had to stop and crouch down. The wind increased even more, howling and gusting at times. "No!" he cried out, but it was too late. The wind took the Scrolls right out of his hand. He watched them fly away, and then he shut his eyes.

Robby wanted to turn around and run back to the safety of the ledge where he'd begun. Slowly he stood, and the idea came into his mind that if he turned back and made it to the cliff, he could open his eyes and find himself back in the woods near his neighborhood. His old life would still be there waiting.

"But I don't want that old life," Robby said aloud. He knew all too well the kind of life it would be. A life of uncertainty, a life of fear—his biological father would see to that, he felt sure. *C'mon, Robby, let's get going.*

He took a step. Then another. The wind shrieked and the bridge swayed, but Robby held the guide ropes and coached himself as he pressed on. *Four years of gymnastics—I've got good balance. Nine years of baseball, football, and soccer—I've got the strength.*

He felt a subtle change in the incline. The bridge had bottomed out and now began to climb. *I'm doing it!* Robby thought excitedly. *I'm going to make it!*

He walked faster, with more confidence, and his hold on the guide ropes wasn't as severe. He even released his grip a couple of times and walked more casually. The incline steepened, and Robby was so pleased with his efforts that he ventured to look over the side. Just once.

His left foot slid off the side of one of the planks. His right knee buckled, and he fell. All Robby's worst fears came rushing back. Frantically, he grabbed the left guide rope with both hands. But his hands slipped off.

As his body fell below the bridge, Robby grabbed the planks with both hands. He felt the tendons in his hands protest, and his fingernails felt ready to rip right off the ends of his fingers. But still he hung on.

And with the wind howling, Robby dangled from the bridge,

trying desperately to hoist himself up. He managed to get a hand between two planks where he could get a stronger hold. Then, using the strength of his upper back, arms, and shoulders, he pulled one knee up to the edge of the planks. But, try as he might, he could not get his knee or foot over the edge because the wind kept blowing.

His muscles ached. Robby knew he wouldn't last much longer. So he pulled with all of his athletic might and yanked his body as high as he could. His right knee found purchase, but only for a moment. Robby struggled, trying to heave himself up, but felt himself slipping. "I can't do this!" he yelled. And then one of his hands slipped off the plank. He let go and fell backward. "King Eliam, help me!" he screamed as his body lost all contact with the bridge.

Robby closed his eyes as he plummeted into the unknown.

A hand found Robby's hand in midair. The grip was absolutely strong and would not let Robby fall any farther. And as if Robby were made of paper, the hand lifted him up and over the guide ropes and placed him securely in the middle of the bridge.

Robby opened his eyes, but there was no one there. *"You are never alone,"* a voice said. And behold, the mist ahead of Robby spread apart, and before him—like a solitary monument—stood a door. Robby raced up the remaining planks and seized hold of the door's large ring. Robby exulted with gratitude, knowing that he had been rescued from his own feeble efforts—rescued and guided at last to The Door Within!

"Thank you! Thank you, my King!" Robby repeated over and over, as the door opened and brilliant light streamed out. It was the glad, golden light of the sun and stars—the very same light that had illuminated the Scrolls and chased away his fears in the dark woods. Robby smiled and entered The Door Within.

PASSAGE

The golden light faded away to a tiny distant point, and a narrow path rolled out like a carpet into the darkness before Robby. Still smiling, he walked up the path, and as he did so, he realized that his senses were behaving strangely. His senses of sight and hearing were dulled, making him feel as if he were underwater. But his sense of touch was alive, and he felt like he could almost feel the texture of the air as it tingled all around him.

Robby held his arms up as he walked, letting the marvelous, peculiar air wash over him. Then the darkness on both sides of him began to flicker. Peculiar blurred images began to appear. Slowly they began to focus.

Dark storm clouds, swirling and brooding, raced overhead. Lightning flashed, shedding eerie flickering light on a sea of armed knights in black armor. This army stretched all the way to the horizon and was as wide as Robby could see. Robby quickened his pace, for he did not want to remain in the midst of such a terrible army. Lightning flashed again. The vision wavered and changed. The storm clouds melted into the deep green canopy of a forest. A great pit opened up in the forest floor, and suddenly the vision took Robby beneath the surface.

A knight appeared there, illuminated by strange gray subterranean light. And before him spread dozens—no, hundreds—of furry brown humps. The humps began to move. They were advancing toward the knight. The knight backed away. As the things grew near, Robby saw a sea of glassy black eyes. Robby turned away from the visions. He kept his eyes on the path as best he could and ran.

In spite of his attempts not to watch, Robby saw images out of the corners of his eyes. The vision flickered and changed again. This time he saw a battle before massive walls of stone. Knights in a great many types and colors of armor fought desperately. Their swords clashed. Arrows flew in swarms.

But suddenly there was something burrowing beneath the knights, and as it traveled it threw great numbers of knights violently into the air. Then, as it neared, Robby caught a glimpse of a large scaly claw reaching out of the crowd of soldiers. Then there were several claws. And each one grabbed a fistful of knights, crushed them, and tossed them aside like broken dolls. Robby felt an unrelenting fear that this creature, whatever it was, was coming after him. He forced himself to look straight ahead, but he could sense the visions begin to speed up—one replacing the next—until it was just a blur.

Robby ran as fast as he could. Just a few feet ahead a shimmering window appeared in the darkness. Robby ran for it and dove, disappearing through the window.

KINDRED SPIRITS

Lady Merewen stood by Kaliam's side on the wide balcony above Guard's Keep. Her silver hair glistened in the moonlight, and her almond-shaped eyes shone with hope.

"Do not fear, m'lord. You chose rightly in this matter. The Blue Mountains must be defended, out of loyalty—and of need. And if our dragon force is quickly victorious . . . it will give Paragor something to think about."

"If?" Kaliam replied thoughtfully. "That is what troubles me. Too often as of late I am left here to stare and wait while my friends venture forth to war."

"There will be war enough for us all before too long," she replied, staring at the shadows of dark mountains in the west.

"Nay, m'lady," said Kaliam, and he turned to her. "It is not war that I desire. But . . . I am averse to ordering good knights into danger, while I remain safe within the walls of the city."

Lady Merewen took Kaliam's strong hands into hers. "There is not a single knight in all the armies assembled here who would question your mettle . . . or your courage." Kaliam's determined expression melted, for Lady Merewen had guessed his secret fear.

"Do not forget who chose you for this position," she continued, capturing Kaliam's gaze in her own and refusing to let go. "You have been called to be Sentinel of Alleble, and King Eliam does not make mistakes."

Kaliam was silent for many long moments. Indecision played upon his brow as he searched her eyes. But then a subtle smile appeared on his lips, and he seemed to have come to an unspoken conclusion. Lady Merewen looked at him questioningly.

"M'lady, you are most extraordinary," he said at last. "But come, it is time now to meet the new Twelfth Knight."

Robby found himself sitting on a chair in the dark. But it was not his room. He turned to his side and stared at a large window that was shuttered except for a crack. Through this narrow portal, Robby saw the twinkle of stars and beneath those, indistinct gray shadows.

He stood and slowly, as if afraid of what he might see, he threw wide the shutters. And then he laughed. Laughed out loud. The kind of joyous laughter he had not experienced in a long, long time. For beyond the shutters lay a wide, sleeping kingdom. Castle turrets, powerful stone walls, keeps and many small cottages lay quiet beneath the stars. But surging with unmatched grandeur, towering higher than many rooftops, plumed the great fountains of Alleble. And something inside of Robby formed the words in his mind, and he whispered, "I've come home."

A sudden knock at a door behind Robby made him jump. "M'lord Robby?" a boisterous female voice called. "M'lord, are you there? Well, of course you must be there. Kaliam said you would be. I suppose the better question is, may I come in? Hullo, Robby?" She knocked again.

"Uh, yeah," Robby called, turning around. "I guess."

The door opened, spilling light into the chamber. And in walked a very round Glimpse woman carrying a rather large tray filled with many covered dishes. She set the tray down on a desk Robby had not seen at first and then went about the room lighting candles.

"There now, much better!" she said, her back still turned as she lit the last candle in the room. "There's some light to eat by. I am Elspeth, and Kaliam sent me to see that you are fed. A growing boy needs his victuals." She turned to look at Robby. "Oh!" she said. "Oh, not a boy at all. A young man."

"That's righ-ight," Robby replied, feeling slightly embarrassed.

"A mite taller than most lads," she said, looking him up and down. "And stronger . . . well, all the better. Come now, have a seat and eat your fill. I have prepared my special stew for you and some biscuits, if you have a taste for them. Sir Kaliam will be here shortly, but if you have questions while you wait, I will do my best to answer them!"

Robby sat down at the desk, and Elspeth removed the cover from a large steaming bowl of stewed vegetables and meat, swimming in gravy. The smell from the bowl awoke the hunger in Robby, and he hastily picked up a spoon and began to eat. There were chunks of potatoes, carrots, and some other vegetable Robby had never seen. It was triangular with one side covered with a thin purple skin. Whatever it was, it was good. But the meat was the best part. It didn't taste like beef. It didn't taste like chicken. It was extremely salty and had some savor that Robby didn't recognize, perhaps from the gravy, but absolutely delicious.

"My mama makes some great beef stew," he said between his last few mouthfuls. "Or at least she did when we lived in Florida, but I gotta tell you, I have never had anything that tastes this good!"

Elspeth beamed and patted Robby on the back. "What a kind lad you are to say such things. My stew is a favorite around here. The Knights of the Elder Guard like it, but no one more than Sir Aelic."

"Who's Aelic?" Robby asked, dabbing up the last of the gravy with a biscuit.

A cloud seemed to fall over Elspeth's jovial face for a moment. "Why, Sir Aelic was as noble a young knight as anyone could know. Sir Aidan's Glimpse twin, you know. He was sorely wounded in the Battle on the Forest Road in Yewland. But now he seems to have just vanished from The Realm."

"Well, that makes sense," Robby muttered.

"What is that you say, lad?"

"Well, back in my world," Robby explained, "I was there when Aidan entered The Realm, and a Glimpse and his twin can't be in the same world at the same time, right?"

"Yes," Elspeth replied. "But how did you . . . oh, silly me. I suppose Sir Aidan must have told you that, you being friends and all."

Robby felt a pang of guilt. It had not been Aidan who told him about the dynamics of leaving one world for another. Count Eogan, a servant of Alleble's greatest enemy, had taught him that . . . and many other things besides. Robby wondered if they knew.

"Where is Aidan?" Robby asked. "Can I see him? He'll be real glad to see me here, I think."

"I am sure I do not know," Elspeth replied, dabbing the scratches on Robby's face with a cool ointment. "If indeed he is back in The Realm, I am glad for it. For Sir Aidan is a valiant warrior. But he has not arrived in Alleble. Of that I am certain. Perhaps Sir Kaliam will know."

"Perhaps Sir Kaliam will know what?" asked a tall Glimpse knight entering the room. He was followed by a beautiful Glimpse with long silver hair. Both of them wore armor and had swords at their sides.

Elspeth bowed. "M'lord, Sentinel!" she said. "And Lady Merewen too, though I suppose I ought not to be surprised." Robby started to stand, but Kaliam motioned for him to stay seated.

"And just what do you mean by you 'ought not to be sur-prised'?" Lady Merewen asked in mock anger.

"Oh, be kind to your servant," Elspeth said, bowing again. "I meant no harm. Forgive the assumptions of an old busybody like me."

Kaliam laughed and turned to Robby. "Welcome, Robby," he said, gesturing grandly with the sweep of an arm. "Welcome to the city of Alleble and into the service of King Eliam the Everlasting."

"The lad from Antoinette's picture," Lady Merewen thought aloud. "Perhaps Antoinette completed her task, after all."

"Who is Antoinette?" Robby asked.

"I wonder Sir Aidan did not tell you," Kaliam said. "Lady Antoinette is a friend of Aidan's from the Mirror Realm—a place Aidan called Colorado."

"Oh," Robby replied. "Aidan moved there. Colorado is far from where I live."

Kaliam nodded. "Lady Antoinette is a skilled swordmaiden. But alas, she has been captured by the enemy."

"Is that my mission?" Robby asked. "Am I supposed to rescue her?"

"Nay, lad," Kaliam replied sadly. "Though every hour that passes while Lady Antoinette is still in captivity scratches at my heart, we are in no position to invade Paragory."

He put his hand on Lady Merewen's arm. She smiled bravely, but she wondered privately if Antoinette would ever leave Paragory alive.

"Where is Sir Aidan now?" Elspeth asked. "Robby says that Sir Aidan has entered The Realm."

"He has?" Kaliam replied with a sideways glance at Lady Merewen. "I find that news somewhat heartening, but Sir Aidan is not in Alleble. Perhaps it is just the difference in the reckoning of time between our worlds. I know that Aidan would not stray from the narrow path unless King Eliam led him to do so—not after what happened the first time he entered The Realm." Kaliam laughed quietly to himself.

Robby looked from Kaliam to Lady Merewen and back. "Why am I here?" he asked.

"To train to be a knight, and if you pass your training, you will be the Twelfth Knight," Kaliam said.

"Twelfth Knight?" Robby asked.

"Yes," Kaliam explained. "Often on special missions, we send forth warriors in teams of twelve. The twelfth knight chosen has special honor. Aidan was a Twelfth Knight. So was Lady Antoinette."

Eagerly, Robby asked, "What is my mission?"

"Impatient to strap on a sword and be off, are you?" Kaliam asked. "I am beginning to wonder if all the beings in the Mirror Realm lack patience. You will discover the nature of your mission tomorrow. But before that happens, you will have much to do . . . training not the least of which."

"Shall I rouse the lad at sunup, then?" Elspeth asked.

Kaliam glanced at Lady Merewen, and the mischievous grin reappeared. "Nay, Lady Elspeth, not at dawn. Say rather, wake him at second bell."

"What?" Robby objected. "I'm going to bed? I just got here."

Kaliam patted Robby on the shoulder. "You have arrived in Alleble in the middle of the night. Rest now, as much as you can. For there is no promise of such comforts as sleep in the future." Elspeth nodded, bowed, and left the chamber. Kaliam followed, but Lady Merewen lingered a moment.

"Should you meet Lady Antoinette one day," Lady Merewen whispered to Robby as she stood under the arch by the chamber door, "you owe her a debt of gratitude."

Robby was shocked. "I don't understand," he said. "I don't even know Antoinette."

"Ah, but Sir Aidan did," Lady Merewen replied. "And Aidan asked Antoinette to seek your Glimpse twin, Kearn, in The Realm—it was in seeking him she was captured."

"Kearn?" Robby replied absently.

Lady Merewen nodded. "Kearn was a powerful captain in Paragor's service," she said with a knowing smile.

Robby felt as if Lady Merewen could suddenly see right through him. "So . . . ," he said, looking at his feet, "you know about me, then?"

"Yes, Robby, I know about you. Antoinette told me some, but Kaliam knew much more than she. But even if they had not told me, I still would have known that you once served the enemy."

Robby blinked back tears.

"In spite of your size and apparent strength," Lady Merewen explained, "there is a fragility about you. At moments you look ashamed, as if you really do not belong here in Alleble. Like you might suddenly be discovered for what you are and be dragged from this city and taken to a much darker place." Tears streamed freely down Robby's cheeks.

"Nay, Robby, I see all too clearly the shrouds that Paragor continues to cast over you in the hopes of reclaiming your allegiance. I see it, because I too wore such shrouds. But let your tears become tears of joy as mine did! I cast off the enemy's feeble webs, and I am confident that here you will find such hope too!"

Robby swallowed and nodded, his square jaw still trembling.

"We shall talk again, you and I," Lady Merewen said. "But for now, sleep. Sleep in such comfort and peace as you have never had before. For, Robby, you *are* home now."

TESTED AND PROVED

It appeared to be a glorious spring day in Alleble. The sun was climbing, and a gentle breeze stirred the great banners hung outside the main gatehouse of the castle. Still, Kaliam felt uneasy that the dragon riders had not returned from their mission in the Blue Mountains, especially now that Robby was in Alleble.

Kindle, the armory keeper, had procured fitting armor for Robby, and Kaliam helped Robby put it on. "So Aidan really defeated an army all by himself?" Robby asked as Kaliam slid the breastplate harness over Robby's head. Kaliam nodded.

"Not exactly by himself," Kindle said with a wink. "Or are you forgetting how Sir Aidan managed to navigate Lady Gwenne and the others through the stampede without getting stomped?"

Kaliam frowned with mock anger. "Yes, well, of course King Eliam was with Aidan in that battle."

"I should say!" Kindle exclaimed with a laugh that made his ample belly shake. He turned back to Robby. "So, why do you ask, lad?"

"I dunno," Robby replied, running his fingers over his new gleaming silver armor. "I guess it's just that things are so different now. Back in my world, when Aidan and I first met, well . . . Aidan wasn't good at much."

"Ah! I see now," said Kindle. "You used to be top knight, eh? And you are worried that Sir Aidan has passed you by? Is that it?"

Robby shrugged. Kindle went on to say more, but Kaliam held up his hand. "To serve in The Realm of Alleble," Kaliam said, "you must put aside all such jealousies."

Each busy with his own thoughts, Kaliam and Robby left the armory en route to the training yards behind the main keep. Kaliam wondered why he had such a nagging uneasy feeling about Robby; Robby wondered if Kaliam held something against him.

The few citizens of Alleble who were out on the avenues nodded respectfully to their Sentinel and his companion. But some of them did more than nod. Three elderly Glimpse women walked by, staring and whispering. Robby heard one of them say, "Is he one of them?" But then the other two ladies shushed her and whisked her away.

"What was that all about?" Robby asked.

"Oh, well . . . they do not often see beings from the Mirror Realm," Kaliam replied. "Especially one so handsome and knightly as yourself." Robby laughed, but he wondered if that was all there was to it.

After many winding passages and several flights of stairs, they turned a corner and Robby gasped. "I have never seen anything like that before!" he said, staring up at the great white stone faces of mountains.

"Pennath Ador!" Kaliam exclaimed. "The Mountains of Glory! It is said that when the first rays of the dawn sun shine between those snowy peaks that great glory will be won by those who are pure of heart!"

"Righ-ight," was Robby's only response. The mountains were dizzying in their immense grandeur, and somewhere in the back of Robby's heart he wondered what it might be like to find some winding path and attempt to scale them.

"Here we are!" Kaliam announced. Robby beheld a network of wooden fences, several archery ranges, and a large field and pavilion that reminded him of a racetrack.

"These are the private training yards of the Elder Guard, the most highly skilled warriors in all of Alleble. Most of them," Kaliam said, glancing northward, "are on a very important mission in the Blue Mountain Provinces. So we ought to have the yard pretty much to ourselves."

"Will you tell me what my mission is now?" Robby asked.

"In time," Kaliam said as they entered a fenced-in ring. "I would test you first on the training urchin, but alas, it is under repair. So we will just have to give it a go the old-fashioned way. King Eliam told me that you have considerable skill with a blade. Is this so?"

"I guess I'm pretty good," Robby replied. "But I don't really know how I compare to the other Knights of Alleble. I was trained—"

"By your father," Kaliam finished the sentence. "He is the human twin of Lord Rucifel, Paragor's right hand. Yes, I know. Rucifel's swordcraft is lethal, but we shall see."

Robby twisted and leaned to test the limits of his armor. "My father said I was a little better than a beginner, but Count Eogan said that I am a gifted swordsman. I think he was just tryin' to flatter me."

"Did you say Eogan?" Kaliam asked.

Robby nodded. "Did you know him?" Robby asked, looking afraid. "He said he was a former ambassador from Alleble."

"I did not know him," Kaliam said. "We have had dealings with

Count Eogan, and he certainly was no ambassador of ours. Masquerading as one of us, Eogan stirred up quite a bit of trouble with our allies. If only I could get my hands on that scoundrel."

Robby looked downward. "You won't see him again."

"How can you be so sure?" Kaliam asked.

"I . . . I killed him."

"Why?" Kaliam asked.

"He tried to stop Aidan from entering The Realm. I had no choice. He would have killed Aidan."

"Oh," Kaliam replied. "Well, I am glad Eogan's treachery has come to an end, but I am sorry for the ordeal you have been through. Just remember, we are at war with Paragor and his allies. What you did was just."

"I know," Robby said, and he turned back to his Sentinel. "But I don't like to kill."

"Neither do I, Robby, neither do I," said Kaliam.

"Sir Kaliam, don't you get used to killing?" Robby asked.

"No. No true servant of Alleble does. We fight to defend our land and our allies. We slay when we have no other choice," Kaliam said.

Robby stared at the mountains. Kaliam's uneasy feeling around Robby had strengthened. *Can I really trust a former servant of the enemy?* The thought just imposed itself in Kaliam's mind. But he immediately shook it away. *After all,* he mused, *I did propose marriage to a former servant of the enemy!* And Robby had shown no signs of duplicity or hidden evil—just the opposite, actually. *Still, I will feel much better when Robby has made the good confession.*

At last, Kaliam dragged a barrel out of the center of the ring. "These are not the finest swords in the land," he said to Robby with a wink. "But they are far better than the first weapon Aidan ever used. Now, choose a blade."

Robby went to the barrel and sorted through the weapons. He took out several—all broadswords—but one at a time he put them back. Growing frustrated, he finally settled on one. He carved a swift two-fisted C-shape in the air and frowned. "Don't you have anything heavier?"

"Heavier than that?" Kaliam asked. "That is a claymore!"

Robby smiled apologetically. "I like the length," he said. "But it just doesn't seem like it'll pack the punch I'm used to."

"What is wrong with the sword?" came a gruff voice from behind the fence, and presently Kindle, the armory keeper, and Lady Merewen appeared.

"The lad has a claymore," Kaliam replied. "And he says it is not heavy enough for him."

"Really?" Kindle whistled. "You must be a mighty lad to wield a heavier weapon than that."

"M'lord," Lady Merewen said, "why not let Robby try your sword? It should be heavy enough."

"It would indeed!" Kindle hacked a laugh. "Last time I tried to handle that, I thought my shoulders would pop from their sockets!"

Reluctantly, Kaliam drew his grand broadsword. He presented it to Robby grip-first and said, "If it is too heavy for you, I will search the other barrels in the yard. I am sure we can find—"

"No, this is great!" Robby said, and he turned and whipped Kaliam's blade toward the fence, stopping within an inch of striking it. "I like this, Sir Kaliam!"

"Yes, I see," muttered the Sentinel. Lady Merewen stifled a laugh, and she and Kindle left the ring, choosing to watch from the safer side of the fence.

Still grumbling, Kaliam chose the claymore and moved to the opposite side of the ring. "Stand you ready?" Kaliam asked.

"I guess so," Robby replied.

The word "Begin!" was barely out of Kaliam's mouth when Robby bolted toward him. He slammed a high stroke against Kaliam's claymore, so hard that the sound made both combatants' ears ring.

But with their blades locked at eye level, Robby shoved with all his might and Kaliam lost his balance. He stumbled backward, and when he looked up, he found the tip of his own broadsword level with his throat. Lady Merewen and Kindle were speechless.

"You cannot fight like that," Kaliam protested. "A knight with a lighter blade would cut you to ribbons!"

Robby considered Kaliam's point. "I guess he could try," Robby replied.

Kaliam gestured and Robby returned to his spot. "Again!" Kaliam yelled.

And again Robby bull-rushed. This time Kaliam was ready. He absorbed Robby's first blow and used it to spin around. The next thing Robby knew, Kaliam had the claymore suspended three inches from the back of Robby's neck. "That was cool!" Robby said. "Can you teach me that?"

Kaliam smiled, pleased to have evened the score in front of his bride-to-be. "There is much I can teach you," Kaliam said. "In time. Let us tilt again!"

On the third duel Kaliam rushed out to meet Robby's charge, and their blades met with a tremendous crash. Kaliam tried to roll off the blow and spin like before, but Robby ducked it and slapped away Kaliam's attack. Their weapons struck again and again, long, sweeping, heavy blows—always followed by grunts from the two fighters. Sweat poured off of them both and the straining muscles of each glistened.

Kaliam began at last to wear Robby down. He backed him into a corner, but Robby did something Kaliam did not expect. He turned the broadsword so that when he struck again, it would not be with the sharp blade, but rather the full flat of the blade. Robby chopped down with all his might on Kaliam's claymore near the hilt. The force of the blow was such that it knocked the blade from Kaliam's hand. Robby thought he had won, but before he could deliver the final shot, Kaliam grabbed the claymore and in one motion rolled and brought the blade point to Robby's back.

"Uh, okay, I give!" Robby said.

Kaliam lowered the sword. "How did I beat you?" he asked.

"I didn't think someone as big as you could move that fast," Robby replied, shaking his head.

"Most cannot," Kaliam said. "Still, you acquitted yourself well with my broadsword. I will see if something like it can be found for you to use more permanently."

"You mean I passed the test?" Robby asked. "I'm a knight now?"

"You have more than enough skill with a sword to be a knight," Kaliam said. "But there is more to it than that. Go now with Kindle. He will take you to Guard's Keep for the midday meal. Afterward, we will meet again, and I will show you your chores." He winked at Lady Merewen. "One of them in particular was Aidan's favorite!"

"Well?" Lady Merewen asked after Kindle and Robby left the training compound.

"Robby has no classical technique," Kaliam replied, absently massaging his forearms. "But what he lacks in style, he makes up for in brutality! He is reckless, almost maniacal with that broadsword. Why, his initial charge is an onslaught of one person! I would gladly have him guarding the walls of our city, and I pity any enemy knight who scales a ladder only to meet Robby and his heavy blade."

"Why do you still have hesitation in your manner, m'lord?" Lady Merewen asked.

"I wish I knew . . . for certain," Kaliam replied, staring into the skies to the north.

"Is there something you guess, then?"

"Tonight, after Robby's Confession Ceremony, I need to speak to him and ask him a question. Then I will have some wisdom and not just a hunch."

"You speak in riddles, m'lord," Lady Merewen said.

He turned to face her and said, "Perhaps it is one of many things I have learned from our King."

She laughed but then pointed over Kaliam's shoulder. "Kaliam, look!"

And there in the skies to the north were hundreds of gray winged shapes. A horn call came on the wind, and it was answered as the trumpets of the city rang out.

Kaliam sighed with great relief. "The dragon riders have returned!"

PENNATH ADOR

This is grievous news!" exclaimed Kaliam. He banged his fist on the table, startling all those assembled in Guard's Keep. "Mallik, is there nothing your resourceful folk can do?"

Mallik's coppery brow was knotted in anger. He wore a sneer of distaste as he spoke. "Paragor's attack was more precise than we ever could have imagined. Some of our cutting tools were spared, but every last one of our wind-carriages was burned to cinders! We are resourceful, yes, but we cannot carve walls without tools—nor transport stone without carriages!"

"In spite of our careful planning," said King Ravelle, "the enemy then stays one step ahead!"

"So it would seem," Kaliam replied. Lady Merewen's light touch on his forearm calmed him enough to sit down.

"The gray walls of Alleble are yet proud and sturdy," said Queen Illaria. "Can they not buffet Paragor's attack?"

Farix answered, "If all the enemy brought to bear on us was his catapults and his fiery projectiles . . . then yes, the walls of Alleble would stand. But the Wyrm Lord's fire is a weapon beyond the strength of normal stone. He would open breaches in our defenses and allow Paragor's foot soldiers to invade."

"And that is our chief fear," explained Kaliam. "Paragor may try to drop his forces behind our walls with his dragon carriages, but our own dragons and archers will limit their effect. But if he is able to break through the walls, we are then forced to abandon our plan of attack to plug holes in our defense!"

"What then is to be done?" Lord Sternhilt asked.

"What indeed?" echoed Kaliam, and he shook his head. "For the Wyrm Lord was a mere shadow of his former strength—shriveled and weak from his captivity—when Clarion fell to him like kindling. Now that he has been nursed to health in the bastions of Paragory, his fire will burn all the hotter. And who can say what powers the firstborn dragon will wield when his strength waxes?"

"It seems we have little hope," said Nock.

"There is always hope," whispered a voice from a hooded Glimpse at the chamber door. And yet each knight in the room felt as if it had been spoken privately in his ear alone. They all turned as the stranger lowered his hood. He had dark feathery hair flecked with gray and brushed to one side where it rippled like willow branches in the wind. Luminous blue eyes with huge dark pupils peered out thoughtfully from under gray brows. A slight smile appeared above his squared goatee, but it was the smile neither of joy nor of madness. No, this Glimpse's expression was in many ways grim, but his smile spoke of confidence and security, an anchor in the room where the sea had become so turbulent.

"Naysmithe!" Kaliam said, and he stood and went to shake his hand. "You are most welcome. Long has it been since you have offered your wisdom in this room!"

"I only repeat such wisdom as I am given," Naysmithe replied mysteriously. "But I say again, there is always hope. The Three Witnesses are coming."

Eyebrows were raised and those at the table broke into murmurs. They spoke excitedly and asked such things as: "How do you
know?" "Are the tales then true?" "Can they save us from the
enemy?" and, of course, "Who are they?"

Kaliam studied the former Sentinel. "Naysmithe, friend and sage
. . . why do you say this?"

"In a time when ancient, legendary evils threaten The Realm,"
he said in that strange penetrating whisper, "the Three will come.
All of Alleble awaits them. And soon I will complete the blades they
will wield. It stirs the soul. Can you not sense it?"

Kaliam was silent. Though he could not explain how he knew,
he could indeed sense the coming of the Three. Later, as he stood
alone on the balcony above Guard's Keep, he stared at the shadows
in the west . . . and wondered.

"Mallik!!" Nock shouted as he sprinted into the dining area of
Guard's Keep. "At last I have found you!!" The hammer-meister
was so startled he spit stew halfway across the table.

"Great moonrascals!" Mallik bellowed, swabbing his bearskin
tunic with a clean cloth. "What in The Realm is the matter?!"

"You will never believe it, my friend!" Nock said. And he
grabbed and tugged on Mallik's thick arm. "Come, you must see!"

Mallik had barely enough time to grab his hammer before Nock
dragged him out of Guard's Keep, down several flights of stairs, and
out into Alleble's late afternoon sun. At last, they cut behind the
gatehouse and made their way to the dragon pens.

There they found evidence that someone had been very hard at
work. All of the pens had been raked clean of dragon scat. Huge,
steaming mounds were piled in the dump zone beyond the last pen.
The dragons all seemed to be resting contentedly on fresh straw. And

that was not even the wonder Nock had brought Mallik to see.

For a young blond warrior with unusual pinkish skin lay upon the back of an enormous dark gray dragon. His eyes were closed, and his head rested between the creature's shoulder blades. The dragon's tail curled protectively over the knight's legs. But what really caused Mallik's eyes to bulge was seeing the four ivory-white spikes protruding from the dragon's tail.

"King Eliam, save us!" Mallik cried. "Is he dead?"

"Nay, my friend," Nock said. "Only sleeping."

"But that is Splinter he is lying on!"

"I know!" Nock said. "Why do you think I came to get you?"

"Who would be so foolish as to sleep on that beast?" Mallik asked. "I would wager my beard he is another from the Mirror Realm!"

"That is Robby," answered Nock. "A good friend of Sir Aidan's. Lady Merewen told me he is to be Twelfth Knight on the mission into King's Forest tomorrow. But hush, we must rescue him without waking the monster."

Mallik and Nock tiptoed to the pen, and Mallik held his hammer high above Robby's sleeping form. "Go ahead," Mallik whispered urgently. "But mind the eyes!"

Being incredibly light on his feet, Nock leaped to Mallik's broad shoulders and walked across the haft of his hammer. Nock hooked his legs around the huge steel head and dangled down until he could reach Robby.

"Robby," Nock whispered. "Robby, wake up!"

Robby shrugged his shoulders, but his eyelids did not even so much as flutter.

"Robby!" Nock said a little louder. "Wake up! You are in danger!" This elicited a growl from Splinter. And finally Robby opened his eyes.

"Oh," Robby said. "I'm sorry! I was fixin' to get back to work, but I guess I must have dozed off." Then he looked strangely at Nock and Mallik. "What are you guys doing?"

"We are trying to save you!" Nock exclaimed. "This dragon is untamed—very dangerous!"

Robby sat up with an amused look on his face. "What, her?" he asked. "She's just a big ole pussycat!"

"Nay, Robby!" Mallik argued. "She is ornery and tempestuous! Trust us. We have seen her aroused."

Robby laughed. "You're joking! I know I'm the new guy, so I should expect it, but c'mon. You could at least come up with something serious!" Robby folded his hands behind his head and made no attempt to get off the dragon's back.

"Grab on to Nock's hands!" Mallik bellowed. His shoulders were beginning to wear down. "She is dangerous, I tell you!"

"Oh, stop!" Robby said as he spun around and straddled Splinter's back. Then he made a clicking noise with his tongue and his teeth. Immediately, Splinter rose on all fours and spread her wings. She brought her nose close and nuzzled Robby's chin.

"Ya see?" Robby said. Nock fell off Mallik's hammer, and the two of them stared.

"I do not believe it!" Nock said. "No one has been able to saddle—much less befriend—that creature!"

Robby made another clicking sound, and Splinter took off from that spot and soared into the sky. She did a shallow loop, scattering loose straw all over Nock and Mallik before finally landing again in her pen.

"How did you do it?" Mallik asked, brushing straw from his armor.

"I don't really know," Robby replied. "I was cleaning her pen, and well, she just kind of warmed up to me. I've been that way with animals for most of my life."

Mallik, Nock, and Robby talked about many things: the goings-on in The Realm, their adventures with Aidan, and the possibilities of Robby's mission. Robby didn't know much about that. Mallik and Nock did, but they would tell him precious little. They did not want to say anything without leave of their Sentinel.

Often their conversation turned to Pennath Ador. They found that the three of them had in common a love for mountains, and in short order they became friends. With the sun beginning to fall toward the horizon, Mallik and Nock needed to leave. "We are due to meet with Kaliam," Nock said. "But we will see you tonight at the ceremony."

"What ceremony?" Robby asked.

Mallik laughed. "Kaliam certainly enjoys keeping the new ones in suspense, does he not?"

"C'mon, you guys," pleaded Robby. "Tell me something!"

"You will see," Nock replied with a wink.

They started to go, but Robby asked, "Before you leave, I was wondering . . . do you know if it would be okay for me to take a little walk at the foot of the mountains?"

"That would be no little walk," Nock replied. "But certainly it is permitted. I often go there myself. There is the beginning of a trail on the other side of the Elder Guard's training compound. The path follows a steep incline through a dense patch of pines and will eventually lead you to the base of Pennath Ador. But do not linger past sundown, or you will miss your own ceremony!"

And with that, they departed.

Robby followed the narrow winding path through the pines, and just as Nock had foretold, it grew quite steep. Eventually, he broke through to the other side of the evergreens. And there it was. *It really looks different up close,* Robby thought. He couldn't even see the snowcapped peaks. Just a sheer face of stone, much of it gray and angular with juts and clefts, and a few large fields of another kind of rock, smooth and white. Robby continued to look up until his neck ached. Standing at the foot of such a giant made him feel very small. Yet Robby felt a sense of peace—a sense of being protected by the great walls of stone all about him. Robby actually walked up and placed the palms of his hands on the stone. It felt cool, but somehow vibrant. Robby smiled.

"You like these mountains, do you not?" came a voice from behind. Robby turned and saw an older Glimpse warrior, clad all in white, sitting upon a stone. Robby hadn't heard anyone approach, but there he was as if he'd been there all along.

"You like these mountains?" he repeated, and Robby found his voice somewhat familiar . . . though he could not say where he had heard it before.

"They're awesome," Robby replied. "Where I'm from, we don't have any mountains like these."

"Yes, I know," the Glimpse replied. "There are no mountains like these anywhere in this world. These are the first mountains born in all of history. They are very powerful."

"When I touched them, I felt . . ." A word came to Robby's mind, but he did not speak it aloud.

"You felt loved."

Robby stared at the old Glimpse. *How did he—*

"Of course the mountain itself does not express love," the Glimpse continued, interrupting Robby's thoughts. "But like all pure things at the dawn of time, they were washed in the love of their creator. In spite of The Schism, there are some who can still feel the pulse of that time. Some who can touch the memory of The Realm undefiled. You are such a one."

Robby stared. The old Glimpse stared back and sat so very still that he almost looked like he was carved from the stone upon which he sat. He was a curious being. Long, straight white hair flowed like a river over his broad shoulders. His mustache and beard were also long, straight, and white. Only his eyebrows were a bit unruly. They too were white, but they were bristly and thick, especially at the bridge of his nose where they seemed almost to meet. His eyes were utterly blue—even in the failing light. And as Robby stared into them he saw a depth of intensity he had never seen before. There was bright, beaming gladness there, but also wrenching sorrow. There was great fatherly pride, but also disappointment. Empathy and indignation. Love and wrath. The only emotion Robby did not see in his eyes was fear.

And there was one other thing that Robby did not see in the old Glimpse's eyes: He did not see them glint a color. Not even once. "Please, sir," Robby said. "Tell me your name."

"My name?" he echoed. "I am surprised that you do not already know it. But come closer and let us talk."

He saw that the strange being was girt with an immense sword, but Robby felt no threat. He stood right before him and waited. At a gesture, Robby sat down upon another stone. They were silent for many moments. Robby's mind was a whirl of thoughts and emotions—like a barely simmering pot that suddenly came to a rolling boil.

"You still have doubts," said the stranger. It wasn't a question.

"Doubts?"

"About all this," the old Glimpse replied, holding out his arms. "About many things."

Robby suddenly felt on the spot. "Doubts, I'm not sure if—"

"It is okay to have them," he said. "A doubt is nothing more than an invitation . . . an invitation to think. So, tell me, what have you been thinking about?"

"My father," Robby whispered. And as soon as the words came out, he wondered why he shared them with this stranger. But his deepest thoughts began to pour freely out as if he were talking to his closest friend. "Well, it's just that Dad's on the other side. I don't think he'll change, and . . . I don't want him to die." Tears streamed down Robby's cheeks, and he choked as he tried to speak again. "There's so much at stake, but he doesn't see. Mama and Jill—them too! I don't know . . ."

"I know the separation that you feel," said the Glimpse. He put a warm hand on Robby's shoulder. "And I never intended for you—for any—to have to feel it like this. But take heart! You are never alone."

"But my family . . ."

"There is yet time for your mother and your sister. But your father made his decision a long, long time ago. He was deceived, and because of his willful refusal to seek the truth, he can no longer see it."

"But there's a chance, right?" Robby asked.

The Glimpse nodded.

"I've got to try, don't I?"

"Very well, Robby," said the Glimpse. And it seemed that the sun had gone down, for the base of the mountain was robed in shadow. "You have decisions to make, beginning with this one: You can abandon your mission here and return to your realm—"

"But I don't even know what my mission is," Robby said.

"You know that you have been given a mission," said the Glimpse, "and that is enough. The choice is whether you will fulfill that mission or return to your world in the hope of bringing your family to the point of turning. Some good will come of either decision, but you must choose tonight."

Robby nodded miserably. "It's . . . it's hard," he said.

The old Glimpse stood. "You demonstrated your trust," he said quietly, "when you entered The Door Within. The only thing you must decide is whether you will continue to trust."

Robby watched as the Glimpse walked slowly to the path that led through the evergreens. He turned and looked one last time at Robby, and he smiled. Then he vanished into the trees.

Robby buried his head in his hands and wept.

Not a moment later, someone put a heavy hand on his shoulder. "Robby?" came a deep voice. "Are you all right?"

Robby looked up and there was Mallik, leaning on his immense hammer. "Nock told me you had probably come this way. But you are distraught. Has something happened?"

"I'm okay," Robby said, standing and wiping the last of his tears away. "It's just that I kind of lost it when I was talking to the old knight about my family."

"Old knight?" Mallik looked confused.

"Yeah," Robby replied, pointing to the path. "I mean, he looked old—still real strong—but old. You must have passed him on the path."

"I passed no one on the path," Mallik said.

"But you must've."

Mallik shook his head. They stood in awkward silence for some time.

"Come, Master Robby," Mallik said at last. "I cannot solve this mystery you have suggested. But perhaps Kaliam can. Now we should go. Many have gathered in your honor. I came to bring you to the main hall on time."

"The ceremony?"

"Yes," Mallik replied. "The very one."

They turned to leave, but Mallik stumbled over a pumpkin-sized gray stone. "That smarts!" Mallik said, laughing at his own clumsiness. "But I suppose it could have been much worse. That stone could have just now fallen from up high and hit me in the head!"

Robby laughed so hard it hurt.

"Hey," Mallik said, with a mischievous wink of the eye. "Before we go, would you like to see something?"

Robby nodded vigorously.

"Right, now stand aside," Mallik said, a grin widening on his face. He snatched up his hammer to a great height. "Now watch the stone. You will see sparks for sure!"

Robby watched the stone just as he was told. Mallik flexed his massive arms and swung his great hammer down. There was a sound that reminded Robby of the icemaker on his fridge at home, and the stone exploded in a shower of green and yellow sparks!

"That was incredible!" Robby exclaimed. "Your hammer can break rocks?"

"The head of this weapon was forged of *murynstil*," Mallik replied. "And my grandsire found a way to flash-temper it to a hardness beyond any stone in The Realm."

"Cool!"

"Well, almost any stone," Mallik corrected himself. "It takes me several swings to break the blue granite of my homeland, but it eventually shatters."

"Can you do it again?" Robby asked.

"We really ought to get back," Mallik said, grinning.

"Please!" Robby said. "C'mon, Mallik. Just one more time."

"All right," Mallik conceded at last.

Robby grinned and stood a few paces back as Mallik went over to the large white stone upon which the old Glimpse had been sitting. "Now this should please your desires!" Mallik said, and again he hoisted his hammer high. With great strength and terrible force, Mallik slammed the hammer down upon the white stone.

There was a thunderous sound that echoed off the face of Pennath Ador. But this time the stone did not shatter. Mallik's hammer bounced and fell out of his hands. He ran in a tight circle, clutching his hands as if burned.

"GREAT MOONRASCALS!!!" Mallik howled.

"Are you okay?" Robby asked.

"Aye, lad!" Mallik replied, picking up his hammer. "I just must have missed the center with my stroke. It does that sometimes. Now stand back."

Mallik took a deep breath and brought his hammer crashing

down upon the white stone. And again the hammer bounced without so much as a tiny spark. Mallik dropped his hammer and screamed at the mountain. Then he ran back and picked up his hammer for a third try. This time when he lifted his hammer, he brought the head so far back that it almost touched the ground behind him. Mallik's eyes bulged as he wrenched his body and swung the hammer in a huge arc.

The hammer's head struck the stone a mighty blow. A sound like a cannon shot bounced off the mountain, and a small chip of white shot into the woods. There had been no spark, but a small lick of fire sprouted on the white stone and danced there for a moment before flickering and going out. Suddenly the top of a small pine tree toppled over and fell—exactly where the chip of stone had gone.

"Did you see that?" Robby asked.

"Aye, I saw it," Mallik replied. "I saw it, but I do not believe it!"

"The old Glimpse who was here said this mountain was the very first mountain, that the white stone is powerful."

"No doubt about that," Mallik said. He whistled. "Why, this rock here is harder than the blue granite from my . . ."

Mallik's voice trailed off, and he stared up suddenly at the massive face of gray, and among that, the huge fields of white stone.

"What?" Robby asked, looking from the white stone by his feet and back to the mountain.

Mallik grabbed Robby by the collar of his tunic. "Hurry! We need to get back to the castle!" And Mallik lumbered off into the pines.

"What?" Robby asked, stumbling after him. "What's going on?"

"Well-done, Robby!" came Mallik's voice from up ahead. "You may have just saved the Kingdom of Alleble!"

THE GOOD
CONFESSION

While rushing up the passage from his chamber, Robby turned a corner and ran smack into a young Glimpse maiden. They tumbled awkwardly to the ground. Clad in his armor, Robby had landed on his back and looked like a turtle.

"Oooh, I knew I should have worn my armor!" the Glimpse said, and she was on her feet immediately, brushing the dust off a long emerald-green gown.

"I'm real sorry about that," Robby said. "It's just that I don't know my way around the castle and—" But when he finally got to his feet and saw her, he forgot what he was about to say. She had extremely long straight black hair that fell in dark locks behind her neck and back. And some draped on either side of her ears.

"Well?" she said, her raven dark eyes smoldering. "Where were you going in such a—" And then it was her turn to be suddenly awestruck. "You, you are not Glimpse-kind," she said, regaining some composure. "But I feel I have met you be—" She took in a sharp breath and put her hands to her mouth. "Kearn!" she exclaimed with sudden recognition. "Nay, but Kearn's twin from the Mirror Realm!"

Robby blushed. "That's me. My name is Robby Pierson." But then he felt obligated to say, "But I'm not like that Kearn guy."

"I daresay you are not!" She laughed. "You are a warrior of Alleble now. Well-met, I say! I am Trenna Swiftfoot." She held out her hand demurely, expecting Robby to kiss it in the manner of a chivalrous knight. Robby took her hand in his and shook it vigorously instead.

Trenna drew her hand back and smiled. "And from what I have heard," she continued, "you are to join me in the ceremony tonight."

"I am?" Robby looked at her questioningly.

She nodded.

"Oh, righ-ight," he said.

There was an awkward silent moment. "Do you know the way to the Great Hall? See, that's why I ran into you—I was lookin' for it, but got kinda lost."

"I will lead you," she said. "Keep up with me, if you can."

"That shouldn't be too hard," Robby replied.

"Oh, really?" Trenna raised an eyebrow, and before Robby knew it, she was gone.

She beat him to the Great Hall—beat him soundly. It was all Robby could do just to keep from losing sight of her and getting lost again. When Robby finally made it to the Great Hall, he was drenched with sweat. Trenna, on the other hand, looked dry and cool. A few Glimpse knights and maidens snickered as they passed by Robby and entered the crowded hall.

"I hope you fight better than you run," said Nock, who had watched the last leg of their race.

"It's hard running in all this armor," Robby said, tugging at the collar of his tunic.

"Oh, making excuses now, are we?" Trenna asked.

"No!" Robby replied curtly. "Well . . . yeah, I guess I am. I want a rematch."

"Anytime," she said, smiling sweetly.

"You two know each other?" Nock asked suspiciously.

"No!" they replied together as if horrified by the notion.

"We, uh, just ran into each other tonight," Trenna clarified.

Nock's intense blue eyes scanned them both.

"Robby Pierson, Trenna Swiftfoot, come forward!" Kaliam commanded from inside the hall. The crowd inside became suddenly quiet. Robby and Trenna walked slowly in, feeling very self-conscious with all eyes trained on them. They met Kaliam in the front of the vast arched room. Robby saw Mallik, Elspeth, Kindle, Lady Merewen, and several other prominent-looking Glimpses—all dressed in shining bright armor.

Kaliam smiled at Robby and Trenna and then turned to the crowd. "Knights and ladies of Alleble, friends from Yewland, Mithegard, and Acacia . . . we gather here tonight to witness the good confession of not one but two who would join our ranks!"

"Hear, hear!" the crowd cheered.

"Huzzah!" Mallik shouted.

"Ordinarily," Kaliam went on, turning back to Robby and Trenna, "this ceremony comes at the end of many years of training and education. But now, by King Eliam's decree in time of war, we perform this with all confidence and surety."

More cheers.

"And ordinarily, this ceremony is for one warrior at a time. But tonight you both have come. For both of you have been released from a kind of bondage: Trenna, the chains of iron you wore in Baen-Edge; Robby, the invisible chains you wore in the Mirror

Realm. But both in bondage manufactured by The Betrayer. On this glorious night we welcome you into an entirely different world where you are free to choose whom you will serve."

Kaliam then turned and Kindle came forward bearing a tray upon which lay two gleaming swords. One was short, thin, and beautifully curved. The other was a broadsword with a wide blade and a dragonwing crossguard.

Kaliam picked up the short sword and said, "Trenna, Robby, kneel before me."

The large room became entirely quiet. Kaliam glanced at Lady Merewen. She smiled.

"Trenna Swiftfoot," Kaliam began. "Steadfast huntress of Yewland, you are not called tonight to abandon all loyalties to your homeland. Nay, serve your queen faithfully. But by your declaration, you have already become a full servant of Alleble by making a confession of allegiance in the presence of Lady Antoinette. So this night, we make public that which you have already declared in private.

"Do you, Trenna, confess allegiance and absolute loyalty to the one true King, the provider of all that is just and good? Even were the hordes of darkness to assail you in hopeless demand of your life—even then do you swear devotion forever to the King? Trenna, say 'aye' only if this is the sincerest wish of your heart."

Trenna looked up, her eyes glinted blue, and she said, "Aye!"

"Huzzah!!" Mallik bellowed. Kaliam glared at his hammer-wielding friend as if to say, "We are not finished yet!"

Kaliam took the sword and lightly tapped it on each of Trenna's shoulders. "Then by the heartfelt confession of your lips, I dub thee Lady Trenna, swordmaiden and defender of Alleble!"

The room erupted in cheers—and huzzahs! And, crying tears of joy, Trenna accepted her sword from Kaliam's hands. Kaliam then turned to Robby. At first, Robby avoided the Sentinel's gaze. *Trenna decided so easily!* he thought. The whole time Kaliam had been speaking with Trenna, Robby had been silently debating. The strange encounter with the old Glimpse in the mountains kept replaying itself over and over in his mind. *The choice is whether you will fulfill that mission or return to your world in the hope of bringing your family to the point of turning. Some good will come of either decision, but you must choose tonight.*

Kaliam took the second blade from Kindle and turned to Robby. "Robby," he said, "you responded to King Eliam's invitation and entered The Door Within. You traveled the narrow path and have come now to make the good confession. This sword . . ." Kaliam held the blade aloft for all to see. "This sword was crafted long ago for a doughty knight who fought for Alleble in the Cold River Battles. It is a fearsome, heavy blade, emblazoned with the image of a dragon. And you have come to Alleble with the ferocity and the passion of such a beast.

"And already, in just a short time, you have struck a blow against the enemy that he will find hard to endure."

Mallik came within an inch of shouting out another HUZZAH, but Nock elbowed him in the ribs.

"And you have shown yourself courageous in battle," Kaliam continued. "Your skills warrant knighthood, so I now require of you . . . the good confession."

Robby shifted uncomfortably on his knees. He wanted desperately to become a knight and serve King Eliam, but he felt another kind of desperation as well . . . and he wasn't sure which would win out.

"Do you, Robby, confess allegiance and absolute loyalty to the one true King, the provider of all that is just and good? Even were the hordes of darkness to assail you in hopeless demand of your life—even then do you swear devotion forever to the King?"

In that moment Robby's field of vision clouded. And he saw his mother, smiling and happy as she often was when they lived in

Florida. She was flattening dough with a rolling pin and looking up expectantly. Then he saw his sister Jill, but she was younger . . . wearing pigtails like she used to before makeup and high school. She was just grinning like she knew the world's greatest secret. Finally, Robby saw his father. They were at the marina in Panama City. He was wearing that Hawaiian shirt Robby had given him for his birthday. He was showing Robby how to cast the fishing rod. Robby couldn't help but think how contented they both looked— father and son. But then the vision changed horribly. The faces, except his, were all still there. But they were grief-stricken, anguished, and fearful. There seemed to be dark water all around them—are they drowning? But wait! No, it was not water. It was oil . . . dark oil, and his mother, father, and sister were in the fountain. Suddenly, fire ringed the fountain and engulfed them!

"Noooo!" Robby screamed. The crowd gathered in the Great Hall gasped.

"Robby?" Kaliam said. "Robby, what is wrong?"

Robby put his head in his hands. "I don't know, I don't know, I don't know," he cried.

"I do." And suddenly Lady Merewen was there. She went to Robby and put her hand on his wet cheek. "You are torn," she whispered.

"I just can't let them die!" he said, looking up at her with desperate eyes.

"Who, Robby?" Lady Merewen asked.

"Mom, Dad . . . Jill—they'll die if I don't go back!" Robby closed his eyes and began to shake.

"Robby, look at me!" she said, and she lifted his chin. And slowly, Robby looked up at her. "Now," she said, "who told you they would all die?"

"He did."

Lady Merewen tilted her head and restrained the anger she was feeling. "Paragor is a liar, Robby!" she said forcefully. "For the longest time, he ruled you by his lies, and now that he has lost you, he wants only one thing: to render you powerless."

"But my family . . . if I don't go back, who will tell them?"

Lady Merewen smiled and put her hand on Robby's shoulder. "King Eliam the Everlasting has many servants," she said. And suddenly, Robby felt another hand on his shoulder. He looked up, and there was Trenna, grinning like a schoolgirl. Yet another hand, a big one, landed on Robby's other shoulder. Robby smiled, for there was Mallik. Nock came next, then Kindle, and another . . . and another. And still many more after that until Robby was surrounded by Glimpses. Their hands chased away the chill, and Robby pictured the eyes of the old Glimpse from the mountain.

"The only thing you must decide is whether you will continue to trust."

"Robby, I offer to you now the good confession," Kaliam said. "Think deeply on this, for you are free to choose. Only answer 'aye' if it is the deepest longing of your heart."

Robby looked up at the glad loving eyes of his new friends, but no, they were somehow more than friends. They were family. *I will trust you,* Robby said in his mind. But out loud he yelled at the top of his lungs, "Aye!"

"Then by the heartfelt confession of your lips," Kaliam announced, tapping the sword blade lightly on his shoulders, "I dub thee Sir Robby, Twelfth Knight of Alleble and servant forever of King Eliam the Everlasting!"

The roar that escaped the Great Hall in that moment could be heard even by those who passed by the castle on the road. The celebration ensued, but for Kaliam, Robby, and many of the warriors gathered there, they could not enjoy much of it, for they had important matters to discuss.

"Can they do it?" Kaliam asked. He stood beside a roaring fire in Guard's Keep.

"My people are masters of mountain and stone," Mallik replied proudly. "If there are any fissures in the tough white rock of Pennath Ador, we will exploit them. Still, it will take an army, and we need to begin now, before my kinsmen arrive."

"What must we do?" asked Farix, and he pulled a rolled parchment and a quill pen from his wide sleeves.

"First, we will need more cutting and wedge tools," Mallik explained, the lust for his craft thick in his voice. "King Brower will bring those that were not destroyed in the attack on Ludgeon. It is a goodly amount, but not enough. These will need to be made with haste and precision—not an easy feat to combine. And they can be made only from the purest veins of murynstil."

Kaliam turned to the armory keeper, who looked lost in thought. "Kindle?"

"Aye," he replied. "We can do that. Naysmithe can make anything from any metal in The Realm. But he will need a team of craftsmen, and every forge in Alleble will need to be stoked. I will see to it."

Mallik nodded. "Good!" he said. "Next we will need to harvest dragon skins—enough to stitch together a flexible pipeline that will reach halfway up the mountains."

"My word," said Elspeth. "I can get the skins, for as you know, our dragons shed their skins often. But what on earth would you need such a length for?"

"Ahhh," Mallik said, a twinkle in his eye. "That is the secret of our craft, but you shall learn it soon enough!"

"What more do we need?" Farix asked, busily scrawling everything on the scroll.

Mallik twirled a braid of his mustache for a moment. "A hundred kettles to boil snow," he said. "Miles of good rope, a forest's worth of timber, fifty sturdy carts with several hundred spare wheels, and as many dragons as we can spare."

"Splinter will help!" Robby chimed in.

"Nay!" Mallik exclaimed. "I would take any dragon in Alleble, save that one. Splinter is your steed now, and you shall need her for your mission."

"Soon, Sir Robby!" Kaliam said, seeing Robby's eagerness.

Robby grinned, for he liked being called sir. *Wait 'til Aidan sees me!* he thought.

"That is quite a list," Farix said.

"This is quite a task," Mallik replied.

"And time is the great unknown," King Ravelle said. "We are hoping to do much without knowing when Paragor will mount his offensive. Have we heard from your scouts on the Cold River?"

"Yes," Kaliam replied. "There is much movement in Paragory. More troops arrive each day, but at least so far, he has not given any indication of when he might attack."

"That is good news," King Ravelle said. "Perhaps we will have new walls upon which to fight, after all! Oh, and well defended those walls will be. Nock and Queen Illaria have been training Yewland's Braves with the arbalest. As is expected, they have taken to them with great enthusiasm! Combining the arbalest with Blackwood Arrows has absolutely devastating effect."

"Excellent." Kaliam stood, clapping his hands. "Well, then, many of you have your orders. See to them, and honor our great King with your work. The twelve I have selected will remain, for we must discuss your mission into King's Forest."

The fire in Guard's Keep was now just glowing embers. It hissed and popped behind the black grate, its warmth nearly spent. The candle chandelier swayed and turned slowly, sending flickering shadows dancing around the room. The chilled night air slipped in through the closed shutters.

All mirth had disappeared. Each knight looked grimly thoughtful. Robby gazed at the other warriors, and aside from himself and Kaliam, he counted only ten. Kaliam stood by the fireplace, staring expectantly at the chamber door. Robby wondered who was missing.

"I am sorry!" came a voice from outside the room, and in sped Trenna—now wearing the bright armor of Alleble. "I did not mean to keep you waiting," she said. "But I would feel out of place among such proud ironclad warriors without my own silver armor."

Trenna quickly took a seat next to Robby.

"Tonight," Kaliam began, "you all met Sir Robby of the Mirror Realm and Lady Trenna from Yewland."

"Never alone!" sang out a Glimpse with bushy eyebrows and a lion's mane of black hair. "And well-met, I say!"

"Yes, Sir Oswyn," Kaliam said, smiling. "Well-met, indeed. For we know them, but they do not know all of us. I shall remedy that presently."

"When tomorrow you take flight over the Mountains of Glory and enter King's Forest, Thrivenbard will lead you." A princely looking dark-haired knight with sharp features and large brown eyes stood briefly and bowed toward Robby and Trenna.

"Thrivenbard's wood knowledge is without equal in The Realm," Kaliam went on. "And of the twelve, he alone has ventured into King's Forest. Even so, Thrivenbard would be the first to tell you that for such a mission as this we will need all the woodland experience we can muster. So Halberad, his apprentice, will join us."

Halberad, a knight clad all in brown leather armor, stood a moment and bowed.

"Like Trenna, the next three warriors were born and raised among the trees in Yewland," Kaliam said. "Nock, Baldergrim, and Boldoak."

The sandy-haired archer stood first and winked at Robby and Trenna. "Hail, Dragonfriend and Swiftfoot," Nock said. "I trust there will be no more races in the forest." Robby and Trenna glanced sideways at each other and blushed.

The two knights who stood next could not have been more different. The one called Baldergrim was tall, slender, and golden-haired, clean-shaven with skin smooth like porcelain and large gray eyes. Boldoak was broad and muscular with unruly shocks of dark hair and a wild beard to match. His skin was weather-beaten and worn, with a large scar prominent on his cheek. Boldoak's dark eyes were barely visible slits beneath his protruding brow.

"At your service," Baldergrim said in a rich, deep voice.

"For the King's glory," said Boldoak, his voice low and gravelly. They both bowed and sat.

"The realm of Acacia, ever a friend to Alleble, sends three of its greatest hunters, Jarak, Locke, and Valden, to help us on this quest." Three warriors stood, each dressed in armor of burnished copper. Jarak, a medium-build Glimpse with clever green eyes and a reddish Vandyke beard, said, "Proud to serve with you!"

"As am I," said Locke, who looked very young with a mop of light brown hair and a sprinkling of freckles upon his nose and cheeks.

Valden was taller than the other two, and had waves of ruddy blond hair, small peaceful eyes, and a narrow goatee. In spite of the kindly appearance, Robby noticed that Valden had a pair of long-handled axes dangling from holsters at his sides. Valden said nothing but bowed just the same.

"Valden does not speak much," said Locke.

"Except in battle," corrected Jarak. "Then, cover your ears!"

"You have already heard from Sir Oswyn," Kaliam continued. "But know now that he is gifted with herbs and medicines."

"I deliver balms that heal for our allies," Oswyn stood and said. "And more explosive remedies for our enemies!"

"Your fire powder is most effective!" said a massive knight with long blond hair. He stood, reached over his shoulder, and brought round a huge, dual-bladed battleaxe. "Sir Rogan, of Mithegard," he said.

Sir Rogan sat down and winked mischievously at Robby. When he did, his eyes sparkled blue a moment. With curious fascination Robby looked from knight to knight. Each of the warriors, though clearly from many cultures and realms, had eyes that flickered blue, the color of devotion to King Eliam. Robby smiled, thinking that somewhere on earth his own Glimpse dwelt. And now, this Glimpse twin would have eyes that glinted blue as well.

After meeting such a collection of gifted warriors, Robby felt very honored to be counted among them. Most of them were trackers or hunters—except Oswyn, who seemed a type of doctor. *They all have a certain job,* Robby thought. *Except Sir Rogan—and me.*

Robby wondered what their roles on the mission would be, but Kaliam interrupted his thoughts. "Somewhere in a hidden village under the canopy of King's Forest lives a very old Glimpse," Kaliam began. Robby looked up with great interest. "His name is Zabediel, and he was the scribe for King Eliam when this world was new."

"Lives?" questioned Thrivenbard. "Surely you mean *lived.*"

"Nay, my friend," Kaliam replied. "For once, it is you who have gone off track. Zabediel was one of Torin's kin, in the direct line of the firstborn Glimpses. To him has been given unnaturally long life. By the word of King Eliam, Zabediel is yet alive."

Looks were exchanged around the room. No one could fathom anyone, aside from the King, of course, having lived so long.

"Zabediel was pleased to record the King's ideas and his

decrees," Kaliam went on. "He did so for many years. But at one point, still long before Alleble came to be, the King saw into the future of The Realm. And what he saw Zabediel recorded on a single sheet of parchment."

Sir Oswyn nodded as if he knew something of Kaliam's tale.

"This scroll remained in King Eliam's keeping," the Sentinel continued. "Even as Alleble was founded and many things in The Realm were born and grew, the scroll was safe. But when The Schism occurred, Zabediel, fearing for his own life, sought refuge in King's Forest. And the scroll . . . well, the King hid that away, for he knew what could happen if one of ill intent knew its contents."

"The Scroll of Prophecy!" said Sir Oswyn. "That is the parchment you speak of!"

"Yes," Kaliam replied.

"But that is just a legend," Jarak said.

"As were the Wyrm Lord and the Seven," Nock said. "And yet they live and breathe—I have seen it."

Jarak fell silent.

"There are many legends in The Realm," Kaliam went on. "Legends laughed off as harvest tales or children's lore. But even the most far-fetched stories can often be traced back to a kernel of truth. I do not know how much of the legend concerning the Scroll of Prophecy is to be heeded, but this much is known to me: It will help us identify the Three Witnesses."

"I don't understand," Jarak said, pinching the end of his tapered red beard. "Who are these Three Witnesses you speak of?"

"Mighty champions," said Sir Oswyn. "Bold-hearted warriors with magnificent weapons. It is said that these three will come to Alleble in its time of greatest need and defend us from the threatening darkness."

"We have our mission, then!" Baldergrim exclaimed, his gray eyes intense and turbulent like a storm about to break. "Let us go and get this scroll. And then we might match Paragor's living legends with our own!"

"We cannot," Kaliam replied. The chamber became utterly silent. They waited for Kaliam to explain. "Paragor has it."

"You mean that is why he cut down the Ancient One?" Boldoak asked. "That is what he stole from the hollow at *Sil Arnoth*'s center?"

Kaliam nodded.

"What would Paragor want with such a scroll?" Sir Rogan asked, fingering the sharp edge of his axe. "Does it not tell of his demise?"

"I do not know if Paragor's demise is a certainty, my friend," Kaliam said gravely. "Some say the Scroll of Prophecy does not tell the way things must be in the end, but rather the way events *might* unfold for good *or* for ill. The destruction of Alleble could be foretold or the way that our end could be brought about. It could be that the prophecy tells both how the Three Witnesses may be found—and how they might be defeated. In any case, Paragor went to great lengths to get the scroll, and now he has it."

"Is all then lost?" Trenna asked, her eyes large and dark. "For you said our mission is to King's Forest, not Paragory."

"We yet have hope, Lady Trenna," Kaliam replied. "For the Scroll of Prophecy was written in a very old language—the same as The Stones of White Fire that surround the Library of Light. Paragor studied long in that place, and I believe he would be able to translate some of the scroll, but not all. And there is only one being left in all The Realm who still speaks that old tongue."

"Zabediel," Sir Oswyn said.

"Does Paragor know about Zabediel?" asked Nock.

"He may," Kaliam replied, shaking his head angrily. "Somehow our enemy has discovered many secrets of The Realm! He learned of the Wyrm Lord, the Sleepers, and now the Scroll of Prophecy. I have often wondered how! It could be that he shrewdly pieced together bits of truth from old legends. Or, perhaps he has employed more clever traitors than we ever imagined. It has even entered my mind that perhaps, on the night of the Betrayal . . . perhaps Paragor saw these things when he looked into the first scroll of Alleble. Ah! It is maddening!" Kaliam sighed. "In any case, we must assume that Paragor knows of Zabediel."

"Right then," Sir Rogan said. "Our mission is to find this eldest of Glimpses before the enemy!"

"Yes," Kaliam replied. "Tomorrow the twelve of you will take flight over Pennath Ador, but you must enter King's Forest on foot. Find the hidden village where Zabediel now dwells, and bring Zabediel back to Alleble. We must learn the mysteries of the Scroll of Prophecy—and keep Paragor from learning them himself!"

"Do you like the sword?" Kaliam asked Robby as the two stood on the balcony overlooking the seventh fountain.

The long broadsword rang when Robby drew it from its sheath. He carved the air with wide two-fisted strokes. "It's perfect," he said. "The weight is exactly what I like, and the whole dragon emblem thing is cool."

"Indeed it does seem to fit you," Kaliam said, admiring the blade. "I thought so when Kindle first showed the sword to me. The dragon on the crossguard, as I said in the ceremony, is especially appropriate given what you did with Splinter. That was one bad-tempered wyrm!"

"Well, I think she and I have an understanding," Robby said with a laugh. "At least I hope so. I'll be on her back, high in the sky, with just one flying lesson!"

"You are a natural, Sir Robby," Kaliam said. "And the way Splinter has taken to you, she will not let you fall. Remarkable, really . . . the way she responds. It is a singularly unique ability." They were quiet for a few moments. The two knights stared out over the sleeping city of Alleble. They listened to the hypnotic rush of the fountains.

Inwardly, Kaliam debated. He wanted to—no, needed to—ask Robby a question, but he was afraid of the implications of the answer. *King Eliam knows what he is doing,* Kaliam reminded himself. Then he took a deep breath and said, "Sir Robby, when you passed through The Door Within, did anything strange happen to you?"

Robby laughed. "The whole thing was strange!"

"Yes, I suppose it was," said Kaliam. "What I mean is . . . did you hear or see anything that troubled you?"

Robby's smile disappeared. "I . . . I don't really know what I saw," Robby explained. "There were scenes all around me, images of things. They weren't from my world, I can tell you that."

Kaliam nodded thoughtfully. He waited a few heartbeats before asking, "Since you have been here in Alleble, have any of these visions come to pass?"

Robby hesitated. "No . . . I don't think so. First, there was a terrible storm—worse than the ones that blow in off the Gulf where I used to live. Then I saw an army and a forest. The last thing I remember—wait, yeah, that's right—there was a battle, and it was in front of a walled city." Robby pointed at Alleble's walls. "It might have been Alleble. I'm not sure. And in the middle of the fighting, some kind of thing with great big claws started tossing knights around like toys."

Kaliam stared out at the fountains and imagined a battle raging. He imagined the coming of the Wyrm Lord and the destruction that ancient horror could cause. He looked at Robby and smiled grimly. Aidan, Antoinette, and now Robby—all of them seeing visions as they passed between worlds. Captain Valithor had been right all along. *And now Antoinette is in the hands of the enemy. And where is Aidan? Is he too now a captive of Paragor?*

"Kaliam?" Robby asked. "Why did you ask me about what I saw? I mean, it seems like you expected me to have seen something."

"Yes, Sir Robby, I did expect it," Kaliam replied, but he did not elaborate.

"Is there something wrong?" Robby asked, growing concerned. "Have I done something wrong?"

"Nay, Sir Robby," Kaliam said, and he put his hands on Robby's shoulders. "You have done everything right since you entered The Realm, but these things that have happened to you—the visions, your ability to tame Splinter, the visitation by the old Glimpse in the mountains—these things may be of great importance. But we must find Zabediel to know for sure."

Robby was on his way to his chamber for some much-needed sleep, when he remembered something else from his visions between worlds. In the forest, there had been a knight. And he became surrounded by many dark, glassy eyes. Robby had no idea if it was important, but he thought Kaliam might know. So Robby sped back the way he had come, at last arriving at the door to the balcony above Guard's Keep. The door was slightly ajar, and Robby hesitated. He felt strangely awkward, and the thought entered his mind that he had no right to just go mucking about in the Castle of Alleble. Then he heard voices. Feeling even more uncomfortable, Robby drew close and put his ear to the narrow crack and listened.

"Is it as you suspected?" one voice asked, and Robby thought it might have been Sir Rogan.

"I cannot be sure," a voice answered. That had to be Kaliam.

"Do you think he knows?"

"No," Kaliam replied. "But we must be careful what we say in his presence."

Robby felt as if a blade of ice had been drawn over his spine. *Could they be talking about me?* he wondered. Robby's eyebrows knotted, and he listened more intently.

"What do you want me to do, then?" asked Sir Rogan.

"Watch him," Kaliam replied. "Do not let him out of your sight, for he may rule the fate of us all."

Hearing footsteps, Robby sprinted away from the door and raced all the way back to his chamber. Moments later, he lay in bed and stared into the darkness. His stomach churned, and he flopped back and forth trying to get comfortable.

Then, like the uninvited whisper of chill wind, a familiar voice came into Robby's mind. *"They do not trust you."*

THE BLACK BREATH

The Paragor Knights carried the screaming prisoners quickly through the catacombs and tunnels deep within the mountains of Paragory. Aidan followed them at a distance, all the while trying to remember the twists and turns so that he could find his way back. The enemy came to a sudden stop, and Aidan ducked behind a ridge of stone that projected from the tunnel wall and quietly drew his sword.

He peered out from behind the rock and saw that the tunnel ended in a kind of cliff overlooking a vast cavern. The prisoners shrieked and screamed. They struggled and fought—even trying to bite their captors. Aidan heard several distinct snapping sounds, and he knew the prisoners had broken their own bones trying to escape. But the knights outnumbered their captives two to one. They were much stronger and wore cruel spiked armor. They shrugged off the frantic blows and dragged a prisoner to the edge. Then, as if the prisoner were a sack of grain, the Paragor Knights tossed him over the edge and far into the cavern. He screamed a terrible, half-choked desperate scream. The scream was cut ominously short.

The Paragor Knights continued hurling the wretched prisoners over the edge, replaying the same scene. And yet Aidan had not heard even one of their bodies hit the ground.

Aidan wept in his hiding spot. He desperately wanted to come to their rescue, but there were too many guards. To rush out there now would be suicide and would condemn Antoinette to never-ending captivity in the holds of the enemy.

So Aidan watched in stunned silence until the Paragor Knights had finished. When they turned and sped back up the tunnel, Aidan had no thought for himself. They could have easily seen him crouching there, but they didn't. They marched right by without even a glance.

At last, Aidan shook off the shock-induced paralysis. He stood, took a few timid steps toward the edge of the cliff—but could not see what lay far below.

The knights had spoken of feeding the Ancient One. *But who or what is the firstborn?* Aidan shuddered, thinking of some hideous creature snatching bodies out of the air. Aidan knew he should run as fast as he could in the opposite direction. But something drew him closer to that horrible cliff.

He slid slowly toward the edge and saw the serrated black crest of an enormous beast. He was not close enough to say yet what it was. But its back was armored with dark, glistening scales, and it seemed there was a ripple of muscle that churned beneath the scales like a wave of convulsions. Suddenly the creature loosed a terrible frightening cry—a wailing shriek that deepened and became a gut-tural roar. Aidan fell backward and clutched his ears. It seemed the whole cavern shook.

After what seemed like a painful eternity, the roar ceased. He heard a sound of wrenching metal and an echoing thud, and then a protracted grinding. Aidan rolled over onto his stomach and crawled to the edge to see what had happened. The cavern had two tall arched doors—like to the Gate of Despair, but slightly smaller. And these doors were opening. Aidan could see the icy wasteland beyond.

Aidan crawled a little closer, and at last he saw the beast in full. It was a dragon four times the size of the ones Aidan had ridden before, filling the cavern with its immense girth. It seemed to be sleeping, for its eyelids were clamped shut. But the creature continued to convulse. Then it opened its jaws and heaved as if it would vomit, but no flame or filth came forth. Instead, dark vapors spewed out—just tendrils at first but then a torrent of darkness. Aidan watched with sick fascination as the liquid shadow flooded out of the creature's jaws and flowed like a dead river onto the Grimwalk. Aidan started to back away, but suddenly the dragon's eye opened. It was a smoldering blood-red, and Aidan felt it could see him prone on the cliff. He backed away as fast as he could, got to his feet, and sprinted back up the tunnel.

After a half-dozen wrong turns later, Aidan emerged from a tunnel into the smoky cavern where the torture cages hung high among jagged stalactites. The Gate of Despair was thrown open, and wide columns of knights issued forth from it. Teams of stocky blackhorne were hitched to siege engines and catapults, and they too were in motion. The dragon riders went to the pens and groomed their steeds for flight. The stronghold of Paragory was emptying.

Aidan saw that beyond the gate the Grimwalk was shrouded in a thickening blanket of darkness—the Black Breath of the red-eyed dragon. Aidan watched as the forces of the enemy marched into the murk and disappeared from view.

At that moment several things happened in rapid succession. Kearn appeared from a passage to Aidan's right. He strode across the cavern floor, barked orders to several ranks of soldiers, and then vanished into a tunnel on the other side. Then the dragon riders began to walk their steeds out of the pens. But they did not go to the main gate, which was choked with massive siege weapons and legions of soldiers. Instead, they led their dragons into any one of a dozen arched gates not far from the passage Kearn had taken.

This is my chance! Aidan thought, and he sprinted across the cavern floor to the dragon pens. But because of the noise of the troop deployment, Aidan did not hear the Paragor Knight who was shouting at him from atop one of the siege towers. "Hey, Blarrak, what do you think you are doing?" Drang yelled. "We do not leave for another hour. You get yourself up here and help me fix this engine right now!"

Drang snarled, banged his fist, and then raced down the switchback stairs of the tower to pursue the errant knight who had the nerve to ignore his commander. But Drang had barely set foot on the cavern floor when a tall knight stepped out from between two siege towers and stood in front of him. This warrior had two swords sheathed on his back beneath a long burgundy cape. The skin of his face seemed thin and stretched just enough to cover the prominent skull beneath. His sunken eyes emanated authority and peril. Drang reflexively stepped backward.

"L-Lord Rucifel," Drang said. He bowed and then stared at the floor. He opened his mouth, but thinking better of it, snapped it shut. Drang knew it was better to speak few words around Lord Rucifel.

"The Black Breath has begun," Rucifel said, his words clipped with anger. "My legions are ready to go forth, but the master sends me to speak to you, Drang. It seems there were some . . . problems . . . on your errand to Yewland. Perhaps you could explain. That is, if you have a moment to spare."

Drang glanced at the dragon pens for a split second and then nodded.

Aidan found the dragon pens as busy as a hive. Riders and dragons were on the move wherever he went. They passed without so much as a glance in Aidan's direction, but even so, he felt conspicuous among them. Aidan went from pen to pen, but could not find Blarrak's or Galdoth's dragon. He felt like he was wasting time.

Aidan looked up at the passage that Kearn had taken, and he wondered how far ahead Kearn had gotten. Aidan gave up looking for the two dragons he knew, but he needed an alternative. After some searching, he found two dragons near the back of the pens. He untied the first, a dark blue dragon with long yellow fangs and a forked tail. It sniffed at Aidan and refused to move. Aidan pulled on its reins, but that just earned him a threatening growl. *Next dragon!* Aidan thought, and he made his way quickly to the other pen.

He was about to give up when he spotted a jagged fence behind the dragon pens. A white wing flailed just above the fence line, then a tail. Curious, Aidan drew closer. As he did, he heard deep rumbling growls, followed by a pained yelp and several oaths.

Aidan walked up and peered tentatively around the fence. He saw four white dragons, their necks tied with cords to iron rings embedded in the floor. He also saw an angry knight walking away and rubbing the back of his arm.

"Uh, excuse me, sir," Aidan said. "Whose dragons are these?"

Annoyed, the knight stopped and turned to Aidan. "They are for slaughter," he said. "That is who they belong to!"

"Why?" Aidan asked.

"What, are you daft, lad?" the knight said. "These are some of the ones we took from the battle in Yewland. Swift as a high gale they are, but useless to us. The ornery things will not let me near them!"

That's probably because they can't stand the stink of you Paragor Knights! Aidan thought, but what he said was, "Could I try?"

The knight looked Aidan up and down. "Your armor looks sturdy enough. Have at it! But do not come crying to me if you get a finger nipped off!" With that, the knight stomped off into the crowds.

Aidan unlatched the fence gate and stepped in. The nearest dragon growled fiercely and bared its fangs at Aidan. *Maybe this wasn't such a good idea,* he thought. Aidan looked around to see if anyone was watching. No one was, so he quickly removed one of his gauntlets and held his hand up for the dragon to smell. Aidan squeezed together his eyes as the dragon's snout came close to his hand.

The dragon snorted, and Aidan jumped. But then, instead of eating Aidan's fingers, it licked them. Aidan patted the steed on the snout, and it ducked its head shyly. He let one of the other white dragons smell his hand to gain its trust. He untied the two and led them out of the fenced-in area. He looked back at the other two, still tied down, and remembered the words of the knight. There could be no other decision. Aidan ran quickly back inside and loosened the cords so that the other two dragons were no longer tied down. "When you get the chance," he whispered to them, "fly home!"

Aidan drew a few stares as he led the white dragons into the thick lines of dragon riders heading for the arched doors. *Nice going!* he berated himself. *Way to stay undercover!* But he knew he really had very little choice. Without the dragon steeds, it would be a long walk to Alleble. Soon enough, Aidan and his white dragons were immersed in the crowd and nearing the doors.

Drang staggered away from his conversation with Lord Rucifel. He was happy to still be breathing, having lied and sworn to escape Rucifel's wrath. But then his thoughts turned to Blarrak. *Wait until*

I get my hands around his thick neck! Drang raged as he scanned the dragon pens. Then a glint of white snatched his attention and there Blarrak was. *Where did he get white steeds?* Drang wondered.

Drang charged across the cavern floor but found himself stuck behind dozens of dragons far back in the line. Still, he watched Blarrak's progress closely.

At last Aidan approached the arched passages. He watched as dragon riders split off and marched into their assigned tunnels. But at the last moment, Aidan drew his two steeds into the passage Kearn had taken.

Aidan waited briefly just inside the passage, hoping that no one had followed him. Then he led the dragons quickly up the wide torchlit hall.

Only a few moments later, Drang stumbled out of the masses of dragon riders and ran up to the tunnel that Aidan had entered. "What are you up to, Blarrak?" Drang wondered aloud as he drew a cruel-looking curved blade and raced inside.

Aidan followed the twists and turns of the passage. He knew that Antoinette was held captive in a high place, a tower perhaps, so he was relieved when the path went steadily up. But as the path steepened, it also began to narrow. After a few minutes the passage was nearly choked to the point where the dragons would not be able to continue. Aidan pressed on, but stopped when he felt a cold draft of air.

The passage forked, and the wind seemed to be coming from the branch that curled down to the right and away. Aidan looked indecisively back to the left branch of the fork. *I'll never get the dragons up there!* Aidan thought. So, hoping he could find some place to secure the dragon steeds, Aidan took the right fork. It sloped gradually at first and then became steep at the bottom. Eventually, the passage leveled out and continued through an ornately carved archway.

Aidan found himself standing outside on a vast railed balcony. He walked out a few paces, saw the dark mountains of the Prince's Crown curling away to the left and the Grimwalk shrouded in a sea of darkness to the right. It was better than Aidan could have imagined—the perfect getaway zone! So, issuing a silent *Thank you* to King Eliam, Aidan quickly tied his dragons to the balcony's iron railing.

Looking up, Aidan saw a dark tower. Roughly cut with a kind of brutal symmetry, the massive tower rose high into the turbulent sky until it was crowned with a collar of jutting black spikes. As far as Aidan could see, there were no windows cut into the tower. He thought there might be one small dark square cut into the very top, but it was very hard to see beyond the spikes and know for sure.

Nonetheless, it seemed a perfect place to keep a prisoner, and Kearn had evidently gone that way. Aidan dashed back up the passage from whence he had come.

From behind an arch, Drang watched Aidan tie the dragons to the railing and stare up at the tower.

So, Blarrak—or whoever you are, Drang thought, looking from the dragons to the tower. *Do you think you will just make off with Kearn's prize? Is that it?*

Drang walked over to the white dragons. "Well, let us see how you do with no dragons to help you get swiftly back to Yewland!"

He went to untie the first dragon, but it growled. Drang tried again, but it nipped at his hand.

"Filthy creatures!" Drang spat. "Well, then," he said, "so you like to play rough. I can play that way. Just let me fetch some of the lads, and we will make a nice little surprise for Blarrak's return!"

Two knights lay hidden in the clefts of rock in the bony foothills just on the western side of the Cold River. The sky was a turbulent mass of ashen gray, and an icy wind shrieked in off the Grimwalk. A thunderous roar rose above the wind, rising to an anguished cry spoken as if pain were its language. Stones shook free and the knights' armor rattled.

"Vygant!" one whispered urgently to the other, who was much higher. "What was that?"

"I do not know, Alaric," he replied, straining to see across the frozen wasteland. "It is a sound like none I have heard before."

"It sure has Fledge spooked," said Alaric. They could both hear the frightened creature's squeals from the cove where they had left her.

"Forget the dragon," Vygant said. "It has *me* spooked!"

"What do you see?"

"Same as before," Vygant replied. "The Gate of Despair is open wide, and there is movement all over the mountains, but still no legions marching forth from within."

"Even so, I do not like this," Alaric said, clambering up next to Vygant. "We should flee at once and get word to Kaliam."

"I am with you in heart," Vygant replied. "But our orders are to watch for Paragor to begin his offensive. We must wait."

"Something has begun," Alaric argued. "I do not think we can afford to—"

"Wait!" Vygant yelled. "Do you hear that?"

"I hear nothing." Alaric looked at him and shrugged.

"No, that is what I mean. The wind has stopped. There is no sound at all."

They both stared across the Grimwalk. The clouds were still roiling. In fact, they seemed closer to the ground and even more disturbed than before. But it was dreadfully silent. Then suddenly, there was something there at Paragor's gate, a bubbling dark mass.

"What is that?" Vygant asked.

Alaric did not answer. They both stared, entranced by the scene unfolding at the gate of the enemy. The mass began to spread almost as if it were liquid, spilling left and right of the gate and saturating the Grimwalk. In moments it became a black wave, surging forward and growing so high that the scouts of Alleble could no longer see the bulk of Paragor's fortress. Silently the wave approached until it was nearly halfway across the Grimwalk.

"It is getting closer!" Alaric exclaimed.

"Okay, we have seen enough to report!" Vygant yelled. The two of them climbed down from their outpost and leaped recklessly the rest of the way down the foothill. Then, tripping and stumbling, they ran for the cove where they had tied their dragon steed. Just before turning the corner, they felt a presence behind them. They spun around just in time to see a wall of black creep over the ridge they had just abandoned.

Tendrils of darkness groped over the stone and reached out as it came. Alaric and Vygant ran, but it was too late. The wave of black washed over them, and they found themselves not in total darkness, but rather in a peculiar twilight. They could still see each other but only in murky silhouettes. And they felt like they were moving in slow motion, almost as if the shadowy air around them had a feathery texture that resisted slightly as they moved.

"What is happening?" Alaric yelled, though his voice sounded muffled and far away to Vygant.

"I do not know!" he replied. "Stay together! Get to Fledge!"

They ran as fast as they could, but the darkness made the landscape nearly impossible to recognize. They found themselves suddenly at the edge of the Cold River, somehow far from the cove and the dragon—their only means of escape. And it was too far to leap across at this point, so they began to follow the riverbank.

Vygant reached and grabbed Alaric's arm, and they stopped abruptly. "Did you hear that?" Vygant asked.

"Listen to the wind howl!" Alaric called back to him.

"That is not the wind," Vygant said. And then they saw eyes in the darkness. Large yellow eyes.

A Superior Foe?

Antoinette heard the jangle of keys. The chamber door swung inward and two guards entered. "It is the only window in this reeking tower," one of the guards said. "Unless you want to walk all the way back down!"

"Not a chance," said the other. The first guard came to Antoinette's cell and shoved the key into the lock. "Move back, Dark Skin!" said the guard, forcing the door open. Antoinette kept her free hands—and her sword—behind her as she backed away. Ignoring her, the guard went to the window.

"Ahrgh!" he said. "Just look at them! We could be with them if we did not have to guard this whelp!"

"What if we caught her trying to escape?" the other asked, loosening his sword from its scabbard.

The first guard turned and eyed Antoinette. "I was hoping you would suggest that." He brandished an iron-capped club. He took one step toward Antoinette, and it became his last. In a blur, she spun inside his swinging arm, and rammed the hard pommel of her sword under his chin. There was an awful crack, and the guard staggered. Then, Antoinette turned the sword and stabbed backward under her own arm. The second guard ran at her, but she side-stepped. And he impaled himself upon the Daughter of Light. In a few heartbeats, both guards lay dead.

Antoinette grabbed the key ring and secured it to her belt. Then she locked the cell door behind her, opened the chamber door, and crept into the hallway.

Beyond the chamber, the hall immediately divided around a wide stone pillar. Antoinette took a few steps up the left side and then doubled back and took a few steps up the right. There were no more guards in sight—just cold iron doors and flickering torches.

Antoinette decided to go left and stole along the wall as quietly as she could. Now and then, the keys would jingle on the ring, and she wished for a moment that she had left them behind. She passed door after door, her heart beating faster at each one. She imagined one of the doors opening suddenly and a cadre of guards rushing out into the hall to capture her. But none did.

At last, Antoinette found what she was looking for: stairs! She descended slowly, the torches casting monstrous shadows of herself on the curling wall before her. From the last step, she peered into the hall. Either there were fewer torches or some had died out, for the hall was much darker than above. Still, she saw no guards, so she pressed on. The hall divided again, but there were three passages. Antoinette shrugged and took the middle one.

She was halfway down that hall when she heard a voice and nearly jumped out of her skin. "Take me with thee!"

She spun around, her sword ready, but there was no guard . . . no knight in dark armor—only a door with a barred window. Looking out sadly between the bars was the oldest Glimpse Antoinette had ever seen. He had large brown eyes deeply set among gray brows and pale, heavily wrinkled skin. He was balding with sickly strands of hair floating like cobwebs near his unusually long stretched ears.

"How did thou escape?" he asked.

"Is it that obvious?" Antoinette replied.

"Thy armor speaks of allegiance to King Eliam." He smiled and his eyes glinted blue.

"You're from Alleble too?" said Antoinette, sorting through the keys for one to unlock the cell door.

"I was," he said weakly. "Long ago. Tell me, m'lady, have the soldiers gone?"

"Most have, I think," said Antoinette. "An unbelievable army! I've got to get back to Alleble. I've got to warn them."

"I must return too. Shall we travel together?"

Antoinette knew the old Glimpse would slow her down, but she could not leave him for certain death. "Of course," she said. "Ah, got it!" The door swung open and out walked the old Glimpse. He was gaunt and frail, and Antoinette wondered what Paragor would want with such a harmless prisoner.

"I am called Zabediel," he said. "Though the young ones call me Zabed. I come from Balesparr, a village hidden deep in the heart of King's Forest."

"I am Antoinette," she said. "Follow me."

"Does thou know the way?" he asked.

"Uh, no," she replied.

"Then perhaps thou should let me lead the way." The old Glimpse brushed past her and ambled up the passage. The two of them made their way through the twisting passages and down several winding flights of stairs. At times, when the path forked or when the meandering path became disorienting, Zabed would stop for a few moments to think. "This tower grows up from the heart of Paragor's main keep," he said after turning back from a dead end. "A wrong turn could lead us to many places we would not wish to go."

Great! thought Antoinette, but still she followed him.

Many turns and dead ends later, Antoinette's pace slowed until finally, she stopped moving. Zabediel ambled on several yards before he realized she had stopped. "M'lady, Antoinette?" he questioned as he walked back to her. She did not answer.

"M'lady?" he said, staring with concern. "Are ye well?"

She mouthed, "What?" Then she blinked and focused on him.

"Are ye well?" Zabediel repeated. "Thou seemed entranced."

"A storm is coming," she said.

"A storm?" Zabed raised an eyebrow. "But we are deep in the mountain. Why does thou think so?"

"I . . . I don't think . . . I know," she replied. "Ever since I was little, I've just known that a storm was going to hit—before it happened. I'd get this strange sort of tingling, and ten, twenty minutes—even an hour later—sure enough, the storm would come."

"And does thou feel this sensation now?" Zabed asked, staring at her anxiously.

Antoinette nodded slowly. "I've never felt it this strongly before," she said. "It hit me so hard, I felt like I couldn't breathe. It's going to be a dreadful storm."

Zabediel stared at her intensely for a few moments more, and then he turned and trotted up the passage. After some time, they came to a place where the path split three ways. The left and the right passages were well-lit and curled away from each other. The middle way led immediately to a long flight of stairs. Zabed looked back and forth and then led Antoinette down the stairs.

They found themselves immersed in the darkness of a very long, narrow hall. Its only torch burned at the far end, so it was very difficult to see. "I do not remember this," muttered Zabediel.

Antoinette closed her eyes and exhaled. "Should we go back . . . try one of those other passages?"

"Nay," Zabed replied curtly. "I know both of those other passages. One leads to the living quarters of three ranks of soldiers. The other leads down deep into the torture pits beneath this city. It would be perilous either way. This should be the right way, but it looks so strange."

Antoinette wondered just how well his aged eyes could see, especially in the shadows. A gust of frigid air brushed by them. The torch flickered and waved suddenly as if it might go out. "Well, you've been right so—"

A crash of thunder struck. They both jumped. Antoinette and Zabed stared at each other, their hearts hammering.

"That was no ordinary thunder," Zabediel said. "For it is no small thing to hear it from within this fortress. I fear thou were right about the storm."

Antoinette nodded and was thoughtful. Just as they were about to set off again, Antoinette froze. She heard something, and it wasn't wind or thunder. It was coming from the other side of the hall. Footsteps. It sounded like footsteps running on stairs.

"Zabed, get back!" Antoinette yelled. She pushed the old sage to a recessed part of the wall just before the stairwell. She leaned just slightly out so she could see. Standing at the end of the hall was a Paragor Knight. His black armor reflected the flickering torchlight, and even from this distance, Antoinette could see that he held a menacing sword.

"M'lady—"

"Shhh!" Antoinette warned. "There's a guard coming."

Aidan's quest to find Antoinette had been reduced to a headache-provoking game of trial and error. There were a dizzying number of twists and turns. He'd already had to double back three or four times to take passages that he'd missed in the unreliable torchlight.

Aidan had passed many cells but found them all empty, and his heart began to despair. But each time, just when he had reached the end of his hope, he heard the voice of his King. *"Seek what was lost."* And each time, Aidan found a new passage heading up.

He took a deep breath and raced up the stairs. At the top, he ducked under a wooden archway and found himself staring up a long, dark hall. He passed the only torch and immediately had the feeling that he was not alone. But Aidan was not going to turn back. Brandishing Fury, he stalked up the hall. In the shadows at the end of the hall, every one of Aidan's senses was on alert.

The Paragor Knight crept closer. Antoinette waited until he was practically right in front of her, then she had no choice but to pounce. She brought the Daughter of Light down with great force, aiming for his head. But by some miraculous effort, the enemy blocked her first strike. Undaunted, she unleashed a flurry of strikes, using her kakari-geiko attack to keep the enemy on the defensive.

The warrior backpedaled with measured steps, maintaining his balance and searching for an opening. Antoinette tried to keep up the pressure, but her arms were getting tired. She sensed motion from behind her. *Zabed! What is he doing out of our hiding spot?*

Just that brief distraction, and the enemy loosed a savage, heavy blow that forced her sword downward. He tried to keep her sword near the floor, and Antoinette got the feeling that she was being set up. Instantly, she leaped backward, knocking Zabed back a few paces. She hoped he was okay, but at least the Paragor Knight hadn't run her through!

The enemy grunted and pressed the attack. He had taken his sword in both hands and rained heavy strokes against her wearying defenses. She knew she was beaten. This was a superior foe.

And then it came—a thunderous blow that slammed the Daughter of Light to the ground. Even though she knew the enemy's attack, his strength was too great and she had no place to leap away again. She could feel him holding her blade to the ground while drawing his sword back for the big thrust. And suddenly, like the shock of a fire alarm going off, a word appeared in her thoughts: *moulinet*.

"Aidan?!" she yelled.

The Paragor Knight thrust forward to kill, but pulled up short. "Antoinette?!"

King's Forest

"King's Forest is very different from the Blackwood," said Thrivenbard to the team of twelve assembled in Guard's Keep the next morning. "But it is queer enough in its own right. While we will not contend with illgrets, wolvin, or the other foul things that were drawn by the will of the Seven Sleepers, there are other hazards. So we must be wary."

"What kinds of hazards?" asked Locke, the youthful-looking Acacian Knight.

"Well, I have not ventured deep into the woods," Thrivenbard reminded them. "But I have been far enough in to know that things grow very big there."

"Perhaps you could define *big*," said Sir Oswyn.

"The trees, for one thing," Thrivenbard replied. "They do not have the beauty or the toughness of those in Nock's Blackwood, but they are tall enough to scrape the sky! And once, while climbing one of these giants, I disturbed a moth the size of a kite!"

"Trees and moths do not seem such a threat," said Sir Rogan. "Is that all there is?"

"Nay. It is what dwells in the trees and feeds upon the moths that I speak of," Thrivenbard said. "Snakes—as long as serpents—with skin that changes hue and texture to match that of the limbs where they dwell. Big enough to lift a knight right out of his saddle, they are. And there may be other things in the depths of the forest . . . things worse."

"Aw! It cannot be that bad!" said Boldoak, absently rubbing the scar on his cheek. "After all, Zabediel was just a scribe, and he survived." This earned Boldoak a smattering of laughs from the other knights assembled there.

"Be that as it may," Thrivenbard went on, "we must still be on our guard. And we cannot forget that Paragor's forces could be in the woods as well."

And at Thrivenbard's command, the knights filed out of Guard's Keep and marched swiftly to the dragon pens.

As Splinter spiraled up into the sky, Robby looked out over the city walls and saw a large caravan approaching Alleble from the north. He applied pressure to the dragon's flank with his right knee. She responded by drifting over closer to Trenna's white dragon.

"May I help you with something, Sir Knight?!" Trenna asked, smiling playfully.

"Uh, verily, you can!" Robby answered, trying to sound noble and heroic. "Perhaps you could tell me who are all those soldiers."

"Those are Mallik's kin!" she replied. "The mighty folk of the Blue Mountains! They come to fortify the walls of Alleble . . . thanks to your magnificent discovery!"

"Why, thank you for thy kind words, m'lady!" Robby said. Feeling awkward in trying to speak more Glimpse-like, Robby decided to stick to his own manner of speech, such as it was. Even so, Robby did not speak again to anyone until they reached King's

Forest. For with Alleble now behind them, the dragon riders made for the gap between the twin peaks of Pennath Ador.

Robby had traveled by plane before. He'd looked out the small windows inside the cabin and been amazed by the way the land below became a patchwork of greens and browns. But nothing could compare to the awesome grandeur of these immense mountains.

Beyond the mountains, Robby saw King's Forest. It was more vast than he had imagined, and it sat upon a mountain itself. The dragon riders descended to the stony foothills just outside the forest, and Robby realized that the size of the trees had deceived him. They weren't growing on another mountain—they were just that tall!

Some of their massive trunks were as wide as a house, and all were covered in huge scales of black and gray bark. They had sparse limbs that reached out like arms with bracelets of dangling moss and wide paws of ferny foliage.

After securing the dragons, Thrivenbard insisted that the knights fan out into a wide row. Then he led them into the forest. "This *is* very different from the Blackwood," said Nock excitedly as he drew near to Robby. "Blackwood trees do not tolerate other vegetation in their midst. But this place is teeming with vegetation! Cedar, oak, fir, and dragonwood—incredible! And look down!"

By their feet were huge feathery ferns and massive patches of some kind of clover with large pink flowers.

"Sorrel," Nock said. "Beautiful, is it not? Oh, how I would like to lie in it!"

Suddenly, Thrivenbard was beside Nock. "Master Nock," he said, "we must all keep our focus on the task at hand. Do not allow your mind to wander." And just like that, Thrivenbard was gone and back to the front line. *Weird, how he does that*, Robby thought.

In spite of Thriven's warning, Robby spent much of the first hour enjoying the natural surroundings. How could he not? There were squirrels the size of dogs, and once Robby and Trenna climbed up on the trunk of a fallen giant and strolled for more than a hundred yards along its length.

The bright afternoon sun filtered down through the treetops and cast glorious golden light on the forest floor and gilded the broad leaves of many of the trees. But the search had turned up nothing. No sign of a village. No sign that anyone had come through the forest recently.

The demeanor of the group had changed markedly after such a long, uneventful walk through the forest. Jarak and Locke amused themselves by telling stories of their hunting exploits in the forests of Acacia. Robby spotted Nock pointing all over the place to a very bored-looking Boldoak. Sir Rogan spoke with Baldergrim and trailed just behind Robby. Even Thrivenbard, who had been so tense early on, had begun to relax a bit.

They came to a section of the forest where the ground cover was a bed of tan pine needles and dead leaves. "Do you notice anything strange?" Trenna asked.

"No," Robby replied, yawning.

"A few moments ago, the wood was alive with sounds," she replied, looking warily up into the treetops. "Now it is utterly silent."

Robby listened. "Yeah, you're right," he said.

Trenna drew her sword.

From up ahead, Jarak suddenly knelt. He reached down into a patch of ferns and held up a strand of gray. "Master Thrivenbard!" he called. "What do you make of—"

He never finished his sentence. Branches snapped. A dark brown blur. And Jarak was gone, pulled into the greenery.

"Hold, servants of the King!" Thrivenbard yelled. "Do not move another step!"

But it was too late. Baldergrim vanished with a sudden grunt.

Locke drew a long curved blade and raced in the direction Jarak had been taken.

"Look to the skies!" Trenna yelled.

"Nay, look to the ground!" Thrivenbard called back. He reached carefully down and parted some shrubs to see what was there. "There are strands of . . . of web strewn across this place!"

Robby froze in his tracks. He stared at it: a twisted strand of gray stretched tight beneath the ground cover. "I see it!" he yelled.

"I do not see anything!" Sir Rogan bellowed. He charged up to Robby's side, but took one step too many. He stepped directly onto the web. Suddenly, from the brush in front of him, a brown nightmare shot forth—but Sir Rogan's axe was at the ready. He swept the broad blade in front of him. They heard a shrill chirping screech, and black blood spattered Sir Rogan, Robby, and Trenna. There at Sir Rogan's feet twitched a long, hairy, segmented limb of brown.

"Spiders!" Sir Rogan spat.

"Thrivenbard, what do we do?" Halberad cried out. "They have taken Jarak and Baldergrim!"

"The webs are a type of tripwire," said Thrivenbard, almost to himself at first. "These spiders live beneath the ground, and they will have taken our knights alive. We must find the burrows without ourselves being caught!"

A bloodcurdling scream came from nearby. Turning, they expected to see another knight being taken away by one of the giant spiders. But to their horror and amazement, they saw a huge emerald-green snake withdrawing up into the treetops with Locke's legs protruding from its massive diamond-shaped jaws. Serpents began to swing down from above, trying to yank knights violently from the ground.

"Defend yourselves!" Thrivenbard yelled. "There are enemies above and below!" Several snakes fell headless, thanks to Sir Rogan's mighty axe. Another snake, this one with jagged golden brown scales, seemed to materialize from the trunk of one of the gigantic trees. It opened its jaws behind Valden.

"Look out!" Sir Oswyn cried. But the snake fell limp to the tree trunk—one of Nock's black-shafted arrows embedded deep in its eye.

Valden waved to the archer and drew in a great draught of air. Then, like a dragon belching forth its fiery breath, he unleashed a deep, guttural yell that rang among the trees and made those nearby clutch their ears.

Valden continued screaming and began to run. A fanged yellow-green snake uncoiled from a tangle of similarly colored vines. It lunged for Valden, but he swung his two axes—one high and one low.

"TRY OUT MY FANGS, BEAST!!!" Valden yelled as his axes connected. The low blade cracked across the creature's snout. The other gashed deeply behind the snake's head. The serpent fell to the ground, and Valden pounced upon it—screaming and hacking until the creature was still.

Arbalests and bows sang out as archers fired volley after volley. Knights hacked at the descending snakes. Others ran and tried desperately to fend off the spiders.

Trenna ran toward a giant snake, but a sudden shadow came upon her. In the chaos around them, only Robby saw her whisked away into the forest depths.

Robby started off after her. Someone yelled, "Wait, Sir Robby!"—but Robby did not stop. He ran as fast as he could, ducking the strikes of several snakes, but when he got to where he thought the spider's burrow should be, he was at a loss. "Where is it?!" he yelled. But it was to no avail. The spider was too clever, too well camouflaged. It and Trenna were seemingly gone without a trace.

Robby stood among the tall trees and looked this way and that, frantically searching for movement—some sign of where they had gone. "Arrggh!" Robby yelled. He'd failed Trenna, dooming her to die agonizingly in the darkness of a spider's lair.

"Never alone."

"What?" Robby asked.

"You are never alone."

"King Eliam, help me," he whispered desperately.

An odd sense of calm descended upon Robby. He looked down at his feet, and his heart began to beat faster. There was a strand of web. *If I follow it . . .* Robby suddenly realized what he needed to do. "Thank you!" he uttered, and raced off.

Heedless of the briers and scratching limbs, Robby followed the thread through the forest as quickly as he could. He did not want to trip the wire until he was ready. At last, he found where the web disappeared under a thin ridge of earth. As Robby looked more closely, he recognized the outline of a wide circular trapdoor.

"This is gonna be close!" Robby said. He stood clear of the trapdoor and found a heavy dead limb. He tossed the limb in a high arc onto the web and waited with his broadsword. Quickly, the trapdoor launched upward. A hideous mass of black eyes, long segmented limbs, and dark brown leaped up from the hole. Robby swung his broadsword as hard as he could and felt it strike something solid. But it gave with a nauseating splatter and came through. Robby looked up and saw the gigantic spider drag its ruined body into the trees and then become still.

His plan had worked—he'd drawn out and killed the spider that had taken Trenna. Now all he had to do was get her out of the spider's lair. He just hoped that Thrivenbard was right about the spiders taking their prey alive.

Robby went to work on the trapdoor, chopping and hacking with zeal. It was stronger than it had appeared, made of many alternating layers of spider silk, soil, and bracken. At last a vast dark hole gaped open in front of him. Robby stepped to the edge and peered warily inside. He saw a deep sloping tunnel lined with gray web.

"Trenna!" he called down into the hole. "Trenna, answer me!"

There was no response at first, but Robby heard a strange clicking sound followed by a swish and a dull thud.

"Trenna, are you there?!" he called again.

At last there came a muffled cry. "Trenna!" Robby cried out. He took a deep breath and leaped down into the tunnel. It was farther down than he thought, and he landed awkwardly, the unfamiliar weight of his armor throwing him forward. He drew himself up and realized just how large the tunnel was. Ten feet high and at least that wide. Robby thought about the spider that he had killed a few moments earlier. It didn't seem quite that large. Robby strained to look down the tunnel, but the light from the hole above traveled down the tunnel only a few yards. From that point on it was pitch-dark.

"Trenna?" he called down the tunnel. There was no answer. Robby held his broadsword out in front and began to advance slowly. The web felt spongy under his feet, and the air was chilly and uncomfortable.

Robby walked down the left side of the tunnel so that he could let his left hand trail across the wall. Every few steps, he would stop and listen. Several times, he heard the same *click—swish—thud* noise again. It was an eerie, almost rhythmic sound, and Robby began to wonder if the spider he had killed was the only spider that lived in this burrow.

Suddenly, the wall on his left ended and he was reaching into darkness. "Trenna?!" No answer. No sound. It was as if his words had been swallowed up as soon as he spoke them. He reached out in all directions with his broadsword and found that the tunnel apparently opened up into a wide space or a chamber. Robby could see nothing, but he had the dreadful feeling that he was being watched.

I hope you're with me, King Eliam, Robby thought as he slowly moved forward. *Never alone, right?* Somewhere to his distant left, there came the *click—swish—thud* sound. Robby stared, but saw nothing. Then, the same sound, but to the right and not quite as far away. And this time, light glimmered briefly in some corner of the chamber.

What is that? Robby wondered, and then he realized what it must be. *Trapdoors. More trapdoors—but then that would mean this is not the burrow of one single spider, but the den of many!*

His heart hammering and sweat pouring down his back, he forced himself to move forward. A few more steps, and Robby had the distinct feeling that there was something in front of him. He pointed the broadsword forward, squeezing the haft in a death grip. He lunged forward just to test and heard an ominous scuttling. It sounded like the crunching of broken glass on pavement.

Robby stopped and stood very still. He stared straight ahead. His mind whirled with a million thoughts—chief among them was that coming into this burrow was quite possibly the dumbest thing he'd ever done in his life.

"Not dumb. Valiant."

Robby smiled tentatively. *Okay, but I don't feel very brave.*

Suddenly, he heard the *click—swish—thud* sound. It came from far behind him, and there had been the briefest flash of light. It was enough at least to see what stood there in front of him—and to temporarily blind him. He'd seen long segmented legs, a pair of large sickle-shaped fangs, and eight black eyes. This spider was much larger than the other he'd seen earlier.

Robby carved the air in front of him. "Get back!" he yelled. He heard the creepy scuttling sound. Then, *click—swish—thud,* and the light flashed again. The spider had reared up. Its forelegs were high in the air and menacing, its sharp fangs and opening jaws fully visible—if but for a moment.

Robby backpedaled, keeping the sword moving. The light flashed again just as the spider pounced. He saw it coming at him in that momentary illumination. Screaming, he slammed the sword from low to high. He struck something so hard, it sent a tremor up

his arms. There came an earsplitting chirping screech. And then
something took hold of the end of his sword.

Click—swish—thud! The light flashed again. The beastly spider
had his sword somehow clenched in its mandibles. All went black
again, and Robby wrenched his blade with all his might. But the spider wrenched back. It lurched quickly to the side, and Robby stumbled heavily to his knees. It heaved back the other way, jerking
Robby off his feet entirely. He crashed to the ground and yelled.
The pain was intense. It was all he could do to hold on to the sword,
but he did. He knew to let go would mean the end.

Somehow he got back on his feet. Robby gave one more weak
pull and was about to give up, when he had a desperate idea. With
renewed strength, he planted his feet and yanked back on the
sword. He strained so hard he felt the muscles of his arms and upper
back begin to pull. As Robby expected, the spider pulled back on
the sword, trying to rip it from Robby's grasp. Robby put all of his
body weight behind a fearsome thrust and drove the broadsword
into the spider's jaws and up to the hilt into the creature's ghastly
throat. The spider died in an instant, its legs spasming, curling, and
becoming still.

Robby glanced to the right at the source of the light. One of the
trapdoors had been flung open. Robby turned back, and in the shadowy light, he could finally see just how monstrously huge the spider
was. Maybe it was a trick of the dim light, but something seemed to
be moving on the spider's abdomen.

"Sir Robby?!" a voice called. He thought it was Sir Rogan, but
Robby did not answer. He stared at the now undulating abdomen
of the spider.

"Sir Robby!" another voice called.

"I'm down here!" Robby called. He recognized Sir Oswyn's voice,
but his eyes were still fixed on the creature. There was something
there. No, several things. Then one came out of the shadows and

Robby understood. It was another spider—a baby—and yet still as large as a great cat and menacing. Another spider came into view. Then two more. A dozen or more crept up from the big spider's abdomen.

Robby twisted his sword free at last from the dead spider's jaws and began to back up. "Sir Rogan!" he cried, the warning evident in his tone. "Sir Oswyn, get down here!"

There seemed to be no end to the baby spiders, and they scuttled over the body and closed in on Robby.

A torch in hand, Oswyn and then Sir Rogan leaped into the spider's den, and what they saw took their breath away. A gigantic spider lay dead in the center of the underground chamber, but dozens more had Robby cornered at a distant wall.

Then all at once, the spiders attacked. One leaped at Robby, but with a swipe of the broadsword, Robby cut it in half. Some pounced from the wall or leaped from the ceiling. Robby was covered with clawing, biting spiders. Each time he batted some off, others quickly replaced them.

Sir Rogan swung his battleaxe like a clock's pendulum, dividing and dismembering spiders. Oswyn joined the fray, his narrow blade carving easily through the teeming spiders. Black blood splattered everywhere.

Finally, they reached Robby, knocking the last spiders off of him as he collapsed in their arms.

"He has been bitten," Sir Oswyn said gravely.

Sir Rogan, with great effort, fended off the remaining baby spiders. "Will he live?!" he called back.

"I cannot say!" Oswyn yelled. "I think so, but we have to get him out of here!"

Then *CLICK—SWISH—THUD!* A flash of light brightened the chamber. Then another, and another. Sir Rogan turned and saw trapdoor after trapdoor open and large spiders coming into the den. "We are caught!" Sir Rogan exclaimed.

"No, not yet!" yelled Sir Oswyn. "A trapdoor, there!" He pointed over Sir Rogan's shoulder, and indeed there was a faint outline of light.

"Trenna!" Robby whispered urgently. He struggled in Sir Oswyn's grasp, attempting to stand.

"What?" asked Sir Oswyn. "Sir Robby, do not exert yourself!"

"No, I . . . I can stand!" yelled Robby. And to their amazement, he planted his feet and pushed himself up with his sword. "Trenna's still down here . . . somewhere! I couldn't find her."

Sir Rogan turned, swept out his great axe, and cut the legs out from under an approaching spider. "We cannot wait!" he bellowed. "The spiders will overrun us!"

"We can't just leave her!" Robby argued. He brandished his broadsword.

"Very well," Sir Oswyn reluctantly conceded. He reached into a pouch on his belt and withdrew two tiny leaves. They were dark green with red fringes. "Eat these," he said to Robby. "A crude remedy, but they will help your body fight the venom!"

Robby put both leaves in his mouth and chewed. His tongue began to sting as if he'd eaten a hot pepper, but his mind and vision seemed to clear almost instantly.

Then Sir Rogan turned to Sir Oswyn. "Do you have any of that powder you put to such use in the Blue Mountains?"

"I have enough!" Sir Oswyn said. "That is, if I guess your plan Sir Rogan." He slid two long tubes from the belt at his side and handed them to Sir Rogan. "But you realize the web lining of this den—of all the tunnels . . ."

"I know," Sir Rogan said. "That is what I am counting on. We may not have another opportunity to rid the forest of so many of them as this. Oswyn, we will find her if we can. But ten minutes only. If we do not emerge, torch this place!"

Sir Oswyn nodded. "Never alone!" he yelled, and then he clambered up through the trapdoor and out into the forest light.

Sir Rogan batted away a spider and Robby ran it through with his sword. They looked up and saw many more approaching rapidly. "We will split up," Sir Rogan said. "We can cover more ground that way, and the spiders will divide their number to chase us."

Robby nodded.

Sir Rogan handed Robby one of the tubes. "Uncork this, and pour out the powder as you search. This web should burn on its own, but if not, this powder will do the trick!"

Robby uncorked the tube and let a bit of the fine white powder spill out onto the floor of the den.

"We have ten minutes to find Trenna," Sir Rogan yelled. "Ten minutes! Whether you find her or not, get out of the tunnels and back to the forest before that time is up!"

He looked up at Sir Rogan and nodded. The two of them sprinted off in opposite directions.

The spiders were on them almost immediately. Robby slashed a small spider out of his path with one hand. But a much larger creature loomed before him. Robby drove his sword into the monster's cluster of eyes. It shrieked and flopped about hysterically. Robby started to run away but stumbled. He felt suddenly very light-headed. He swayed for a moment, then righted himself. He knew the spider venom was working on his system, but he would not let himself succumb.

He grabbed up the tube of fire powder and ran to another part of the underground chamber. He had no idea how much time had passed, but he hadn't found Trenna, so it didn't matter.

The tube of fire powder was empty, so Robby cast it aside and continued his search. After several dead ends and finishing off a handful of spiders, Robby ran down a long tunnel and came upon a trio of spiders at the tunnel's end. Then he heard a voice and his heart soared.

"Get away from me, insects!" Trenna yelled. Her curved blade whistled through the air, and she hacked a foreleg off of one of the spiders.

"Trenna!" Robby yelled.

She looked up and saw Robby. "Sir Robby!" she exclaimed.

Robby went after the spiders with renewed vigor. He attacked one of them from behind. Before it could turn to face the new threat, Robby carved a mortal gash in its abdomen. Another, the largest of the three, was more clever. It sprang at Robby, knocking him off his feet. The creature scrabbled on top of Robby and sliced open Robby's forehead with one of its claws. Robby yelled, but the spider was too close for him to swing his broadsword. So he kicked out with both of his legs, launching the spider into the air. Robby rolled and wheeled his broadsword around as the spider charged.

The spider reared and pounced, but Robby was too fast this time. He hacked off the creature's fangs in one sweep of the sword. Then he leaped to the side and hacked at the spider's exposed midsection.

Robby turned to Trenna, who had finished off the last spider. "Took you long enough!" she yelled, but she was not angry.

Far away up the tunnel, they heard a tremendous *WHOOSH*, followed by a howling wind.

"What is that?" Trenna asked.

They both stared up the tunnel.

A harsh orange light raced up the tunnel toward them.

Robby grimaced. "We're trapped!"

THE HIDDEN VILLAGE

Thrivenbard saw Sir Oswyn by a broad hole in the ground from which dark smoke poured.

"Sir Oswyn!" Thrivenbard called. "We have beaten back the serpents, and the spiders have drawn off! We . . ." His words trailed off when he realized that Sir Oswyn was despondent.

"What has happened?" he asked.

Oswyn looked up, misery in his eyes. "Robby, Trenna, Rogan— they have all died by my hand," he said.

"How can that be?" Thrivenbard asked.

Sir Oswyn explained what had happened. "Sir Thrivenbard, while we were in the den, spiders began to pour in from every trapdoor—"

"That explains why the spiders withdrew," Thrivenbard said with wonder.

"I gave them a little longer than the ten minutes. I did not see them come out here, but there are trapdoors throughout the forest. I thought they would use a different door. But I have been waiting here, and still they do not arrive. I fear they were in the tunnels when I . . . when . . ."

Thrivenbard looked at the black smoke pouring out of the hole, and then he understood.

"I should have waited longer," Sir Oswyn said.

"Waited?" Thrivenbard objected. "And if you had? How many more of our team would have been dragged to an evil end under the ground?"

Sir Oswyn stood slowly and nodded.

The rest of the team assembled. They had lost Baldergrim of Yewland, but his kinsman Boldoak had escaped. Sir Jarak of Acacia had fallen, but Valden returned with Locke. Both had been bitten and required medical attention from Oswyn. But Sir Rogan, Robby, and Lady Trenna were still missing.

The team from Alleble pressed on deeper into King's Forest, and each time they came to a smoking spider's burrow they called for their missing comrades. But each time they heard nothing but the whispers of things burned and smoldering.

The sun was foundering in the west and the forest darkening when at last they came to a path among the giant trees. "Many iron-shod feet have traveled this way," Halberad said, stooping low. "Do you think Paragor's forces have come before us?"

"If they have," Thrivenbard replied, "I hope the serpents and spiders wreaked havoc upon them." But Thrivenbard did not laugh. He was bitter and angry. He had led his team into the dangerous snares of the forest's creatures.

"If Paragor's troops entered this wood," Nock said, "then it was by some other path than this one. They are reckless and destructive—as we saw in the Blackwood. This path was trodden by a rank of soldiers both orderly and well-disciplined."

"If not the enemy, who else might have come this way before us?" Halberad asked.

"Zabediel entered the forest alone," Sir Oswyn said. "Or so the accounts say. And yet, we are looking for a hidden village. A village sounds like more than one Glimpse to me. How could both be true?" No one knew or even had a guess. Nonetheless, they followed the path, and it led them deeper and deeper into the shadowy trees.

As they walked, Nock took a sudden interest in the high limbs of the trees. He strode forward to be near Thrivenbard and said, "There are scouts in the trees."

"Yes, numbering near a hundred so far," Thrivenbard replied. "Their camouflage is excellent, so I may have missed some."

"Their woodland skills are far superior to Paragory's," Nock said.

"And yet, I am not at all sure that they are friends," Thrivenbard replied. "In any case, we shall soon find out."

The path led the team from Alleble into a clearing. Only a few of them had noticed the watchers in the trees, but all felt a sense of present danger. When they came to the other side of the clearing, Thrivenbard discovered a large gray stone embedded in the ground like a grave marker. It was roughly square, chipped and gouged, but bore only one symbol: it looked like a letter Υ with its right arm split so that a smaller branch angled off to the left.

Thrivenbard held up a hand. "Stop!" he yelled. "Sheathe your weapons and be still!" The warriors did as they were told. They stood staring up into the trees and wondered what new danger might be upon them. In a moment a wooden spear with a sharp iron head nearly as long as a sword blade stabbed vertically into the soft ground near the stone.

"Hold, trespassers!" came a shout from the trees, and a stout warrior landed softly beside the spear. He wore dark cloth armor that striated his shoulders and chest, and mail made of tiny black rings. Upon his back he wore a long quiver filled with a dozen or more spears like the one in the ground.

His face was crisscrossed in paints of gray, black, and dark green. His eyes glinted green. He smiled, grasped the spear like a staff, and approached Thrivenbard. "I am called Warriant," he said, "first vanguard of Balesparr the Wood Realm!" He whistled, and similarly clad warriors fell like rain and surrounded the Alleble Knights.

"Had you passed The Stone of Challenge unwelcomed," Warriant said, "you would have felt the prick of our bales before you even saw the Baleneers who threw them. But you waited. For that courtesy, I thank thee. I judge by your eyes that you come from Alleble. Now speak swiftly and honestly. What business brings servants of King Eliam into this wood?"

"I am Thrivenbard, leader of this team. We have come on a mission of dire importance for all The Realm. We seek an old Glimpse named Zabediel."

A murmur traveled like a wave around the circle of spearmen. "Peace!" Warriant cried out. "Do not cast your judgment on these servants of King Eliam!"

But he turned then and looked shrewdly at Thrivenbard. "I know of Zabediel," Warriant said. "But tell me, why have you come bearing arms thusly? Mean you to take Zabediel by force?"

"Nay!" Thrivenbard exclaimed. "That is not the way of our King. We would ask Zabediel to come willingly, or at least to offer advice in our time of need. We are armed because we feared that our enemy, the Prince of Paragory, might seek to stop us from fulfilling our quest."

Deep in thought, Warriant quietly stared at the knight. At last he spoke again. "Alas, Thrivenbard," he said. "You have come far too late to achieve your quest. But please come and take counsel in the holds of Balesparr. There we may both discover the answer to many things looked for, and perhaps find help to achieve our mutual goals."

"Too late?" asked Thrivenbard.

"Yes," Warriant replied. "For two seasons ago winged Death-reapers from Paragory descended from the sky. They slew a third of my Baleneers and took our sage Zabediel away!"

It was fully night as the Baleneers led the team from Alleble down the winding path into a deep valley. The forest filled with sounds: the eerie trilling of owls, the short, high-pitched bark of the forest coyotes, the crescendo of chirping tree frogs, and a strange knocking sound that echoed from the treetops. Even the Glimpses of Yewland were amazed at the music of the night.

The path went under massive curling roots and more than once crossed over the noisy brook that coursed beside it. The Baleneers talked in hushed tones as they walked, until at last they rounded a bend and saw undulating palisades of varying heights. At the head of these was a tall gatehouse where many lanterns hung.

Warriant led them there and rapped upon the door with his spear. A gray-headed Glimpse leaned out of a narrow window, and his beard hung nearly halfway down the wall. "Speak the password!" he called down gruffly.

"Aelbark, you know full well who I am," Warriant said, trying to be patient. "Now open the gate."

"Sure'n I recognize thee, Master Warriant," the gatekeeper replied. "But as a vanguard, you should know the daily password."

Warriant smiled apologetically at Thrivenbard, and then glared up at his gatekeeper. "Aelbark, you open the gate this instant, or I will tie your beard in a knot and hang you from the Tree of Celebration!"

Aelbark laughed, then disappeared from the window of the gatehouse. They heard the long, grinding sound of the gate's wooden bolt being withdrawn, and then at last the gate opened.

"Look, friends from Alleble!" said Warriant. "Look upon the Wood Realm of Balesparr! Few from your city have beheld it!"

Balesparr's cottages and keeps poked up like thick mushrooms or moss-covered stones among the massive curling roots of the forest's towering trees.

As they entered, any chill from the outside forest left them, for Balesparr was a city of light. Candles of every imaginable color burned in every window. Lanterns hung on the corners of avenues and byways, and hardy fires burned in public hearths wherever two or more streets met. Glimpse men, women, and children looked with wonder upon the visitors. Some spoke in whispers and pointed. Others shied away at a glance.

When Warriant came to a certain street corner, he said, "Thrivenbard, as leader you will join me. Also, is there a Sir Oswyn traveling with you?"

"I am Sir Oswyn."

"Then I request that Sir Oswyn join us," Warriant said. "And anyone else you would like. My Baleneers will take the others to their barracks where they may sup and rest from their journeys."

Warriant dismissed his soldiers to their barracks and then led Thrivenbard, Nock, and Sir Oswyn to a massive cylindrical building. Its stony face had many high arched windows, but only one grand door. They entered and Warriant said, "Welcome to the main hold of our city. Here we shall discuss many things, but first, I return to you a few things you have lost."

Thrivenbard stared at Warriant questioningly, but no details were forthcoming. They followed a long curving hallway and arrived in a wide room with a high ceiling. In the center of the room was a very large fireplace where a merry fire crackled and flickered. Facing the fire were three tall chairs.

"You have come at last," came a gruff voice from one of the chairs. And a familiar face leaned out from the chair and looked their way.

"Sir Rogan!" Os yelled. "By King Eliam's provision! You live!"

"Of course I am alive," he grumbled. "No thanks to you! I said set fire to the spiders' den in ten minutes, but the flames raced in by nine—according to my count!"

"I waited twelve!" Sir Oswyn exclaimed. "How did you—"

"I was on a patrol with a squad of Baleneers when one of the spiders' trapdoors began to tremble. I prepared to strike when a hand suddenly appeared from beneath the ground! We wrenched open the door and pulled Sir Rogan out just ahead of the flames," said Warriant with a laugh. "He was a sorry sight, what with his hindquarters on fire!"

A female laughed from one of the other chairs, and Lady Trenna appeared, followed by Robby. Their armor gleamed as if it had just been polished. Sir Oswyn ran up and hugged all three.

"I thought I had cooked you all," he cried. Then, studying them all a moment, he asked, "Are all of you well?"

"We seem to be," Robby said.

"I now know Sir Rogan's tale, but how did you escape?" Sir Oswyn asked.

"I found Trenna at the end of a long tunnel," Robby said. "The fire came, and there was no trapdoor there . . ."

"So we made our own," said Trenna.

"How do you know?" Robby asked. "I don't remember anything after we killed those three spiders . . . that and the fire coming. I don't see how—"

"My memory is a blur," Trenna interrupted. "But our swords were fouled with mud and grime. There was dirt in our hair and under our fingernails . . . that had to be what happened."

"But why wouldn't we remember?" Robby asked.

"They have been going on like this for quite some time," Warriant said with a laugh. "Spider venom does strange things to the mind. And the two of them took about as much venom as a body can withstand and still live. When we found them, next to the exit they had dug, they were beginning to fade. Skin green, muscles seizing—most unpleasant to look upon. Fortunately for them, it is customary for all Baleneers to carry with them a spider poison remedy. It effectively washes the venom from the blood, and the victim sweats it out. It is very fast-acting."

"Would you show me this remedy?" Sir Oswyn asked eagerly. "My herblore is substantial, but I know of nothing that strong for spider venom."

"Of course," Warriant replied.

"I am grateful to have these three back," Thrivenbard said. "But Warriant, were there any others?"

Warriant shook his head grimly. "All of our patrols are back," he said. "They found no one."

Warriant summoned several Baleneers, who brought in a large table, more chairs, and enough bread, cheese, and drink to feed twice their number. After they had taken something to eat, the conversations turned to serious matters. Thrivenbard told Warriant about the growing threat of open war with Paragory. He told of the rise of the Wyrm Lord and of the release of the Seven Sleepers. And he told of Alleble gathering all its allies to make a final stand against the enemy.

"But you did not enter the forest to enlist the aid of Balesparr," Warriant said after Thrivenbard's tale was told.

"Nay," Thrivenbard replied. "We did not know that such a force existed."

"You sought Zabediel," said Warriant.

"Yes," Thrivenbard replied. He looked with indecision at Sir Rogan.

Warriant smiled and put his hand on Thrivenbard's shoulder. "Ah . . . ," he said. "You are not sure if you should speak further on this matter. For my eyes sparkle green, and Balesparr is not an ally of your kingdom. Am I right?"

Thrivenbard looked at the ground.

"I see that I am," Warriant said, but there was no blame in his voice. "Perhaps it would help you to know that I already know something of your situation. And I have guessed even more besides. See if what I say is not close to the mark. You sought after Zabediel because he was of old the scribe of King Eliam. And in an age long before Alleble and Balesparr, Zabediel recorded a prophecy that would concern the fate of all The Realm."

The knights from Alleble were still as if stone.

"When the Wyrm Lord spilled the innocent blood of King Eliam's noble servant Torin," Warriant continued, "and The Realm was divided, Zabediel, being kin to Torin, sought refuge in this forest and founded the village of Balesparr. This Scroll of Prophecy was hidden, but now Paragor has it and seeks to use it to bring his dominion to this land. Your hope, however, is that Paragor's wisdom is limited—that he could not make full use of the Scroll without Zabediel translating the language. You came for Zabediel for two reasons: first to protect Zabediel, keeping him from falling into the enemy's hands; and second, to learn all that you could about the prophecy so that you yourselves might use such knowledge to defeat Paragor!"

Thrivenbard was bewildered. "How do you know all of this?"

"Zabediel told us much," Warriant replied. "But much of this we learned from our time living in many other places. You see, Balesparr is a realm made of Glimpses who have turned away from the lands where we were born. It is a refuge, a place for those weary of politics and warfare. A place where we can thrive and grow without the threat or fear of wickedness. A place where evil has no influence. But alas, no place is safe forever. Paragor found us, and we have been reminded of bloodshed. And . . . he has taken our Zabediel, the founder of all that we live and believe."

"I am sorry," said Thrivenbard. "Both for your loss and for my mistrust."

"Your caution is justified in times such as these," Warriant said. "But Balesparr can be trusted."

Thrivenbard exhaled and shook his head. "Then I tell you this: We hoped that Zabediel could tell us how to find the Three Witnesses."

Warriant frowned. "Zabediel spoke often to those he trusted of why he fled into the forest and why he must remain hidden until the end of his days. And while he spoke about the nature of the Scroll of Prophecy, he did not tell us what it said exactly. Who are the Three Witnesses?"

"Many in Alleble believe that when the threat of darkness is greatest, three warriors will come and lead Alleble to victory, but we do not know how to find them," Thrivenbard said. "Alas! Ever Paragor seems one step ahead of us. He stole the Scroll of Prophecy and now he has taken Zabediel. I fear now that this mission was futile, that the lives of my comrades have been lost in vain."

"Nay, not in vain," Warriant said. "Your coming to Balesparr may yet yield some hope."

"I do not understand," said Thrivenbard.

Warriant explained, "When Paragor invaded this place, he made bitter enemies. He murdered hundreds of our Glimpses, stole away more than just our leader, but the refuge that defines our way of life, as well. We can no longer hide from the troubles that confront the rest of The Realm. Paragor seeks to overthrow Alleble and enslave the free Glimpses of The Realm, and Alleble calls to all its allies to fight back. As first vanguard of Balesparr, I offer you three thousand Baleneers. Will you have us?"

Thrivenbard grinned and extended his hand. "Yes, Alleble will have you!"

"Excellent!" Warriant exclaimed. "I must go now to the barracks. We must prepare for war!"

THE SCROLL
OF PROPHECY

Antoinette pushed the Paragor Knight halfway back up the hall-way so she could see better and then ripped his helmet off.

"Owww!"

"Aidan!" Antoinette cried, hugging him. "It's really you!"

"Yeah," Aidan replied, bewildered by the sudden turn of events. "It's really me. Antoinette, I was looking for you in a cell. What are you doing running around—" Then Aidan noticed a very old Glimpse stepping out of the shadows. "Who's he?" Aidan asked.

"This is Zabediel. He was in a cell near mine."

Zabed looked at Aidan very suspiciously. "A Paragor Knight from the Mirror Realm?" asked Zabediel. "Can thou be trusted?"

"I'm an Alleble Knight," Aidan said. "I took this armor from a Paragor Knight so I could move around unnoticed within Paragor's army."

"When did you return?" Antoinette asked.

"Not long ago. I was with Robby fighting Count Eogan, and all of a sudden I just kind of got pulled in on The Thread," Aidan said.

Zabediel moved toward Aidan, staring at him as if he was studying him.

"The Thread? Oh, I don't care how you got here . . . I'm just glad you came," she said.

"I had to come," Aidan replied. "It's my fault you got captured, isn't it? I asked you to look for Robby's Glimpse."

"It's not your fault. You didn't tell me not to follow Kaliam's orders. It is I who placed many in danger in my quest to find Robby," she said sadly. "But I found Robby's Glimpse. He's Kearn!"

"I saw him too. Do you know where he is?"

"I don't know. I'm not sure, but I think Kearn just disappeared."

"Disappeared?" Aidan asked.

"Yeah. One minute, he was there in my cell, and the next— gone!"

"That's what happened to me," Aidan said excitedly. "But that would mean that Robby is . . ."

"Someplace in The Realm," she said.

"Antoinette, we have to get to Alleble," Aidan said, taking her hand and starting down the hall. "I've got to talk with Kaliam. Come on, I have two dragons I left on a balcony below." They ran back the way Aidan had come, taking odd turns, and spiraling ever down.

"Wait!" Zabed's strained voice came from behind. "I . . . I must rest."

Aidan and Antoinette would not go on without Zabed, so the three rested.

Antoinette sat with her arm around Zabediel's slight frame. "Even with your dragons," she said, "I don't know how we'll get past Paragor's forces."

"Easy," Aidan replied. "We'll just fly above them."

"Aidan, you don't understand. We might get by Paragor's ocean of soldiers, dragons, and catapults, but he's set free terrible monsters also: giant wolf creatures called the Seven Sleepers and a powerful dragon called the Wyrm Lord. Oh, Aidan, you have no idea what he can do!"

"We have to try. I have something . . ." Aidan reached into his armor, unbuttoned a flap on his tunic, and pulled out the scrap of parchment he'd found in the Blackwood. He held it up and showed Antoinette. "King Eliam led me to this scroll, and Paragor wants it. I don't know what it says . . ."

"The Scroll of Prophecy," whispered Zabed. He gently took the piece of yellowed parchment from Aidan's hand. "These are the words of King Eliam the Everlasting, uttered prophetically at the dawn of this world."

Aidan and Antoinette stared at the old Glimpse. "How . . . how do you know that?" Antoinette asked.

Zabediel smiled. "I know, m'lady Antoinette, because I was there when King Eliam spoke these words."

Aidan's mouth fell open. "But that would make you—"

"Older than time," Zabediel said with a laugh. "And so I almost am. I am in the line of Torin, Pureblood, the firstborn in all The Realm! I walked with King Eliam when all things were safe and beautiful, and I heard him speak the fate of this world. It was I who wrote his words down in the most ancient of tongues, and I alone of living Glimpse-kind can read all of what is written here."

"What does it say?" Aidan blurted out.

"Such knowledge is a heavy burden to bear. It is because of this that Paragor ripped me away from my wooded refuge and subjected me to agonizing tortures. Ye see, this is but the final piece of the Scroll of Prophecy that Paragor now commands. He stole it from the heart of Sil Arnoth, the firstborn tree of all The Realm. But old Arnoth was more clever than Paragor supposed. Even in death, he would not relinquish it all. The longer portion that the enemy now holds is incomplete. He suspected this for a time, but I think—thanks to my own efforts and to Aidan's—Paragor is now content with what he has. And we must hope that he will continue to believe that."

"What do you mean?" Antoinette asked.

"The Scroll of Prophecy tells many things," Zabediel explained. "For Paragor it tells what his itching ears want to hear: how final victory over Alleble might be achieved. He is wise in his cunning and well-learned in ancient tongues. Between what he was able to decipher on his own and what he was able to torture out of me, Paragor has unleashed the Wyrm Lord and the Seven Sleepers. They are a bane to this world, and two thirds of the final disaster that Paragor longs to visit on all Glimpse-kind."

"Two thirds?" Aidan said. "I don't understand."

"No," Zabediel said, holding up the parchment and smiling grimly. "And neither does Paragor. For he does not know what is written on this, the last part of the prophecy. And he does not realize how the end he foresees could be his own."

"Will you tell us the prophecy?" Aidan asked.

"I will," he replied eagerly. "For, unless my wisdom is far astray, the prophecy concerns you both."

Aidan and Antoinette stared at each other and then back at Zabediel.

"'Hear now, you called ones of the King,'" Zabediel read from the scroll. "'Hear King Eliam the Everlasting's prophecy—in its entirety—as it has not been spoken since the beginning.'"

Aidan and Antoinette lost all sense of where they were when Zabediel began to recite the prophecy from memory. The walls of the passage peeled back, and the flickering torch blazed anew and became a distant sun rising over a pristine green world. All was serene, but a bruised sky on the western horizon signaled a storm was coming.

Laugh and be glad, realm from my hand.
Wind and trees, sing songs.

Mountains rise and smile at the sky.
My children, grow and be strong.
Gifts I have given thee, and gifts will I give
To the firstborn and all of your kin.
A path of light I have laid out before thee,
And the greater prize, choose from within.
Alas, my children, among thee,
In the darkness, a deed will be done.
Covetous wyrm ire will burn like white fire,
And innocent blood will run.
Wind and tall trees will fall silent.
Mountains will scowl and shudder.
The sky will turn black and
My children will weep
For the realm torn asunder.
From Torin's Keep, the dragon will fly,
Swift on the wing, away from my eye.
Into the deep forest where
The first wolvins dwell,
He will teach them his secrets and
Persuade them to lie.
No forest will hide, the blood-red stain
Of their unfortunate choices.
And though they lay quiet beneath the boughs,
I still hear their voices.
Traitorous wyrm! I see from afar.
The whole realm groans around thee.
In the Shattered Lands your
Consequence stands
Entombed beneath a molten sea.
I will call the Seven, out from their den,
And though they beg and weep,

A sepulcher of trees will be their doom,
And evermore they sleep.
From the sorrow, new hope will spring.
Glimpse-kind will fill all the lands.
Alleble will be my beacon.
Seven fountains where the waters dance.
All will know of my kingdom,
And I will watch over all.
From near and far and the Mirror Realm,
Many will answer my call.
I will choose my favored one
And give him the sword of the pure.
Yet his loyalty like a castle wall
Will but for a time endure.
His will be the black desire
To make the wyrm's choice his own.
Innocent blood will spill again,
A fountain left as dry as bone.
The Betrayer will be cast out,
But in the darkness will reign.
He will prey on the weak and weak-minded,
And rule with a scepter of pain.
In secret, his armies will swell,
Bloated by vengeance and greed.
The firstborn wyrm will rise again,
And the Seven will no longer sleep.
In Alleble the bells will peal
When the Herald comes forth
And calls the name of Three Witnesses
In the kingdom's darkest hour.
Heroes, seers of visions,
Travelers of both Passage and Thread,

Warriors of the Mirror Realm
Become The Betrayer's dread.

The Child of Storms, the Dragonfriend,
The Seeker of the Lost,
Will raise their swords in battle
And dare to risk the cost.
They will charge into the darkness,
The Black Breath of the wyrm.
And shine like bands of sunlight
In the coming final storm.
But when all efforts have failed,
And The Betrayer has taken the throne,
The Witnesses will be brought alive
And two destinies will be shown.
They must face the offer
To see the victory in his eyes.
The Betrayer he must turn them
Or else must take their lives.

"That is the end," Zabediel explained, and his voice returned to normal. "The end as Paragor knows it. I have gone through great pain to convince him that there is no more that could affect his rise to power and Alleble's fall."

The torchlight flickered and thunder rumbled ominously.

"The prophecy makes it clear that Paragor will capture the Three Witnesses. And as far as his arrogant imagination is concerned, he believes that when he does, his victory will be assured."

"But the prophecy . . . it doesn't end there," Aidan said. "You haven't read from the parchment I found."

"No, it does not end there, Sir Aidan," Zabediel confirmed. "And let all The Realm rejoice because it does not. There is more,

and there is, I think . . . hope. I read it now to you. May you understand it well."

When the Witnesses decide,
Former deeds may be undone.
The Seven Swords may be unveiled.
Worlds once divided become one.

"That's it?" Aidan blurted out. "When the Witnesses decide?
Decide what?"

"You will know when that time comes," Zabediel answered.

"But it says 'Former deeds MAY be undone.' That doesn't
sound very certain."

"I did not claim that the prophecy would guarantee victory,"
said Zabediel. "To think that it does would be to err like Paragor. I
only said the last part of the prophecy offers hope, and it does."

"But what are the Seven Swords?" Antoinette objected.

"There, Lady Antoinette, my wisdom fails," said Zabediel.
"Perhaps that is a question for someone else to answer."

Thunder slammed and reverberated in the stone walls of the
hallway.

"The storm," whispered Antoinette. "Zabed, can you run now?"

Zabed nodded. "I fear we must run or we all will perish."

A Greater Mission

All through the night, Warriant, the first vanguard of Balesparr, mobilized his soldiers to help the citizens of his village prepare for evacuation. Thrivenbard promised he would send a fleet of dragons back to bear them to their new homes in the Kingdom of Alleble.

Baleneers led Thrivenbard and the remaining Knights of Alleble to their dragons on the edge of King's Forest.

Now, as Thrivenbard, his knights, and a large contingent of Baleneer spearmen passed through the gap between the mountains, Thrivenbard was lost in thought. He was grateful Warriant had sent his spearmen to help defend Alleble, but the Alleble commander's thoughts still lingered on the ones who would not be coming back—the warriors who died in that perilous forest. And, of course, the fact that Zabediel was now in the hands of the enemy was even more bad news for the followers of King Eliam.

His thoughts were interrupted by a thunderous crack. From high above, the dragon riders from Alleble saw newly erected scaffolds and platforms, nested in various crags upon the western face of the mountains. There was another earsplitting crack, followed by a great grinding sound.

"Witness the craft of King Brower and his kin!!" Thrivenbard called out in a loud shout.

They watched in rapt amazement as a huge white section of stone detached itself from the mountain's face and slid slowly down until it disappeared into a cloud of snow and debris at the foot of the mountain. The dragon riders swooped down beyond the drifting cloud and found thousands of Glimpse craftsmen in teams of fifties and hundreds gathered around massive segments of that same brilliant white stone. Some of the Glimpses wielded immense hammers and pounded on enormous wedges and chisels. Still others were busy with serpentine hoses, spilling gallons of snowmelt wherever metal met stone.

"Look!" Robby pointed, drawing even with Trenna as they soared over the copse of evergreens and the training compound behind the castle. And below the dragon riders, a steady train of long wagons crept slowly along a newly cleared path. The wagons were drawn by dozens of stocky blackhorne and their payload: more huge sections of white rock. Some were cut in vast sheets, others into massive triangles.

Trumpets blared, for the heralds had seen the return of the team from King's Forest. And all the dragon riders looked up and were astonished by the sight before them. Protected by dizzyingly intricate networks of scaffolds, and rising so high that they hid the western horizon from view, were immense new battlements made of the pure white stone from the twin mounts of Pennath Ador. Not nearly complete, but clearly well in progress, the walls and towers stood gleaming in the morning sun.

"By the King's grace!" Sir Oswyn sang out. "They work fast!"

"Elspeth, all of our remaining allies have arrived. King Brower's folk are working like frenzied ants upon the walls. And the scouts on the

Cold River have not returned with any news of threat. Do you have everything you need for the dinner celebration this evening?"

"Yes, m'lord."

"There is one more thing I request of you, Elspeth—but you must keep it as a secret."

Curious, Elspeth stepped closer to him. "M'lord."

"Merewen and I shall marry at the celebration this evening," he said, handing her a piece of parchment. "Would you be sure all of the people on this list are invited to join us in the King's Garden?"

Elspeth grinned. "I will personally see to it, Sir Kaliam. We shall all have a merry time tonight. Yes—"

A sharp knock at the door interrupted Elspeth.

"Sentinel Kaliam!" a voice called. "Thrivenbard has returned from King's Forest! He awaits you with news in Guard's Keep!"

Kaliam took his place next to Lady Merewen at the head of the table in Guard's Keep. Gathered there as well were King Ravelle, King Brower, Queen Illaria, Lord Sternhilt, Robby, Trenna, and a dozen other prominent Glimpse warriors.

Thrivenbard stood and told the tale. He spoke of the battle with serpents and spiders and the lives that were lost there. He told of the finding of the hidden village of Balesparr and of their promise to fight for Alleble against the enemy. And last, he told of Paragor's daring attack on Balesparr where he took Zabediel, the aged scribe, and flew away with him to the dark mountains in the west.

"How long ago did this happen?" Kaliam asked. His eyes were vacant, and his face wore a stunned expression. "How long ago did Paragor take Zabediel?"

"Two seasons, according to Warriant," Thrivenbard replied.

"Two seasons?!" Kaliam exclaimed. "That would put it before the battle at Mithegard!" Kaliam was silent a few moments, lost in thought. "This Warriant fellow," he said at last. "You say his eyes glint green. Are you sure you can trust him?"

Nock spoke up. "Sir Warriant is an honorable knight. If Paragor was his master, we would all be dead now. When we approached the hidden village, Sir Warriant and his Baleneers surrounded us in a clearing. They waited among the treetops with their sharp spears at the ready. It would have been like catching fish in a barrel."

"Besides," Sir Oswyn chimed in, "if Sir Warriant was an agent of the enemy, he could just as easily have had eyes that glint blue to deceive us."

"No, these are Zabediel's folk," concluded Thrivenbard. "He is no enemy of Alleble."

Kaliam stood and paced the front of the room. "Two seasons," he muttered to himself. And then to the group, "If it is as you say, then it answers many hard questions but leaves me still with one that troubles me even more. We can now guess that Paragor had the Scroll of Prophecy and Zabediel before our journey to Yewland. It must be that the Scroll revealed the location of the tomb of the Wyrm Lord in the Shattered Lands, as well as the Sepulcher of the Seven Sleepers in the Blackwood. This is how Paragor is able to stay ahead of our plans."

"Those are the answers," Lady Merewen said, looking with concern to Kaliam. "What troubles you still?"

Kaliam looked directly at her and then at the group assembled before him. "What I still do not understand—and forgive me for questioning the wisdom of our King—but, if Paragor took Zabediel months ago, the King must have known. Why, then, would he wait and send us on a mission that could not be achieved?"

"Perhaps there was a greater mission," Thrivenbard said as he stood. "M'lord Kaliam, I struggled with this same thought as I mourned the loss of many of our team. Why send them to their doom if Zabediel is not there to be rescued? But then I realized that while we have lost some of our finest warriors, we have gained thousands in return. And the spears they wield are swift, as silent as the grave, and deadly accurate! I wonder how many lives the Baleneers will save by going to war on our side."

Many expressed agreement with Thrivenbard as they left the afternoon meeting. Two warriors remained seated near Kaliam: Robby and Lady Merewen.

"I liked what Thrivenbard said about King Eliam," Robby said. "I haven't known him long—the King, I mean—but that's kinda the way he is. I mean, I've wondered for a long time about why things happen the way they do. I wondered why my dad left—abandoned us when I was little. But if he hadn't, we might never have moved to Maryland. I might never have met Aidan. And then I wondered why Aidan had to move, but he needed to talk to his grandfather—needed to hear about Alleble so he could try to get the truth through my thick head.

"So many things had to happen just the right way to get me here!" Robby wiped the tear off his cheek. "Y'know, I was thinking that maybe one of the reasons King Eliam waited so long to send a team into the forest was because of me. I learned a lot in those woods. I learned that some things are worth risking my life for." He thought of Trenna and her radiant smile. "And I also learned I hate spiders!" Robby and Kaliam burst out in laughter.

Kaliam put his arm on Robby's shoulder for a moment. "Thank you," he said.

"I didn't do anything," Robby replied.

"Yes . . . yes, you did."

Robby grinned and seemed to stand a little straighter. "I'll see you, m'lord," he said. "I'm gonna go play with Splinter."

"Do you still question?" Lady Merewen asked just after Robby left.

"I do not question the King's judgment, no," Kaliam replied.

"But I can see doubt lingering in your eyes," Lady Merewen said, taking his hand.

"You have a gift, m'lady, for seeing beyond my words," Kaliam said, smiling a little sadly. "The doubt you see is not doubt of the King. I doubt myself."

"Why so?" she asked. "Alleble's armies number nearly as many as our enemy now that our allies have all come—and add to that a legion of adept spearmen! The new walls will be complete in a few days. You have prepared as well as may be."

"You encourage me, Merewen," he said. "But Paragor wields the Wyrm Lord and the Sleepers. He has also the Scroll of Prophecy and Zabediel, the only one left alive who could interpret it fully. Without that wisdom and knowledge, how can I possibly know for sure who the Three Witnesses are?"

DRANG'S GAME

The torchlit passages in the heart of Paragor's stronghold twisted and turned like a den of serpents. "Please tell me you aren't lost," Antoinette said when Aidan stopped suddenly at a fork in the path.

"Quiet, I'm thinking!" Aidan barked.

Zabed placed a withered hand on Aidan's shoulder. "What place does thou hope to find?" he asked.

"It's a huge balcony," Aidan said. "On the northern side of the great tower. I tied the dragons there."

"Does thou mean the tower crowned with thorns?"

"Yes!" Aidan exclaimed.

"Then take the passage on thy left," Zabed explained.

There came a strange rumbling from below. It grew louder, and Aidan recognized the sound as the tromping of many iron-shod feet. Paragor had not emptied his fortress completely after all. "Soldiers!" Aidan shouted. "Antoinette, they know you've escaped! We must hurry!"

They could hear shrieks and the shouts of many voices, distant but growing ever closer.

"The rats in this cursed hold will smell us out, I fear," Zabed growled. "I have told ye the prophecy of thy scroll. You have no longer need of me. Leave me behind."

Aidan looked at Zabed, who was starved from his long imprisonment, thin and frail with age.

"Maybe there's another way," Aidan said, and he handed Fury to Antoinette. Then he grasped Zabed's wrists and carefully slung him onto his back.

"Nay, lad!" Zabed protested. "Leave me be! I will slow thou down to the demise of all!"

"Zabed, I won't leave you," Aidan said, hefting the sage and taking a few steps. "C'mon, Antoinette!"

Aidan ran surprisingly fast, bearing Zabed's extra weight more easily than he had thought he could. The passage curled and then sloped downward. Aidan whispered a quick *Thank you* to King Eliam and charged on. Antoinette, Fury in one hand, the Daughter of Light in the other, raced after him.

Heavy footfalls fell in the passage behind them. *Too close!* Aidan thought. *They'll catch us before we can—* Then he saw it. The passage opened up at the bottom and strange gray twilight fell upon the stone beneath a wide arch. Aidan knew that arch. The balcony and the dragons were just beyond it!

"It's just ahead!" he cried. "Hurry!" Just then an arrow swooshed over Aidan's shoulder, struck the ceiling of the passage ahead, and clattered to the ground. Angry screams blared from the passage.

Aidan dashed down the hill. The arch was closer. Almost there. Suddenly, Zabed groaned. His arms stiffened and then went limp in Aidan's grasp. Zabed's gray head fell on Aidan's shoulders.

"No!" Aidan exclaimed. "Zabed?!" But the old sage did not answer. Aidan surged beneath the arch into the ethereal gray of night in Paragory. But the moment Aidan stepped on the stone of the balcony, his feet slid out from under him. He skidded as if on ice and fell backward. His weight came down hard on Zabed.

Antoinette was right behind him. She lost her footing as well, flailed to keep her balance, but crashed to the stone. Her sword and Fury clattered across the balcony. Antoinette pushed herself up from the ground. Her hands felt wetness. She stood awkwardly and looked at her palms. Even in the shroud of gray night, she could see glistening blood. *Blood!* Antoinette looked around. They were in a great wide pool of blood.

Aidan struggled to his feet, turned, and saw the two white dragons he had brought from the stables below. They were slain, their long necks hewn and scored with many jagged wounds. And sprawled unnaturally near the dragons were five dead Glimpses. Paragor Knights—each of them gouged deep by dragon claws or bitten.

Then Aidan saw Zabed, facedown in the blood. A cruel black shaft protruded from his shoulder, and he lay very still. "No! Zabed!" Aidan yelled, as he staggered toward the fallen sage. A dozen Paragor Knights appeared in the shadows on the downslope of the passage, but Aidan did not see them. He knelt next to the old Glimpse and felt for a pulse. There was none.

Antoinette grabbed her sword and dove behind one of the dead dragons. "Aidan!"

But Aidan seemed lost in a fog. He held the frail hand of the old Glimpse and thought of Captain Valithor, the Glimpse twin of Grampin. Aidan had held Valithor's hand as he died, pierced like Zabed with an arrow meant for Aidan.

Antoinette watched the enemy advance under the arch. In a moment they could hack Aidan to bits with their curved swords. "Aidan! Snap out of it!" she cried. "Aidan!"

An arrow glanced off Aidan's shoulder, and he fell backward. Finally aware of his own peril, he scrabbled in the blood, snatched Fury, and dove behind the other fallen dragon steed. Sickening wet thuds followed as a barrage of black shafts drilled into the fallen white dragons.

"How many?" Aidan called out.

"At least a dozen," Antoinette answered. "There may be more coming. I don't know."

Aidan grimaced. The balcony wall stood behind them, and beyond that, there was a hundred-foot fall to the jagged rocks of the Grimwalk below. Twelve against two and nowhere to go.

Never alone, Aidan thought as he slowly rose to look over the dragon carcass. The enemy was there, but they were not advancing. Not yet. It seemed more to their taste to try to pick off their prey from a safe distance. After all, they were in no danger from return fire.

"I see your game, Blarrak!" came a voice. "If that is who you really are!"

Aidan peered over the dragon carcass. It was Drang!

"Yes, I know your game!" Drang yelled. "But I play it better than you! Now give up Kearn's prize, for I am several moves ahead of you!"

Another volley of arrows streamed in. Many stabbed into the dead dragons, others hit the balcony wall and fell at Aidan's feet. "Antoinette, the dead Paragor Knights in front of the dragons—do any of them have a bow?"

Antoinette looked at Aidan strangely, then she nodded and peered around the dragon. The dead knights had only swords, no, wait! There was one bow. It lay beneath the Paragor Knight farthest from the fallen dragon in front of her. Antoinette ducked back and called to Aidan, "There is one bow. I can get it, but I'll be exposed."

"No you won't!" Aidan said. "Be ready." Aidan suddenly stood up, and ran to the right of his dragon cover. He slashed Fury as he ran, and the enemy trained their bows upon him. At that moment, staying low, Antoinette sprinted from behind her dragon.

The arrows flew at Aidan, and he dove to the ground and rolled. One shaft struck Fury's crossguard and fell away. Several others bounced off the balcony wall. Aidan stood again and leaped for cover, but not before a black shaft struck him in the upper arm.

Aidan hit the ground, and struggled to tear off the armor on his arm. He could feel the tip of the arrow on his skin, and he knew if it penetrated, the poison from even a scratch could kill him. At last the armor came free. The tip had gone clean through the armor, but there was no blood on his arm. He was safe.

"I got it!" Antoinette called.

"Do you know how to shoot?"

"Yes, actually, I do," Antoinette replied. But could she remember all that Nock had taught her in that short lesson at Torin's Vale?

Aidan grabbed every fallen arrow he could find, and even plucked a few from the dragon's body. These he tossed over at Antoinette's feet. Antoinette fitted the first shaft to the bowstring. She sat still for a moment, rehearsing the movements. *Eye on the target, draw the bowstring to your ear, pull back a little more until the string releases itself . . . and, oh yeah, expect to hit the target!*

Then she stood suddenly. She spotted a broad warrior standing near the arch. She aimed, drew back, and the arrow was gone. She had been aiming for his chest, but the shot was a little high. The arrow plunged straight into the Glimpse's neck. Antoinette lined up another shot. Another arrow flew, and another enemy fell. But the enemy fired back, and Antoinette dropped to the ground for cover.

Lightning flashed, illuminating the balcony, and Aidan saw a pair of knights crawling across the bloody balcony. Thunder rumbled overhead. Aidan yelled, "Get the two on the ground!"

He watched as Antoinette fired at the two prone figures. Her first shot drilled into the closest knight. His head hit the balcony with a dull thud. The other warrior got up and tried to run, but fell within a few steps as an arrow pierced his armor and plunged deep between his shoulder blades.

"Wow! Who taught you to shoot?" Aidan asked.

"Nock!" Antoinette replied with a wink.

Aidan looked up over the dragon. There were two Paragor

Knights left: Drang and a big galoot of a warrior who didn't seem to know which end of the arrow to put onto the bowstring.

"I'm out of arrows!" Antoinette said, drawing the Daughter of Light. "But I think we can take them!"

"Okay," Aidan called back. "I'll take the big guy, but if you can, leave the other guy alive. He may know how we can get out of here."

"Uh, okay," she said. "I'll try!"

The giant looked up and saw Aidan coming. He tossed away his bow and pulled a huge double-bladed battleaxe from his back. Aidan soon found out that whatever skill the giant lacked with the bow, he more than made up for with the axe. The giant's first strike almost took Aidan's head off. He ducked just in time, but had no time to mount a counterattack. He had to roll into the blood to avoid a devastating chop from the giant. He rolled to his feet. Lightning flashed, and Aidan saw rage flickering on the giant's face as he pressed the attack.

Aidan leaped over a low axe stroke and then dodged to the side, but not far enough, and the axe blade slid over his leg armor. "Ah!" Aidan yelled. His thigh burned hot.

This is not good! Aidan thought. The dragons' blood was so slippery that it was hard to sidestep the warrior's wide axe slashes. And he was afraid to try to block the axe with Fury. If the axe broke his sword, Aidan would be left weaponless.

Then the giant came running with his axe held high. Skidding in the blood, Aidan ran too, but he ran away from the giant toward the balcony. The giant was right behind him, ready to bring the axe down when Aidan ran out of room. At the last possible second, Aidan swerved to his right, grabbed the tail of one of the dead dragons, and slid. He slammed into the balcony wall. The massive Paragor Knight tried to pull up at the last second, but slid in the blood. The balcony wall hit him about waist-high. He flipped over the edge and disappeared with an angry scream.

Aidan got up and saw that Antoinette had done her part. She had disarmed Drang and had him pinned to the stone wall with her sword tip stuck in his shoulder.

"Oww!" Aidan said, limping as he approached the two. He yelled at Drang, "Was it you who killed the two white dragons?"

Drang glanced at Antoinette's armor. "Servants of Alleble, eh? I have nothing to say to the likes of you!"

"Antoinette," Aidan said, rubbing his injured leg, "persuade him."

Antoinette twisted her sword blade just a tiny amount. Drang yelped with pain. "Ahhgg! All right! No, I did not touch the dragons. M'lads did it! Ahh, stop!"

Antoinette stopped turning the blade. Lightning flashed and thunder rumbled as an icy breeze washed over the balcony.

"You ordered them to do it, though," Aidan said. "Right?"

"Right!" Drang laughed. "And now the dragons are gone, mine included—not one left! Looks like you'll have to walk back to Alleble!"

"Antoinette."

She turned the sword.

"Yeeeggg!" Drang yelled. "I have a horse! Stabled down below. She is old, not very strong, but she is yours."

"A horse?" Aidan yelled. "That's it?"

"All that is left! Now stop, please!"

Antoinette removed the sword from Drang's shoulder. He slumped to the ground. They tied Drang up and left him there on the balcony. Aidan led the way to the stables within the mountain.

But as they ran, Aidan thought about Drang's parting shot. "Go ahead, Dark Skins!" he had yelled. "Go ahead, ride my mare all the way to Alleble!" He laughed. "By the time you get there, there won't be anything left."

A Time for
All Things

Kaliam stood near the three-tiered fountain in the courtyard where he had proposed to Merewen. He was thankful for the bright afternoon sun overhead, though he knew that in a matter of hours, that would change.

King Brower, Mallik, and the rest of the Blue Mountain folk had worked day and night on the new walls. And now, just two days later, the walls were nearly complete. But still, Kaliam wondered if it would be enough. He remembered all too well the carnage at Clarion . . . and Yewland. The Wyrm Lord and the Seven Sleepers—they might turn the tide of the battle alone.

"Kaliam," a voice said. "It is time to prepare for your wedding." Turning, Kaliam saw Sir Oswyn standing at the door and nodded.

The guests had gathered in the garden. Sir Oswyn stood directly in front of the fountain. Kaliam took his place near the center, near

Farix. Then all turned and looked. Between the trees, shrubs, and statues, they saw brief glimmers of white. And then, at last, Lady Merewen appeared riding a tall white unicorn. Her luminous violet eyes sparkled. A circlet of tiny white flowers rested above her brow. Her gown seemed to shimmer like cloth made of both white diamonds and deep blue onyxes. Draped across her shoulders and under her brilliant silver hair she wore the black velvet hand-embroidered heirloom sash that Kaliam had given her. Kaliam grinned. The unicorn stopped beside Kaliam, and he helped Merewen down.

Oswyn read from a scroll. "Children of The Realm!" Sir Oswyn's great voice rang out. "King Eliam the Everlasting calls you to this celebration to bear witness this day. If you are willing, so say you Aye!"

The crowd spoke as one voice. "Aye!"

"Very well then," Sir Oswyn said with a broad smile. "May King Eliam and all the glad souls in the Sacred Realm Beyond the Sun witness this event also. And may all the blessings of our mighty King be upon you all."

From his pocket Oswyn produced two halves of a golden coin.

"Kaliam and Merewen, I offer you each a half of this betrothal coin. If you accept, that means you agree to betroth your life to each other before King Eliam and these witnesses gathered here. Do you accept this coin?"

Kaliam and Lady Merewen answered together, "I do."

Sir Oswyn placed one half in Lady Merewen's hand and the other half of the coin in Kaliam's hand. Turning to Kaliam he said, "Lord Kaliam, take this half as a—"

But Os never finished the sentence. Kaliam interrupted, saying to Lady Merewen, "I gladly take the coin, but I will never need a reminder of what you are to me and what we are together." Then he took the coin, joined hands with Lady Merewen, and kissed her.

The crowd erupted in cheers far louder than Sir Oswyn's plea, "Wait, Kaliam, you are not supposed to do that yet!" At last, Oswyn laughed and said, "In that case, by the power granted me by King Eliam, the provider of all that is just and good, I declare that you are husband and wife! Let the merrymaking begin!"

In another corner of the garden, far from the merrymaking, King Ravelle sat alone on a stone bench. He looked up forlornly at a statue on the corner of a row of trees and hedges. It was the image of a maiden who appeared to walk forward and hold out her hands as if releasing a dove into flight.

"It is a marvelous statue," came a voice from the path to King Ravelle's right.

He looked, and his mouth fell open. "Ariana!" he exclaimed. "My wife! Of all the unlooked-for joys on this day!"

She took him into her arms and they embraced. "I should never have left you," she said. "You were a foolish, pigheaded warrior, but I was equally stubborn."

King Ravelle laughed aloud. "I hope we are wiser now."

She smiled.

"I searched for you; where did you go?" he asked.

"Many places. Eventually I found refuge in Balesparr."

"The hidden village?" he asked.

"Yes. Come, Ravelle," she said, her eyes glinting bright blue. "We have much to talk about."

As the celebration continued, Kaliam entered the courtyard where all the Knights of Alleble and their allies were assembled.

"There is a time for all things," Kaliam said loudly. "There is a time for singing, and we of Alleble sing each month at the fountain to remember the dawn where King Eliam returned to us and cast out the enemy. There is a time for weeping, and we have all wept bitterly for our losses at Mithegard, Clarion, Yewland, Ludgeon, and most recently at Balesparr."

Looks were exchanged. Many nodded, and some tears fell.

Kaliam's expression darkened. "Our enemy of old sits now on our doorstep. He has committed unspeakable evils and stands ready to do more. But I say we deny him!"

The crowd cheered. Some raised fists high.

"Our enemy has brought an army larger than any he has wielded before. An army built by deception, greed, and wanton violence. He is coming here to increase his force of slavery, but I say we deny him!"

The cheers grew louder, and a buzz grew in the crowd.

"Our foe has released ancient evils—names many thought were merely harvest tales for frightening children. But I assure you, they are real. The Seven Sleepers, the Wyrm Lord are under Paragor's command, and he intends to bring down our strong new walls, but I say . . ."

"DENY HIM!!!" the crowd answered together. But no voice was louder than that of King Brower from the Blue Mountains.

When the noise quieted down somewhat, Kaliam went on. "The enemy was cast out by the one true King. And Paragor now comes to claim a throne that does not belong to him, but we say—"

"DENY HIM!!!"

Kaliam's eyes smoldered. "I began by saying there is a time for all things. A time to sing, a time to cry, a time for peace—" Kaliam drew his sword and shouted to the crowd, "There is a time for all things, yes? But now I say it is TIME TO FIGHT!!!"

The crowd went into an uproar. Shouts went up: "Deny Paragor!" "Defend Alleble!" "Fight now!" and "Man the battlements!"

The crowd's shouts were so loud, they did not hear the rumbling thunder in the storm clouds gathering overhead.

An Old Friend
Well-Met

The uncanny darkness generated by the Wyrm Lord covered the Grimwalk and extended in every direction as far as the eye could see. A turbulent storm continued to churn overhead. After leaving Drang, Aidan and Antoinette searched for a way to escape from the caverns inside the Gate of Despair. This proved to be long and difficult, for Paragor had left behind teams of sentries, and several times they were nearly caught. But for their efforts, they found no dragon steeds, only Drang's horse. It was a black mare, old and tired from abuse, but it was the only thing they had.

Antoinette wanted to leave right away, but knowing firsthand the icy dangers of the Grimwalk, Aidan insisted that they find something to keep themselves warm for their long ride. Eventually, they packed or wrapped themselves in anything they could find: stable blankets, leather tarps, strips of oily cloth.

At last, the two Alleble Knights led Drang's horse through a small side door on the far side of the caverns where the siege towers had once stood. They emerged into the strange twilight world created by the Wyrm Lord's Black Breath. They could see within the shroud of darkness, and it was still frigid cold on the Grimwalk.

"How good are you at riding?" Antoinette asked.

"I seldom fall off," Aidan said.

"Okay, I'll take the reins," Antoinette decided. "What should we name her?"

"You want to name Drang's horse?"

"She's not his anymore. Any ideas?"

"She looks so tired," Aidan replied. "Like she's really weather-beaten, y'know? Maybe something like Stormy, Thundergallop, Black Lightning, Stormchaser—"

"Stormchaser?" Antoinette exclaimed. "I like it! In a way . . . we are chasing a storm."

Soon they were racing across the icy Grimwalk on Stormchaser. The bitter cold forced them to keep their faces covered up, and they did not speak.

They had not crossed even half of the Grimwalk before the tiring horse stumbled on a rut in the half-frozen ground, almost throwing her riders. Antoinette slowed Stormchaser to a trot, then a walk—until eventually Antoinette and Aidan were forced to walk beside the poor creature. Finally, the beast was barely moving.

Antoinette tried in vain to find some dead shrub or twisted root that the horse could eat. "There's nothing out here!" she exclaimed, kicking at a patch of ice.

They walked along, leading the horse for a few more minutes, but finally she would not move another step.

"Do you smell that?" Antoinette asked. "It smells like pennies."

"What?" Aidan turned and ran to Antoinette. "We have to get moving!" he yelled.

"But the horse," Antoinette argued. "We can't just leave her!"

"We have to!" Aidan said, urgently trying to pull Antoinette along. "The Stilling has come!"

"Stilling?"

But before Aidan could explain, Stormchaser's front knees buckled. Then she lay motionless on the snow, her eyes open.

"She's gone, Antoinette!" Aidan screamed. "It's part of Paragor's curse on this place. We have to leave now, and we have to keep moving, or it'll happen to us too!"

Aidan looked ahead into the murk. He thought he might be able to make out a ridge of rock a few hundred yards away.

"C'mon!" he yelled. Their muscles burned, but they pushed themselves on. And suddenly, they were there at the ridge of stone. It was closer than it had appeared. Another trick of the Black Breath, Aidan figured. He searched over the craggy rock for a cave, but there were none to be found. There was, however, another find. Wedged between some rocks, they found a buttoned leather pouch.

"Open it!" Antoinette said.

Aidan took off his gauntlets and practically tore the pouch open. His hands shaking, he reached inside. "It's food!" he yelled, pulling out a strip of dried meat. He tossed it to Antoinette and found a piece for himself. It was rock-hard, but after gnawing at it for a while, they were able to bite down.

"This is so good," Antoinette said, chomping on a second strip.

They each managed to wolf down five or six strips before Aidan closed the pouch. "We need to save some of this for later," he said, standing up.

"Wait, Aidan," Antoinette said. "I don't want to get up yet. Let's just rest a second."

"No, we need to keep moving, remember?" But Aidan's muscles ached worse than he thought they possibly could. Running in armor over uneven terrain with air so cold they could barely breathe had taken its toll. A short rest sounded good to Aidan. He sat down next to Antoinette and slowly pulled his knees up to his chest.

"Cold . . . ," Antoinette whispered. "So cold."

Aidan took a layer of cloth off his head and draped it over Antoinette's shoulders.

"Thank you, Aidan," she said, and those were her final words.

Aidan curled up next to her, struggled to keep his eyes open, but succumbed at last and was still.

When Aidan woke up, he couldn't see and he couldn't move. He was surrounded, wrapped tight in something dark and warm. He struggled, but it was like being held in a vise. He wasn't going anywhere.

"Good morning, young Aidan," came a loud raspy voice that seemed to vibrate through whatever it was that surrounded Aidan. "I trust you had a good night's sleep, hmmm?"

Wait! I know that voice! Aidan thought. "Falon?"

"Yes, Aidan," came the reply. "You remember old Falon, do you? Hmmm?"

Suddenly, the grip loosened, and Aidan fell backward. He landed in the palm of a large, dark three-taloned hand. And Falon's huge fang-filled face hung right there in front of him. "I did not think we would meet again," she said. "But I am glad."

"Antoinette!" Aidan cried out.

"I'm over here!" Antoinette said. Falon uncurled another part of her long serpentine body, and there was Antoinette, smiling like it was her birthday. "I finally get to meet Falon the Great! Her son Faethon guards King Eliam's treasuries, and he is pretty impressive, but nothing compared to his mother! She saved us, Aidan," she said. "We fell asleep on the Grimwalk."

"Not a very wise thing to do," Falon said. "It was fortunate for you that I was in the area. When I found you, you had both begun to turn blue. But Falon's coils warmed you right up, hmmm?"

Aidan sat bolt upright. "But Falon, you're out of your lair. You're out in the open! How is that possible?"

"Ah, you remember!" Falon laughed. "Yes, normally, to be out under sun or moon would spell the end for old Falon. But this mist, this dark canopy, is over everything from Mithegard to Alleble. I found that I could endure it."

"What were you doing on the Grimwalk?" Antoinette asked.

"When I discovered that I could move about," Falon explained, "I decided to pay Paragor a little visit. I owe him much, young Antoinette, for he and his brood have all but destroyed the race of mortiwraiths . . . taking the blood of my kind for their poison. But when I came calling to his little castle, Paragor was not at home. Pity. And there were very few of his knights about either."

"Paragor has taken his armies to attack Alleble," said Aidan. "Oh, no! How long did we sleep?"

"Since last night," Falon replied. "It is hard to tell in this bleak mist, but I deem that it is near midday."

"Falon, we've got to get to Alleble!"

"Paragor is there, you say?"

"Yes," Aidan replied. "He has a massive army."

"But that's not all, Falon," Antoinette said. "He has monsters—the Seven Sleepers and the Wyrm Lord."

"The Wyrm Lord, really?" Falon said, laughing mischievously. "I thought King Eliam found a nice warm spot for that old dragon."

"He did," Aidan replied. "But Paragor let him out."

"Dangerous creature, that one," Falon said. "But then again, so am I."

"Will you take us?" Aidan asked. "Will you take us to Alleble?"

"I would do this even if I was not hungry," said Falon. "But I am starving, yesss, famished! And I have an old score to settle with Paragor."

The Coming
of Darkness

From their team's vantage point Mallik and Nock could see the
world was roofed with a dark, swirling mantle of storm clouds. The
turbulent clouds extended above the city, but the shadowy pall below
advanced only within a hundred yards of the main gate. Lightning
crackled overhead, illuminating the city and the pale faces of many
warriors in an eerie green light. Thunder rolled and crashed.

"What is it?" Mallik asked, staring out from a great height on
the parapet of the new city walls.

"It is certainly not like any storm I have ever seen before," said
Nock, and he adjusted the leather straps across his shoulders. He
was not used to wearing two quivers—his usual quiver filled with
Blackwood Arrows for his longbow on his back and now a smaller
hard leather quiver full of bolts for the arbalest at his side.

"Paragor's devilry, no doubt," said Sir Rogan, fingering his axe.

"Well, let him come," Mallik said. "He will find the walls of
adorite hard enough to break his teeth on." Robby and Trenna
laughed.

"Adorite?" asked Thrivenbard, his eyebrow raised.

"So named by King Brower," Mallik replied. "Delved by my kin from the face of Pennath Ador, this white rock is the hardest stone in all The Realm. Adorite it is called, the *glorystone*."

"I have heard it called by another name," said Halberad, "as I ran errands among your people at the foot of the mountains. They called it *faercrag*. What does that mean?"

Mallik laughed. "That is *fire rock* in the old language of my people."

Halberad nodded. "Ah, I should have guessed!"

"Now, I do not understand," came a quiet voice from behind.

"Ah, Sir Valden," said Thrivenbard. "You were so quiet I did not notice you standing there."

"Just wait until the fighting starts," Robby said, grinning. Valden's peaceful eyes narrowed, and he glared at Robby. When Robby's smile disappeared, Valden grinned and they both laughed.

"To answer your question," Mallik explained, "some call the white stone fire rock due to its peculiar reaction to blunt force. Often when we struck the rock with our picks and hammers, it would spark. And—"

"That is not unusual," interrupted Sir Rogan. "There are other stones that do that . . . flint, slate, and such."

"To spark? Yes, that is common," Mallik said. "But you did not let me finish. The adorite does more than spark. On an especially hard strike, a lick of white fire would appear. Its heat was intense— a few of my brethren were burned. But then we learned to flush the stone with snowmelt as we worked!"

The knights continued to talk casually among themselves, but while the smiles and laughter were brave, they were also full of apprehension. None of them had seen anything like what they were witnessing. And they knew that somewhere in the heart of that darkness, Paragor and his armies were coming.

Near another part of the battlements, Kaliam and Farix led Warriant and all three thousand of his Baleneers up an avenue. The Glimpses of Alleble and all of the citizens of their allies stared out at the newcomers. They were fierce in countenance and wore peculiar shingled armor on their chest and shoulders, but none save boots on their legs.

Perhaps their legs are too big? some thought, for indeed, the warriors from Balesparr had massive thighs and calves that bulged out of the tops of their cloth boots. They looked very powerful—and menacing. Each Baleneer had a very long quiver slung on his back. These were crammed full of the terrible long spears that they called bales.

They came to a wide ramp to the right of the main gatehouse and halted there. Kaliam turned to Warriant. "Queen Illaria and King Ravelle have stationed their archers near every tower upon the battlements," he said. "Send one team of your spearmen to join every two teams of archers. Two thousand on the walls and the others in reserve. We will house them in the barracks behind the walls and along the main thoroughfare where the fountains are. If the walls fail, they will need to cover our retreat."

"It will be done as you say," Warriant replied. "But, if I may, we should take the reserves and go to the tallest towers and high places of the city. We can be very effective at great heights."

Kaliam nodded. "Then choose what heights you may."

Warriant raced off, shouting commands to his forces.

"You know," Kaliam said quietly to Farix, "there is something in Warriant's gaze that is disturbing."

Farix nodded. "I have seen it too," he said. "Not troubling in the sense that he might betray us. But something wild."

"Yes," Kaliam agreed. "Like an untamed animal that has just been let out of a cage."

All of the defenses of Alleble were in order. The storm continued to churn above, but the lightning and thunder were not as fierce as before. Kaliam and his commanders stood on the main battlement above the gate to the city. Robby paced back and forth . . . waiting.

"This is not Paragor's usual pattern of attack," said King Ravelle. "He hits hard first, and attempts to overwhelm with brute force. That is what he did in my city."

"And in Clarion, Yewland, and the Blue Mountains," Kaliam agreed. "Why does he wait?"

"Perhaps not all of his forces are in place," offered Lord Sternhilt. "We have not yet seen so much as a single Paragor Knight."

"And yet, I feel he is out there," Kaliam said.

"In that murk, who can tell?" said Farix.

"There is one way to find out," said Warriant.

"You do not mean to go down there?" Lady Merewen asked. "It is perilous beyond that curtain of darkness."

"You sound as if you have been in there," Warriant said, scoffing at her cautions.

"I have, Sir Warriant," she replied. "In the Blackwood this darkness surrounded us. It changes your senses, and evil things lurk there. We were fortunate to have survived."

"Apologies, m'lady," Warriant said. "I will stay alert."

"You mean you still plan to go?" Lady Merewen asked.

"By Kaliam's leave, yes," he replied. "We will go in just far enough to find Paragor's position. My people are stealthy. We will be careful." He looked questioningly at Kaliam.

Kaliam nodded slowly. "You have my leave," he said. Then he turned to King Ravelle. "Send a squad to man the gates. Shut them behind as soon as they leave, but be prepared to open them at a moment's notice!"

Warriant turned and looked at Kaliam strangely. "Gates?" he asked. "Who said anything about gates?" And with that, he nodded to a group of his Baleneers, and to the terror of all, they leaped off the battlements.

Kaliam and the others rushed to the parapet just in time to see them land softly on their feet. The other Baleneers, the ones who still stood high on the walls, turned and grinned.

Kaliam turned to Farix. "I cannot believe they just did that."

The Baleneers did move stealthily, making swift dashes from tree to tree over the plains. At last, they passed silently into the gloom.

Those atop the walls watched them as if through a veil, until they had gone too deep into the murk for anyone to see them. A great silence settled over the ramparts as those who watched waited.

Then came a sound as if from far away. It was like the echo of screams. And then again, louder and more terrible. Agonized, wrenching screams—some cut short suddenly. Others wailed until a few figures ran out of the gloom.

"The gates!" Kaliam yelled. "Open the gates!!"

Immediately, the triple portcullis lifted, and five knights ran inside. "Close the gates!" Warriant yelled.

"But there were others?" asked the guard.

"Close them now!" Warriant commanded. "The others are dead."

ENEMY WITHIN
THE WALLS

Of the five who fled the darkness and made it back into the city, Warriant was the only one still standing. The other Baleneers were taken into the barracks for medical attention.

"What happened?" Kaliam yelled. Warriant looked up, a maniacal, angry glint in his eyes.

"Wolvins!" Warriant yelled. "The biggest I have ever seen. They tore my men apart in front of me. I put a bale into the chest of one of the creatures. It bit off the end and kept coming."

"The Sleepers!" Farix exclaimed. "Sound the alarm! Paragor's armies are here!"

But out of the shroud, before the bells of Alleble could be rung, a piercing wail arose. It began as a shriek that drove knights to their knees and then lowered to an unearthly rumbling roar that shook the walls with its thunder. From the edge of the darkness a volley of a hundred flaming projectiles soared into the turbulent sky. A hail of arrows followed, fired from unseen longbows. And then thousands of soldiers in dark armor streamed out from the murk. They carried battering rams, tall ladders, and grappling hooks and assaulted Alleble's walls in a hundred places at once.

The fiery missiles landed beyond the gates, some reaching almost as far as the first fountain. They crushed cottages and small keeps, leaving hot fires wherever they fell. Several landed in the midst of companies of Alleble Knights running to support those upon the walls. Hit by arrows, archers and knights fell from Alleble's walls into the teeming broods below.

But Alleble was ready for this first attack. Legions of knights within the walls pumped gallons of snowmelt from the enormous vats used days before in the crafting of the walls. Fires were doused as soon as they sprang up, and the knights were ready for ten times that first wave.

And atop the walls, Queen Illaria, King Ravelle, and an infuriated Warriant gave the orders for their teams to open fire. Nock and some of the archers began with their new arbalests. They loosed a first volley of darts—these made from the sturdy timber of the Blackwood—and the enemy's front line dropped as if a great mat had been ripped from under their feet. The archers were stationed two-deep so that after firing, the second archer stepped forward while the first reloaded. The Paragor Knights raised their shields, but that mattered little, if but to throw off the archers' aim. The bolts launched from the arbalests hit the enemy's shields and passed through them as if they were made of paper. And the ground nearest the foot of the castle walls became littered with the enemy's dead.

The Baleneers focused on the enemies who came with ladders and grappling hooks. They were used to spearing wild game from the high limbs of trees in King's Forest, so this range made it easy for them to pick off the enemy. They heaved their sharp bales down with great might. Those enemies on the ground blinked and found themselves pinned to the earth with a spear through their chests.

Others who were unfortunate enough to be climbing the ladders took a spear in their forged helmets.

The volleys of flaming projectiles continued with little effect. Some hit the adorite walls of the city and did no damage to the walls but caused a great tongue of white fire to flash outward and cling to the enemy while it burned. Paragor Knights fell smoldering to the ground.

For hours, Paragor's armies clamored before the walls of Alleble, but that was all they could do. Kaliam looked with awe at the new walls erected by Mallik's folk from the Blue Mountains. The walls proved tougher than anything the enemy had to throw at them. Battering rams shivered and cracked upon them. Grappling hooks could gain no purchase, and slid down to fall upon the heads of those who had thrown them. And with Yewland's archers and Balesparr's Baleneers defending the parapets, Paragor's great siege towers could not get close enough to the walls.

But Kaliam knew better than to relax. He knew only too well that the enemy had a devastating weapon at his disposal. He looked out over the wall into the murky darkness breathed into existence by the evil Wyrm Lord.

"Kaliam," Farix shouted as he ran up, "what are your orders, my Sentinel?"

"Farix, good. I am glad you have come," Kaliam said, pointing out into the shadows. "What do you see?"

Farix stared into the gloom. "I see a thousand knights on foot," he replied. "They have also pendulum battering rams, and siege towers, but beyond that, I can see nothing."

"That cursed darkness! It hides the enemy's designs. We see only those within range of a short bow, but what lies beyond? And where are the Wyrm Lord and the Seven Sleepers?"

"Perhaps Paragor is waiting to release them at the time of greatest opportunity," Farix said.

"Now is the time of greatest opportunity!" Kaliam shouted out in frustration. "The Wyrm Lord in his weakest state razed Clarion to the ground, and together with the Sleepers, they devastated our combined forces in Yewland! By now Paragor has no doubt nursed them back to full strength. Why does he delay?"

Farix was silent.

"We must be ready," Kaliam said. "Farix, go and find Kindle and make sure he has his force of spearmen near at hand. And see to it that Mallik and his folk fill the turrets should any of their siege engines win through to the walls!"

"Yes, Sentinel," Farix said, and he vanished down the stairs.

Kaliam stared out over the enemy into the darkness. He paced the parapets until he could bear it no longer. He raced along the wall, ducking into and out of massive turrets, until he came to one of the guard towers near the main gate.

As Kaliam approached, seven sentries ran to him and stood at attention. "What news?" Kaliam asked.

"The gates hold," answered the first guard in line, a clean-shaven Glimpse who wore a gleaming conical helmet. "In fact, it has barely been assaulted since the battering rams were turned back."

Kaliam went to the wall and stared down between two stone merlons at the enemy. There were knights as far as the eye could see in that gloom, but they were armed with swords and milled about almost casually.

"We sent the archers to the outer walls," the sentry continued. "They are needed more there to repel the siege towers."

"Yes, good," Kaliam replied. But he was not so sure. He looked again down at the enemy. As thick as ants on a carcass they were, but they had no ladders or devices for scaling, no great rams for smashing the gates. Why would the enemy abandon the gates? It was the weakest point of entry. "You have done well," Kaliam said at last. "But do not be caught unaware by a lull in their assault. Send word to bring a host of archers back to the gate. I feel the enemy will strike here again."

The sentry nodded and sent one of his knights racing along the wall. Then he and the others returned to their posts.

"What is Paragor's plan?" Kaliam thought aloud. He turned and looked behind him, up Alleble's main thoroughfare, past the Seven Fountains to the castle. He longed to speak with the King. Surely he would know what to do. But King Eliam had gone to the Sacred Realm, a place where his Sentinel could not follow. And there had been no report of his return. Kaliam would have to lead the defense of the kingdom himself.

Suddenly, the sound of metal grinding against metal ripped through the din of the siege. Kaliam whirled around. "What are they doing?!" The enormous deadbolt arm of the main gate was being drawn back. He pointed to the sentries. "Go!" The sentries dashed from their post and flew down the spiral stairs to the causeway leading to the gatehouse.

Still the great murynstil bolt continued to slide back. Shouts came from the enemy knights on the other side. Kaliam went to the parapet and saw that they were aimless no longer. Hundreds had gathered at the gate, and to Kaliam's astonishment, they were forming ranks. Kaliam looked back along the walls, and there, running swiftly along the parapets, was Nock, and he led a great team of archers.

"What is happening?" Nock asked when he drew near.

"There is evil afoot!" Kaliam exclaimed. "Someone has begun to withdraw the great bolt to the gate!"

Nock and the others stared.

"I sent a team of guards to the gatehouse, but—" Kaliam looked back to the gate just in time to see the last of the bolt slide away from the guides on the portcullis. He felt a tremor of fear creep along his spine, for slowly the gate itself began to rise. "Nay! This is not possible! Nock, I must go myself to the gate! But see, the enemy is forming on the other side—lining up—as if they might simply walk in!" Kaliam locked eyes with Nock, and in that moment, he was not speaking captain to knight, but friend to friend. "Do not let the enemy enter our city!"

"They stand in line to perish," Nock said, motioning to his team.

Kaliam's broadsword unsheathed, he sprinted down the stairs and across the causeway to the gatehouse. He paused at the ramp and watched. The triple portcullis continued to rise. It was nearly high enough for the Paragor Knights who clamored there to squeeze through. *I will put a halt to this!* Kaliam thought as he hurried up the ramp.

But Kaliam stopped short. There before him was a trail of twisted bodies. He recognized the Glimpse warriors strewn about the road like broken toys, and their eyes were frozen open in fear.

"What madness is this?!" Kaliam exclaimed. Few weapons could inflict this kind of damage—Mallik's hammer, perhaps. And that led Kaliam to a very disturbing thought. Could one of Mallik's folk, the Glimpses of the Blue Mountain Provinces, be a traitor like Acsriot or the false ambassadors?

Kaliam held his broadsword in front as he climbed to the top of the ramp. And there, turning the giant chain-driven wheel that raised and lowered the triple portcullis, was a single knight. *That is impossible!* Kaliam thought. *It takes three stout warriors to turn that wheel!*

The knight stopped and stood to face Kaliam. Dressed in the armor of Alleble, he smiled grotesquely at Kaliam before walking toward him. And as he drew near, he seemed to change. It was as if with each step, he grew larger. Then Kaliam saw his eyes. They flashed blue at first, but then they flashed red. The warrior began to convulse . . .

FALON'S WRATH

The wind whooshed through Aidan's and Antoinette's hair as they clung to Falon and watched her myriad legs rise and fall rhythmically like pistons. They had long since seen the Cold River come and go, and Aidan knew Alleble was close.

The storm overhead was beginning to intensify. Lightning bathed everything in putrid shades of green. Thunder rumbled and crashed. "Thingsss go ill with the city," hissed Falon. "Paragor has been busy . . . too busy."

Aidan and Antoinette saw the silhouette of Alleble, but there was fire and smoke. And surrounding the entire city like a pool of oil was an army larger than either of them had ever seen. "Look! Look at the walls!" Aidan said.

"They're white!" Antoinette yelled. "When did—?!" But then she looked off to the side. "Oh, no! There's a huge crack in that wall!"

"Falon, hurry!" Aidan cried.

"Do not fear," Falon said. "They will pay for all they have done."

At last, they came to the edge of battle, and Falon slowed to a stop. She stretched out a foreleg and Aidan and Antoinette reluctantly climbed down.

"Falon, what are you doing?" yelled Aidan.

"We can't stop here!" Antoinette exclaimed. "You've got to take us to the gates!"

"Patience, young warriors," Falon said, and she brought her broad face close to them. "The forces of the enemy are thick here like a carpet of ssspiders. Allow old Falon to clear a path for you. Wait here for now, hmmm? Things are about to get nasssty."

Robby felt kind of useless as he marched around on top of one of the southwestern walls. He couldn't throw a spear or fire a bow. And the enemy never made it to the top of a ladder—the Baleneers made certain of that!

Suddenly, a trumpet sounded. Robby turned and looked to the north. There was frantic activity at the area nearest the main gate. He started to run toward the gate. *I can't believe this!* Archers choked off the passage along the parapets on both sides. And the massive Glimpse warriors from the Blue Mountains were blocking the castle towers. Robby spun around in restless circles, not knowing what else to do. Then a ladder clattered to the wall right beside him. Robby leaned over and looked down. He saw two enemy knights rapidly ascending.

But before Robby could do a thing, a warrior hurled a spear down upon the climbing knights and then gave the ladder a mighty shove. It flew backward and landed in a sea of enemies.

Robby drew his broadsword just as another ladder appeared on the wall a few yards away. A Paragor Knight appeared, his head just cresting the wall. Robby ran and went to kick the ladder, but the weight of his armor gave him more momentum than he could handle and he overextended his leg. The Paragor Knight fell backward off the ladder, but for a horrifying moment Robby had one foot on the castle wall and one foot on the ladder. He leaned toward the ladder, grabbed a rung, and held on, riding it as it fell into a crowd of enemy knights.

Robby shook his head and realized he was more or less unharmed. He sprang to his feet and saw why. There were at least a dozen dead Paragor Knights lying beneath the ladder. Quickly, Robby dove just ahead of a slash that would've taken his head. He rolled and came up with his broadsword ready. Several enemy knights stood facing him. Robby knew there were some closing behind him also, so he did what he did best: he bull-rushed the knights in front of him and swung his heavy broadsword with all his might. He slammed the first enemy with the first blow, smashing a dent into his helmet. Then he sidestepped a thrust and knocked the second knight down with a kick. The third knight tried to circle around to get behind Robby, but Robby was too quick. He spun and swept the legs out from under him.

In just a few moments Robby had taken out three of the enemy soldiers, but many more were charging up to take their place. There could be no winning this battle behind enemy lines. Robby backed toward the wall of Alleble, and the enemy closed in.

Then something drew the knights' attention. They turned from Robby and saw rows and rows of knights turning their heads and looking into the gloom. A huge shadowy shape came forth, and enemy knights were grabbed up and launched violently into the air, cartwheeling into their own forces. In just a few seconds hundreds of knights had been destroyed. *The vision!* Robby remembered in a rush. *It's happening!*

The knights scattered and tried to get away, but it came upon them with lightning speed. A large serpentine creature with huge slanted yellow eyes rose and began grabbing up Paragor Knights in each of its huge claws. The monster hurled them away and raced toward Robby. Robby backed away in fear, slamming into the wall.

He closed his eyes and suddenly felt himself being lifted from the ground. The taloned fingers of the beast clenched in. Robby screamed and dropped his broadsword. He expected any second to be cast into the air or smashed into the wall.

"You are not a Paragor Knight, are you, hmmm?" Robby felt warm breath wash over him. He opened his eyes to a squint and saw nothing but huge yellow eyes and jaws filled with teeth as big as knives. "I sssee that you are not! It is a good thing for you that Falon's eyes are still keen."

Several Paragor archers fired upon Falon from what they thought was a safe distance. Falon didn't even glance in their direction. She simply slithered the back end of her body around behind them and crushed them in her coils. "Pesky, aren't they?" she said with a mischievous laugh. "Now then, who are you?"

"My name is Robby," he replied. "You aren't going to eat me . . . are you?"

"Eat you?" Falon smiled. "Nay, young Robby. I have already had my fill of these black-armored folk. Not terribly tasty . . . no. But, perhaps I will go back for more later."

Robby felt a chill run up his back.

"Wait," Falon said. "My eyes may not be as good as I claimed. You are not Glimpse-kind! You are from the Mirror Realm, hmmm?"

"Righ-ight!" Robby nodded. "I'm from Maryland."

"The land of Mary?" Falon asked, scratching her chin with one of her talons. "Never heard of that, but I have met others from the Mirror Realm. You do not by any chance know Sir Aidan, do you?"

"Aidan!" Robby's eyes lit up. "Yes, he's my best friend!"

"Your best friend? Really?" Falon smiled. "Oh, this is getting interesting now, isn't it, hmmm?"

"Is he here?"

Falon nodded. "I left Aidan and Lady Antoinette in a valley behind the enemy's flank, out of harm's way . . . for the moment."

"But I thought," Robby stammered, hardly believing his ears. "I mean, Aelic was near death, . . . and that means—"

Falon looked at Robby strangely. Slowly she lowered Robby to the ground. "Pick up your sword, young Robby," she said. "Where we are going, I have a feeling you are going to need it."

THE FINAL STORM
UNLEASHED

Kaliam knew that before him stood the Wyrm Lord, changing from a large Glimpse to his true self. Kaliam raised his broadsword and charged. The Wyrm Lord lifted up his claw and backhanded Kaliam off the ramp, sending him crashing into some short trees nearby. Now in his true form, the monstrous dragon with dark scales, a long crested neck, and wings that spread and blotted out all the sky was looking down at Kaliam. The Wyrm Lord reared back and inhaled. A loud horn rang out and the wyrm craned his neck, and in that moment, a black-shafted arrow plunged into the creature's right eye. He shrieked, grabbed the arrow, and yanked it free. The eye closed and did not open again. Then the Wyrm Lord stirred his great wings and took to the air.

The next face Kaliam saw was much more pleasant. "Would you like a hand?" asked Nock.

Kaliam stood and asked, "That was your shot?"

"I owed him one from the time we met in the forest," Nock said, pulling Kaliam up to the ramp.

Kaliam ran to the wheel. "Nock, help me close the gate!"

Nock ran over to help pull the wheel, but before he arrived Kaliam yelled, "It is no use! The wyrm has fused it with his fire!"

Then they heard a noise like thunder. "Horses!" Nock yelled. "We are too late! Paragor sends his mounted troops!"

They ran down the ramp and saw the gate raised high and hundreds of dark horses pouring in. "Quick, to the parapets!" Kaliam shouted. And as they climbed to the gatehouse wall, the wind began to howl. Lightning crackled and struck a nearby tower. They looked from the parapets out over the plains of Alleble; the clouds billowed and churned like the contents of a cauldron.

"The storm is breaking upon us!" cried Nock.

Kaliam and Nock stared into the storm and saw shapes materializing out of the clouds . . . winged shapes.

"Paragor releases his dragons at last!" Kaliam exclaimed.

And the sky became filled with shapes of dragons. Upon each dragon rode a warrior whose helmet was in the shape of a skull. Each wielded a long staff with a sickle-shaped blade at the end.

Kaliam heard Sir Warriant yell from the walls, "The Deathreapers have come! The Deathreapers!"

Kaliam and Nock sprinted along the parapets as the Deathreapers descended. The Deathreapers swooped down and slashed with their scythes, hewing anyone within their reach.

"Nock, where are our own dragons?" Kaliam asked.

"I do not know," he replied. "But I will go and find out. Never alone!"

"Never alone!" Kaliam repeated. He looked back at the enemy pouring into the gate. He saw the lightning split the sky, and the Deathreapers swarming in overhead. Alleble's defenses were crumbling. He drew in a deep breath, hefted his broadsword, and ran across the walls. *Where is Lady Merewen?*

❦

Falon came to a stop just beyond the southern flank of the enemy. Robby clambered down off of Falon's foreleg to see two knights: a soldier in the dark livery of Paragory and a warrior of Alleble, standing side by side. "Aidan?"

"Robby!" Aidan yelled, and he ran to his friend.

"Aidan, did you join Paragor?"

"What?" Aidan asked, dumbfounded. And then he looked down. "Oh, the armor! Uh, that's a long story! But I'm with Alleble. Robby, this is Antoinette Reed."

"So we meet—," Robby said.

"I hate to break up thisss reunion," Falon said, "but we have something important to do." Falon held out her foreleg and Aidan, Antoinette, and Robby climbed up.

"Yes!" Aidan exclaimed. "Take us to the gates!"

"Nay, Sir Aidan," Falon replied, shaking her massive head.

"But, Falon, you said—"

"I changed my mind," Falon replied curtly. "The enemy at the gates of Alleble does only the bidding of its master. I intend for us to go after Paragor himself."

❦

The lookout on the balcony above Guard's Keep loosed a trumpet blast, and the combined dragon forces of Alleble and its allies soared up from behind the castle. They had been waiting for the signal, waiting for Paragor to send his dragons into the skies.

Trenna's stomach did a flip as her white steed streaked straight up to get over the castle and then swooped down into formation. Queen Illaria led the team, most of whom flew with her in the

Battle of the Blue Mountains. In seconds, they saw the enemy circling above the thoroughfare of Alleble like vultures.

When the Paragor dragons saw the force of Alleble approach, they wheeled about to face them. Trenna fitted a black shaft to the bowstring and took aim. The first enemy rider came into view, but just for a brief moment. The sight of the rider's skull helmet threw off her aim. He dove quickly and Trenna's shot went wide.

Just then, another enemy rider flew in from the side. He brought his scythe down hard, but Trenna drove her steed out of the way. There were more of them than she thought. Every time she attempted to turn and shoot, several enemy riders attacked and forced her to evade. But Trenna was not to be outdone. She urged her dragon to fly right into the path of several enemies and then turned to run.

"Come on!" she cried, looking over her shoulder. When they followed, she smiled. Trenna's dragon was far swifter than those of her enemy, but she let them close the gap. "You think you are going to get me!" she said, and then she turned her dragon and led them right past the southwest wall.

Nock heard the trumpet blast and saw the dragons come swooping down from over the castle. "There they are at last!" he yelled. "Archers, spearmen! Our dragons have joined the fray!"

Nock ran to the nearest tower and ran inside. He went to a huge cabinet and replenished his supply of Blackwood Arrows. On the way out, he saw that a siege tower had lowered its drawbridge. A huge warrior was coming across it. Nock fitted a shaft to the string and was about to fire when he realized it was Mallik and not an enemy. Nock ran over and greeted Mallik just as he stepped back onto the walls.

"Oh, hello, my archer friend!" Mallik said. "What brings you to my side of the party?"

"I almost put an arrow in your hide!" Nock answered. "What were you doing in that siege tower?"

"Oh, just fixing a few things," Mallik said, a mischievous smile curling beneath his coppery mustache. "Watch!"

Mallik turned and took a mighty swing with his hammer, bringing it down on the edge of the drawbridge. The whole siege tower began to shake, and then it collapsed upon itself in a great cloud of debris.

"How did you do that?" Nock asked.

"Remember," Mallik said, "we Blue Mountain folk are good at building things, but in the process, we learn how to knock them down!"

They laughed, but then Mallik turned and pointed. "A white dragon is coming this way. Is that not one of your kin?"

Nock looked, saw the chase, and called over two more archers. Trenna brought her steed down right in front of the archers with the enemy directly behind her. They let Trenna pass, but not the Deathreapers. The archers timed their shots perfectly and loosed their shafts.

When Trenna looked back, there were three riderless dragons following her. The technique worked so well, Trenna tried it again. The archers upon the walls picked off five more enemy riders. But eventually the Deathreapers grew wise. They had watched Trenna and knew what she would do.

Two waited in ambush high above the parapets for Trenna to soar in front of the walls. She did so exactly as before. And just as before, she looked over her shoulder to see if her pursuit had been eliminated, and then she started to wheel about. The two Deathreapers who had been lying in wait streaked down toward Trenna. She didn't see them until it was too late. The enemy riders kept Trenna between them and swept down their scythes for the kill. In a split second when she recognized the threat, she tried to pull away. The blades missed Trenna but clipped both of her dragon's wings. The loyal white steed tried valiantly to maintain control, but it could not generate the lift it needed. Trenna's steed fell awkwardly about a hundred feet and slammed into the roof of a cottage.

"No, Trenna!" Nock had watched from the walls. "Come, Mallik!"

"Do you think there is a chance?" he asked.

"I do not know," Nock answered grimly. "But we must try."

THE THREE WITNESSES

Falon carved a bloody streak through Paragor's forces. Aidan, Antoinette, and Robby, shielded by Falon's enormous bat-wing ears, held on for dear life. Archers opened fire on her, and a strange horn rang out, but there was no slowing the mortiwraith's charge.

At last, she came to the foot of the hill and began to climb. "Ready your weapons, young ones!" she called back to them. Huge guards were at the fence where the torches stood. They rushed down the hill swinging battleaxes and massive spiked clubs. Falon brushed them aside, incurring dozens of deep wounds, but still she climbed. She drove over the ring of torches and then slowed to a crawl. She held out her foreleg to let her riders down.

"It is best that you stand on your own two feet from here," she said. "Stay close behind me, hmmm? I will shield you as much as I can, but be wary." Falon clambered up the incline. Careful to avoid her giant footfalls, Aidan, Antoinette, and Robby followed right behind.

The top of the hill was a huge expanse, but in the exact middle was an enormous carriage drawn by a massive blackhorne. There was a warrior seated upon the front of the carriage. He was clad in shining black armor and wore a red cloak that flapped heavily in the gusting wind. At his side was a long sword, and in his hand was a heavy mace that swung like a pendulum when he stood.

"Hail, Falon firstborn," said the warrior. His voice was rich and melodic. "After your efforts on behalf of Mithegard, I have so looked forward to our meeting." Thunder rumbled and the storm clouds swirled slowly over his head.

"You have always known where I dwell, Paragor," Falon replied. "I wonder why you never visited my little labyrinth. We could have had such fun . . . in the dark, hmmm? But it was kind of you to veil the sun and moon so that I could come to you."

"And it was kind of you to do so much of my work for me," Paragor said as he tilted his head to see the approach of Aidan, Antoinette, and Robby. "Very kind . . . you have even brought me back those I did not know I had lost. Antoinette, I take it you grew weary of the confines of your cell?"

Antoinette's tongue cleaved to the roof of her mouth, and she said nothing.

"You will not harm these little ones," Falon said, growling. "Your business is with me tonight."

"Save your bluster, mortiwraith!" Paragor said, suddenly commanding. "My business is of my own choosing. If these three are of interest to me later, what is that to you?"

Aidan's skin crawled and he stared at Antoinette. Robby looked at them quizzically.

Falon emitted a low, rumbling growl that shook the hilltop. She bared her fangs and hissed, "Paragor! You have stolen from these three as you have stolen from me—all in the name of a crown you will never wear! You owe us a price in blood, hmmm? And we have come to collect!"

"Enough of this!" Paragor exclaimed. He whirled his mace above his head, and suddenly it caught fire. The clouds above him swirled faster. A shriek cut through the wind.

"The Wyrm Lord!" Antoinette cried.

From the darkest blotch in the clouds a large winged shape flew. He dove right for Falon. She reared up like a cobra waiting to strike. Aidan, Antoinette, and Robby raced out of the way.

The Wyrm Lord crashed into Falon like a comet and the two rolled backward down the hill. They came apart at the bottom. The Wyrm Lord loosed a stream of fire at Falon, but she coiled away. Then Falon snapped her tail section like a whip, and many of her talons slashed across the Wyrm Lord's armored chest. The Wyrm Lord shrieked but recovered from the wound faster than Falon expected. The firstborn dragon unleashed a horrible spout of fire. Overcome by the blaze, Falon rolled backward down the hill and lay in a heap.

"No!" Aidan yelled, and he drew Fury from his sheath and turned to Paragor.

But Paragor swung his flaming mace faster and faster. The clouds above began to funnel. They swirled down and engulfed the mace and Paragor's arm. The flames from the mace spiraled up into the clouds. And Paragor began to laugh. "Leave them alive!" he cried. "We have business later!"

The tornadic clouds surrounded Paragor and lifted him high in the sky. Then the Wyrm Lord swooped down and carried him in the direction of Alleble.

"Leave them alive?" Aidan thought aloud. "Who is he talking to?"

Then they heard the steady march of many soldiers. Aidan, Antoinette, and Robby found themselves staring at a surging mass of Paragor Knights, a thousand or maybe a legion strong. The ring of soldiers closed like the tightening of a noose. There was no escape.

Kaliam quickly found Lady Merewen. She ran to him. "What news, m'lord?" she asked.

"The main gate is lost," Kaliam said. "We have managed to contain Paragor's horsemen, but they may break through the ranks and win the fountains—especially if the Seven Sleepers are loosed in the city. But no one has seen them since Warriant's venture into the murk. The battle in the skies is slowly tilting in Paragor's favor. He has so many riders, and they wield fear along with their blades."

"It is time then," Lady Merewen said, taking his hands into hers.

"It is time. But, m'lady," Kaliam objected, "what if I am wrong?"

"It is the King's will, my husband," she said. "You will not be wrong."

"But without the Scroll of Prophecy? There is so much more—"

"You have known in your heart without the Scroll! How often have you told me of their visions?"

"But—"

"Cast away the doubts!" Lady Merewen implored him. "Did not King Eliam say that one would come who would call them? Kaliam, you are the Herald of the Three Witnesses!"

Kaliam shook his head to argue, but there came over him then such a tangible sense of peace that all doubts fled. Kaliam nodded, embraced his wife, and departed the barracks. He sprinted through back ways and hidden avenues until he came to the bell tower behind the northern wall. Aside from the ninth level of the Library of Light, the northern tower was the tallest vantage in the city. Kaliam raced up the staircase and found himself in an open-air room with a huge bell and a balcony on both sides.

He looked out over the kingdom. The strange ethereal darkness of the Wyrm Lord was beginning to dissipate, and he could now see the size of Paragor's army. Kaliam was amazed. Already there were more than a thousand enemies within the walls, but there were still tens of thousands teeming, railing to get in. And somewhere out in the shadows lurked the Seven Sleepers, the Wyrm Lord, and Paragor.

"King Eliam," the Sentinel said aloud. "By your power, I herald the Three Witnesses to come forth and be known throughout The Realm."

Then Kaliam took hold of the chime rope in both hands and gave it a tremendous tug. The bell sounded a clear note that traveled through the city and out into the plains. And to Kaliam's astonishment, it seemed as if the battle halted below. Fires still burned, smoke trailed into the sky, and dragons still flew, but the fighting had stopped. Kaliam felt as if the eyes of The Realm were on him.

Kaliam stepped to the edge of the balcony with no thought for what might come out of his own mouth. "Children of Alleble and of The Realm!" he said, and his voice resonated and traveled like that of the bell. "I speak as Herald for the mighty King Eliam of Alleble. I speak with his authority. And I speak with his conviction. Today, I call forth the Three Witnesses of Alleble! I call, and they shall come forth and rid the land of darkness!"

It became deathly silent—even the storm seemed to calm.

"I call forth Lady Antoinette the Child of Storms! I call forth Sir Robby the Dragonfriend! And I call forth Sir Aidan the Seeker of the Lost! Come forth, Witnesses! Throw down evil and declare truth by the might of King Eliam the Everlasting!"

The Paragor Knights had tightened the noose around Aidan, Antoinette, and Robby when the bell tolled. All heads turned toward Alleble, and it seemed that the entire Realm was suddenly hushed. A bell-like voice rang out from within the kingdom, and all wondered how it could be heard from such a distance. Aidan, Antoinette, and Robby knew it was the voice of their Sentinel.

When Robby heard his name, the sword began to tingle in his hand. "I am the Dragonfriend," he whispered.

"I am the Child of Storms," Antoinette whispered.

"I am the Seeker of the Lost," Aidan whispered.

The Paragor Knights froze at the call but soon regained their wits. They brandished their weapons and closed in.

Suddenly, Robby yelled out, "I am the Dragonfriend!" He raised his sword in the air and charged the Paragor Knights, confident that King Eliam was with him. It looked absurd to the enemy: one lone knight rushing recklessly toward more than a legion of foes. But before Robby reached the first enemy, there came the noise of many wings flapping. And up from the back of the hill flew a hundred dragons. No one knew from whence they had come, but they slammed into the ranks of the enemy, obliterating their front line.

Antoinette stepped forward, trusting King Eliam, and declared, "I am the Child of Storms!" And she held her sword aloft. At that moment, lightning streaked down from the sky and struck Antoinette's blade. But it was not the sickly green lightning that had come from the prior storm. This lightning was as pure white as the white stone of Pennath Ador. Antoinette raced toward the enemy knights, and they charged up to greet her. She swept her sword across them, and electricity jumped from the blade, striking each enemy in turn.

Aidan put his hand inside his tunic and felt the parchment touch his hand. "I am the Seeker of the Lost!" he cried out. And then he charged at the enemy knights, and they were sorely afraid.

In only a few moments, more than a hundred enemy soldiers were laid low. Three of Robby's dragons came and bore the Three Witnesses away to the city of Alleble.

BATTLE AT THE
SEVEN FOUNTAINS

W hat has happened?" Kaliam asked the moment Nock and Mallik emerged from the stairs.

"Lady Trenna and Queen Illaria," Nock replied, "their dragons fell in the aerial assault—"

"And King Brower," said Mallik. "He was overcome as he defended the gate."

Suddenly, a mournful howl rose over Alleble's outer walls. Sir Warriant looked out from their vantage point atop a wide turret near the fountains. "What is that sound?" he asked. "Wolves?"

"Worse," said Thrivenbard. "They are the Seven Sleepers!"

"If those beasts are coming now," said Warriant, "it was wise, Kaliam, to order the knights on the front walls to fall back to the fences." Kaliam nodded, but pensively looked upon the fences.

In the days before Paragor's attack, the crafty Glimpses of Yewland and the Blue Mountains had erected special palisades. These fences they made tall with extremely sharp points on top and no gaps between poles so that, unless airborne, none could see

284

beyond them. They stretched north to south all the way across the main thoroughfare of the city.

"Will they see what we have planned?" Nock asked apprehensively. He pointed to the Deathreapers still in a chaotic dogfight with the combined dragon riders of Alleble high above the city.

"Nay," Lady Merewen replied. "The riders of Paragory do not have the keen eyes of Yewland's Braves. And Queen Illaria's riders will keep them too busy to search behind our palisades."

"I hope you are right," Kaliam said.

Suddenly, the shriek of the Wyrm Lord shattered the silence.

"The walls!" cried Mallik. There was a tremendous flash and an agonizing cry, but the wall split and began to crumble. "I hope the faercrag killed that foul serpent!" Mallik groused. Then something grabbed the first murynstil portcullis at the gate and tore it from the stone. Then the second was gone . . . and the third. The combined forces of Alleble gasped, for Paragor now wielded fire hot enough to melt adorite and might strong enough to tear murynstil!

With the gate torn and a wall thrown down, legion after legion of Paragor's main army entered the city of Alleble. Seven huge yellow-eyed wolvins came too. But they did not press forward like Paragor's infantry. Rather they stalked behind the legions of Paragor's Knights, restless, chomping, salivating, wanting to attack, but restrained by an unseen hand. Then the Wyrm Lord perched on one of the towers. He shrieked and clawed at his eye. Then his body shook and it began to wreathe itself in garments of darkness. But he too seemed to be waiting. Behind all of this came one lone, defiant warrior. Standing on the rubble of the wall, he held up a flaming mace.

The legions of knights who had been marching forward saw their master's sign and suddenly broke into a dead run.

Kaliam had taken up a position with Nock, Mallik, and many of his commanders—and waited for exactly the right moment. Kaliam nodded and Nock launched one flaming arrow into the sky toward the fountains. It was the first signal.

"They are still coming full-bore," said King Ravelle. "How arrogant they are to think they could just stroll in unopposed."

Kaliam watched closely as the enemy drew within fifty yards of the palisades.

"Almost there," he whispered.

"Come on!" Mallik urged.

The clamor of the enemy was like that of a stampede. Paragor Knights spread as wide as the road and were thick all the way to the front gates. They came recklessly, laughing at the wooden palisades before them.

"They will snap like toothpicks," yelled some of the enemy.

"We will trample them down!" answered another.

"Now, Kaliam!" yelled Sir Rogan.

"Nay! A second more!" Kaliam said.

The enemy knights were twenty-five feet away from the palisades. Twenty. Fifteen. Ten.

"Now!" Kaliam yelled. And Nock released two fiery arrows into the sky.

The very second the two arrows went up, the palisades—the entire length from one side of the road to the other—slammed down. But not flat. These palisades had been fashioned with hundreds of hanging legs that extended when the fence fell and kept the razor-sharp points of lumber at right about waist height.

Moving too fast to stop in time, and pushed from those behind, the first line of Paragor's infantry, almost five hundred soldiers across, drove into the deadly palisades. In one moment nearly a thousand Paragor Knights died or were wounded so severely that they could not fight.

The horror did not end for the Paragor Knights, for behind the palisades stood the bulk of Alleble's remaining armies. They had lain in wait, choking all the back ways, alleys, and side streets—the cottages, shops, and keeps. And at the sign of the first flaming arrow, they had poured behind the palisade like floodwaters. The cavalries of Alleble and its allies Mithegard and Acacia attacked.

Warriant gave the signal and his Baleneers began a deadly rain of spears upon the enemy knights. But thousands more—knights conscripted into Paragor's service, the armies of Candleforge, Frostland, and Inferness—entered the fray. And in spite of Paragor's losses, his was still the larger army.

Paragor's infantry—buoyed by the advance of their reinforcements—turned to face their enemy. Shining sword raked against jagged curved blade. Heavy hammer collided with massive blunt club. And bright, twin-edged axe clashed against the arced scythe blade. Greater was the skill of the defenders, but the numbers of the enemy made up for that.

As Paragor's archers advanced they began to take up positions on the keeps, walls—even the rooftops of cottages. Soon streams of crimson arrows soaked in mortiwraith venom arced overhead and fell among Alleble's forces. Those hit fell dead in their tracks.

The tide had turned in Paragor's favor, and the forces of Alleble and its allies began to be pushed back and overrun.

Kaliam was horrified, and he made ready to join the fray. "Look!" Lady Merewen yelled, and pointed toward the sky.

It was three dragons. They flew over the smashed gate, over Paragor, and just over the heads of the enemy army. And Kaliam saw and yelled, "Behold, all of Alleble: the Three Witnesses!" Just at the hearing of the legendary name, the soldiers of Alleble felt a surge of confidence. And they held at the palisades, not allowing even a single enemy to break through and gain the fountains.

Robby was the first to enter combat. He drove into the middle of a regiment from Frostland. The landing crushed many, and at the wish of her master, Splinter lashed her head and tail about until a clearing had been made. Robby dismounted, heedless of the enemy beginning to close around him. He turned and held a hand to the sky. The dragons beneath Paragor's Deathreapers swooped suddenly as if reaching the end of an invisible chain. Then they began to fly erratically, swerving, diving—even soaring inverted! Most of the Deathreapers could not hold on. They fell out of the sky, flailing violently until they crashed into the city. The now riderless dragons plowed into Paragor's forces, wreaking havoc upon the army they once served. Alleble's dragon riders were now in control of the skies above the city, and they wheeled about and dove into the battle as well.

Antoinette leaped down from her steed and held the Daughter of Light aloft. Spidery veins of white lightning crawled across the underside of the roiling clouds, and an intensely bright streak shot down to strike Antoinette's sword. Sparks flickered and surged up her blade, but by King Eliam's power, the electricity did her no harm. The enemy would not fare so well. Antoinette charged off the edge of the palisades into battle.

A brutish warrior from Candleforge was the first to challenge her. He raised his massive club, intending to pulverize this young girl in one move. He rocked on his feet and brutally swung his club at Antoinette. But there was a strange flash of white light and a sudden breath of oily smoke. When his vision cleared, he saw Antoinette standing unharmed. As his vision began to gray at the fringes, he saw that his club had been split. It was the last thing he saw before he died.

Aidan drove his dragon steed almost sideways at the ranks of Paragor's archers. Then he raked his sword across the backs of the archers' necks as he careened through their ranks. A few turned, but too late. An entire rank of archers went down.

Paragor unleashed the Seven Sleepers. They snarled and bounded into the road, charging the forces of Alleble—heedlessly trampling

Paragor's Knights as they went. A team of Alleble's infantry slashed at one wolvin's face, rending and gouging it with angry red streaks, but the wolvin seemed not to feel it. The Seven roamed the road, laying low scores of Alleble's knights. And at last, they broke through Alleble's forces at the palisades and charged toward the Seven Fountains.

At Paragor's command, the Wyrm Lord spread his wings wide and took to the air. He flew beneath the turbulent clouds like a dark blotch of smoke. The firstborn wyrm spewed streams of his lethal breath into the ranks of Alleble's forces, incinerating dozens and leaving behind scoured trails and charred bodies. Alleble's dragon riders came at the Wyrm Lord from all sides, but he batted them aside as if they were gnats.

Kaliam turned to the warriors assembled near him. "Stay in teams," Kaliam said. "No less than three, for none of us alone can contend with a Sleeper or the Wyrm Lord. Mallik, Sir Rogan, and Nock, stay together. Thrivenbard, lead Warriant and Sir Valden. King Ravelle, Farix, and Oswyn, defend the fountains!"

"Now is our time!" Kaliam exclaimed. "Our armies are outnumbered by the enemy! Our odds are grim at best." Kaliam's eyes were ablaze, and he stared from knight to knight before he continued.

"But we do not put our faith in odds or in numbers—nor even in the prowess of our weapons. We put our faith in the might of King Eliam, who alone defeated death! We serve a King who gave everything for this kingdom—not sparing even his life! And now . . . it is our turn. Draw your weapons and do not hide them again until victory is assured. Nothing can be spared. When the sun rises between the Mountains of Glory, let there be glory given to the King. Glory and a free Alleble—whether we all live or not!"

"NEVER ALONE!" Stirred by their Sentinel's words, the warriors of Alleble, Mithegard, Acacia, Yewland, Balesparr, and Ludgeon charged into the field of battle.

"Words well spoken, m'lord," Lady Merewen said, drawing near to Kaliam.

"M'lady Merewen," Kaliam said. "Do you think that the two of us together can defeat one of the Sleepers?"

"Together we can," she said. "Or together we shall die trying."

Kaliam nodded confidently and looked to Alleble's main gate. Paragor was no longer there.

⟨⟩

Mallik, Nock, and Sir Rogan came upon one of the Sleepers as it preyed upon several fallen knights. Mallik rushed in and smashed his hammer against the creature's hindquarters. It flopped awkwardly to the side, but turned quickly. The Sleeper bared its fangs and growled at its attackers.

"Okay," Mallik said. "So maybe that was a wee bit rash!" And then, Mallik stared. This wolvin had gouges on its neck crusted black with dried blood. "I know you, beast," Mallik said, "and I owe you a little something for Aelic!" Sir Mallik raised his hammer and took a step toward the creature. He stopped short when he saw Nock gesturing.

Nock signaled something to Mallik and Sir Rogan. They nodded, and Mallik took off running. The wolvin's yellow eyes flashed and it raced after Mallik, who was not particularly fast. He dodged and turned corners, occasionally swinging his hammer at the creature's face just to slow it down. All he needed to do was give Nock and Sir Rogan enough time to get into position. The creature was nipping at Mallik's heels as he made a final turn and raced back the way he had come.

Nock stood atop one of the broken sections of the palisades. He took aim and fired a Blackwood shaft into the creature's left eye. The wolvin howled but kept coming. Nock's second shaft found the

Sleeper's other eye. Blinded, it could not see Sir Rogan spring up and sweep his axe low, lopping off the wolvin's forelegs. It faltered, crashed, and slid to a stop right at Mallik's feet. Mallik raised his hammer and brought it down heavily on the beast's head.

"Now there are six!" he yelled.

Thrivenbard, Warriant, and Sir Valden raced after a group of ten Paragor Knights. They chased them into a wide avenue behind the keeps off the main thoroughfare. There, the enemy knights split paths and sprinted down three narrow passages that stretched between a group of small cottages.

"Those are dead ends," Thrivenbard said, looking at his two comrades.

"Verily, they shall be," said Warriant, hefting a bale. When he turned, his eyes were wild, but also . . . they glinted blue.

"Sir Warriant!" Thrivenbard cried out. "Your eyes! You have chosen!"

"How could I not?" Warriant asked. "I have seen the ways of the enemy, and I know the valor of King Eliam by the deeds of his people! Now, Thrivenbard, take the three on the left-hand passage. Valden, the right. That leaves the four in the middle for me!"

"Do you now lead us, spear-meister?" Thrivenbard asked slyly.

"Nay, master woodsman," Warriant replied. "But you owe me one for not putting a bale in your foot that evening near my village. I say this makes us even."

Thrivenbard grinned. "Sir Valden, what do you say?"

Valden said nothing, but he nodded and raised his two long-handled axes.

"Agreed, then!" said Thrivenbard, and the three warriors split and raced into the dead-end alleys.

They emerged victorious a few moments later. But there was no time to celebrate as a Sleeper leaped down on Valden, its jaws snapping perilously close to Valden's neck. Valden hacked at the creature's chest with both his axes, all the while yelling like a madman. Warriant drove a spear into the creature's side, and at last it rolled off of Valden. The wolvin turned, snarled, and lunged for Thrivenbard. The tracker rolled out of the creature's path, but still its claws gouged a hunk of flesh out of Thrivenbard's arm. Warriant came to his aid, but the wolvin hit him in the back with one of its heavy paws, sending Warriant flying against the wall of the other cottage. He fell in a heap. Then the monstrous creature turned its yellow eyes back to Thrivenbard.

"BACK, YOU FILTHY CUR OF PARAGOR!" came a thunderous, roaring yell. Valden had finally found his feet—and his voice! He stood and faced the monster as if daring it to move. The creature pounced. In that moment, Valden threw one of his axes at the wolvin, missed its head, but buried the blade into its humped shoulder. The wolvin bowled Valden over, howled in pain, and fled.

"You will not get away that easily!" Sir Warriant yelled, taking off after him. Thrivenbard and Valden ran around the corner of the cottage and saw Warriant landing on the back of the creature, while holding on to Valden's axe and his own spearlike handles. The wolvin shook and bucked, trying to throw Warriant off, but he would not relent. He clambered up the creature's back, grabbed the nape of fur behind its ears, and twisted. The wolvin turned as if steered and came running back toward the cottages.

"I will finish this!" Thrivenbard yelled. And he drew his two long fighting knives and raced toward the wolvin. Thrivenbard and Warriant made eye contact just long enough for Warriant to understand what to do. He violently steered the creature into a turn. Thrivenbard was already there holding his knives to the wolvin's throat as he slid beneath it. The wolvin took two or three clumsy steps before collapsing in the middle of a wide alley.

Warriant leaped off the beast. He wiped his hands and turned to the others and said, "Well, that was not as bad as I thought!" But Thrivenbard and Valden were not looking at Warriant. For there, angrily sniffing the body of their dead companion, were three more gigantic wolvins.

SHADOW'S BANE

I'm sorry, girl," Robby said. He knelt by Splinter and stroked the crest on the back of her head. "You did your best." She nuzzled his hand weakly, laid her head to the stone, and went very still. Robby looked up over the nearby armory at the turbulent sky, searching with wet eyes for the Wyrm Lord. He was there, banking slowly above the forces of Alleble, raining fire on top of them without challenge. The remaining Sleepers had led Paragor's surging forces for the first time past the fallen palisades. Alleble's armies were slowly being forced back, and the battle raged among the Seven Fountains. Robby shook his head. *Some legendary hero I turned out to be.*

Suddenly a shadow loomed behind Robby. He rose and turned, sweeping up his heavy broadsword. "Whoa, Sir Robby!" exclaimed a heavyset Glimpse warrior. He had a corona of black hair that blended indistinguishably with his beard. And he wore the armor of Alleble. "Lower the sword, lad! I saw what happened with your steed—thought you might have been hurt."

"Kindle?" Robby asked.

"At your service," he replied. "Are you all right then?"

Robby nodded his head slowly. "I'm not hurt."

"Then you best get moving," Kindle said. He lifted a huge battle-axe with a wide blade and started to back away. "The enemy does not take a break to mourn!"

"Where are you going?"

"To the fountains, lad!" Kindle replied. "The dead are piling up, and I would sooner join them than let one rotting Paragor rat foul the water of our glorious fountains!" And with that, Kindle was gone.

Something snapped, and Robby turned round just in time to see the last large chunk of the armory door torn from its hinge and tossed aside by an enormous wolvin. The creature hesitated a moment, stared back at Robby, and disappeared into the armory.

Sword out in front, Robby stepped over pieces of the door and other debris. In the flickering torchlight inside, Robby followed the trail of wreckage: suits of armor lay in scattered heaps, barrels of weapons were overturned, and display tables were crushed. As he wound his way through the aisles and closer to the front of the armory, he felt a disturbing, heavy presence beyond the fear of the creature he was tracking. Robby emerged from behind a tall tapestry and found himself bathed in flickering candlelight. Before him, several enemy soldiers hurried about, lighting more candles. There in the midst of them was Paragor. And at his feet, lying half-curled like a pet, was the wolvin.

"Hail, Dragonfriend!" Paragor said. His voice, which had seemed so haughty and maniacal before, now sounded calm and reasonable. In the wavering candlelight Robby fancied that he saw a great and noble king in shining silver mail seated upon a marvelous ornate chair in a grand throne room. On his lap lay a sword and a scroll. Then, the image was that of Paragor again—though the sword and the scroll remained.

Robby said nothing, but his heart raced and sweat trickled cold down his back.

"Come now, Sir Knight," said Paragor in a light, friendly tone.

"We used to speak often of many things. Will you not come and speak with me now?"

"You are a murderer," Robby whispered.

"A warrior, yes," Paragor replied, holding up his sword. "And I have killed the enemy, just as you have. You wield your blade well, thanks to my servant's training."

Robby looked down at his blade and was silent.

"This is the eve of final victory," Paragor said. He stood from his seat and walked among the candles. "Tomorrow, I will sit on a different throne. And you will sit at my left hand."

Robby trembled. "I won't join you," he said weakly.

As Paragor turned, his dark red cape flourished behind him. He drew within a sword's length of Robby and said, "My dear Robby . . . you have never left."

Robby's mouth fell open.

"Oh, you stepped outside of my protection for a time," Paragor continued, walking over to examine a lush red velvet display that hung on the wall. It was empty, but there seemed to be sunken impressions, indentations suggesting that seven swords had once hung there. "But I do not hold that decision against you," he said, pacing. "I would expect nothing less from a young wolf like yourself. But search deeply . . . you know where your true allegiance lies."

Robby raised his blade and stepped toward Paragor. The wolvin raised its eyelid and growled. "You lied!" Robby exclaimed, ". . . about everything."

Paragor turned and smiled. "Lied?" He raised an eyebrow. "About what? Giving you power? About making you a warrior, a conqueror, a leader? You had all of those things at your fingertips. It was you who turned them aside. But though you have been unfaithful, I have not taken back my promise. All those things still wait for you."

"Enough!" Robby yelled. His head throbbed. "You lied about

Alleble. It was you who betrayed King Eliam. You went behind his back and murdered him in cold blood! I saw what you did!"

Paragor's smile diminished. "You saw what I did?" Paragor echoed. "You were not there. You could only have seen visions."

Robby's head pounded so badly, he could barely think.

Paragor laughed, but suddenly his voice grew low and serious. "Now, Sir Robby . . . I have many powers. But among them is not the power to make you see visions. Only King Eliam can do that. Would he not show you what he wanted you to see? You would never know the difference, unless you were there as I was."

"You're a liar!" Robby screamed. The pain in his head became unbearable. "I trust King Eliam and only him!"

Paragor smiled, turning his back to Robby. "Can you trust him? What of his servants among the Elder Guard—even his new Sentinel—have they trusted you?"

Robby remembered listening outside the door at Guard's Keep and hearing: *"Do not let him out of your sight."*

"And can you trust King Eliam? Has he ever come to you in person as I have? And where is he now? Have you seen him taking up arms on the field of battle as I have? Your King Eliam is a coward, and everyone knows you cannot trust a coward!"

"NO!!" Robby yelled, and he lunged to thrust his sword into Paragor's back, but the wolvin suddenly roused and its jaws clamped down on Robby's arm. The pressure became too great, and his sword clattered to the ground. The creature released his arm. Paragor turned and swiftly took up the sword.

"That was a mistake," Paragor said. "My patience grows thin. Tomorrow, at sunrise, I will offer you one last chance. I hope then you will make a better decision."

The word *decision* hung in the air. And Robby's mind went suddenly back to the old Glimpse who spoke with him at the foot of Pennath Ador. He too had spoken about decisions. And then, Robby felt chills. He understood! "Wait!" he said to Paragor. "I have seen King Eliam! He spoke with me once—like he'd known me his whole life. And . . . he made me an offer too. He offered me hope."

Paragor scowled and nodded to someone behind Robby. Robby went to turn, but something struck him in the back of the head. Robby fell into darkness.

With her back to the sixth fountain, Antoinette held up her sword as a mass of Paragor Knights slowly closed in on her. But no lightning came down. She looked up for a moment and saw white veins of electricity spidering toward a central point, but they were cut off. Brighter green lightning clawed out of the churning clouds like the root of some creeping vine. It crossed the white lightning and choked it until it was gone. Antoinette lowered the Daughter of Light, but when she looked back to the enemy, they parted, revealing a path. And walking slowly up the path was a tall Glimpse warrior. He had long blond hair and held a wide-bladed sword at his side.

"Kearn?" she mouthed. He drew closer and stopped just a few feet away. He sheathed his sword and smiled. It was Kearn, but how this could be, Antoinette had no idea. That would mean Robby had left The Realm. She turned to look near the second fountain. It was the last place she remembered seeing him. But there was no sign of him or any of his dragons. Antoinette heard a sudden fierce growl and something hit her hard. She slammed backward into the stonework at the base of the fountain and slid down. She felt tremendous pressure on her rib cage. Her mind swimming and her vision blurry, she squinted and saw the snarling teeth of one of the Sleepers. She turned to look for her sword, but it had fallen far out of reach. There was a flash and a wave of heat. A stream of fire streaked down from the sky, and a shadow passed overhead. All Antoinette could do was turn her head. Shaking and barely able to breathe, Antoinette looked back. Her sword was gone, and she heard laughter.

The wolvin took its paws from her chest armor, and Antoinette tried desperately to fight off unconsciousness. She focused somewhat and saw a Glimpse warrior there, but it was not Kearn. There was a resemblance, but this knight was much older. His skin looked stretched, and his eyes were sunken. He carried a sword in each hand, and he wore a ghastly smile.

Rucifel! Antoinette thought. Then everything went dark.

From far across the road, Aidan saw the wolvin appear from nowhere and pounce on Antoinette. As he drove his dragon steed to breakneck speed, he watched helplessly as the Wyrm Lord unleashed a wicked flame. *He burned her alive,* Aidan thought, but then he saw the Wyrm Lord take to the air with a limp knight in his grasp.

"Antoinette!" he cried, and he spurred his dragon steed to follow. But the dragon beneath him suddenly shrieked and faltered. It crashed twenty feet to the road, and Aidan flew out of the saddle, landing in a heap near a large catapult that rested upon a hill. Aidan shook his head. He saw that the scrap of parchment had slipped out of his armor. He snatched it up and stood. And there in the middle of the battlefield, Aidan came face-to-face with an old enemy.

"Rucifel!" Aidan cried, and he raised Fury.

"I am pleased that you remember me." He grinned, baring his teeth like a skull.

"Where has the Wyrm Lord taken Antoinette?" Aidan demanded.

"To the same place I will take you!" Rucifel hissed. "Now, drop your sword."

Aidan took Fury and swiped at Rucifel, just missing his ear.

"Then," Rucifel said, beginning to whirl his two weapons, "we will do this the hard way!"

Rucifel's blades came at Aidan from every direction, forcing him back. Aidan blocked and leaped, sidestepped and ducked. Rucifel pressed on, hammering away at Aidan's blade. Aidan stumbled to one knee. As he stood, he glanced at the slope behind him.

The first sword missed Aidan's head by an inch. It slammed into the massive catapult's wheel, stuck for a moment, and jerked free. In that breath of time, Aidan batted away the second sword and threw himself down the hill.

This foe was beyond Aidan's skill. His only chance was to get away, to escape. Aidan looked down at the torn parchment in his hand. Aidan did not understand all of the Scroll of Prophecy, but he knew from Zabediel's pleas that the scrap was important, and that he must not let the enemy get it.

As he ran, Aidan glanced over his shoulder. The knight in dark armor crashed down the hill, gaining rapidly as he pursued Aidan. His cloak trailed behind him like a gray wing, and he swung his two swords in arcs, carving the wind. The blades came closer . . . and closer.

Before Aidan could run another yard, the knight in dark armor fell upon him. Aidan turned, fended off a blow, then ran a few steps; turned again, sidestepped one blade, and barely blocked the other.

"Where will you go?" rasped a voice that seemed to reach for Aidan. "Your kingdom is in ruin. All is lost!"

The enemy's taunts threatened to strangle the small hope that lingered in Aidan's heart. But Aidan would not give in. Aidan blocked another savage blow from the enemy and slashed away his second blade. Again, Aidan lunged away from his foe.

Suddenly, he saw his chance. Beyond the next hill a horse struggled, its reins tangled around its dead rider's arm. Drawing from his final reserve of strength, Aidan charged up the hill and dove for the horse. It shrieked and staggered under the sudden weight but did not fall. Aidan swept his sword up and cut the tangled reins. He thrust the parchment under his breastplate and slapped the horse hard on its hindquarters.

"Go!" Aidan screamed.

The beast reared briefly but then surged ahead with such force that Aidan nearly fell. He could not reach what was left of the reins with his free hand, so he clutched the horse's neck with all his might.

Aidan looked back. The knight in dark armor was now far behind and had given up pursuit. Just as Aidan allowed himself a grim smile, something hit him—hard—in the back, knocking him off the horse. He heard a sharp snap and felt the air forced out of his lungs.

He lay in a heap, his face to the ground. A dull pain throbbed in his right arm. Dizzy, he spit dust and debris from his mouth and looked up weakly from the ground. Out of the corner of his eye, he saw an enormous black wing in the gray sky.

Finally, Aidan got to his feet and saw his plight. The outer walls of Alleble had been breached, fires burned everywhere on the main thoroughfare, and the fountains could barely be seen in the wind-driven banks of black smoke. Paragor's infantry, a massive force in black armor, closed in on Aidan. *I didn't think it would end this way,* Aidan thought.

He held Fury in his left hand and clutched his ruined right wrist to his chest. *But I will not be felled easily!* Aidan stared at the enemy and a grim smile formed upon his lips. He held Fury out menacingly and turned in a circle so that all who approached could see its point.

But suddenly, just as they came within reach of Aidan's sword, the enemy soldiers stopped and began to fall back. To Aidan's astonishment, they turned completely and fled in all directions. But Aidan did not smile. He did not sigh with relief. And he did not drop his guard, for he felt a presence behind him.

There rose a winged shadow. Ten times in size it was, compared to the knight who stood alone to face it. The firstborn dragon, the Wyrm Lord, now in his fullness of strength, stared at Aidan and bore down upon him with all his malice-filled thought. He spread his great black wings wide, raised his muscular forelegs high in the air, and roared so loud that Aidan's ears rang.

But Aidan would not falter. This wretched creature was the cause of so much pain. It had consumed whole kingdoms. No, Aidan would not cower or run from this foul thing. He would face the Wyrm Lord. And with fury and vengeance bubbling inside him, Aidan would smite this thing if he could.

The Wyrm Lord flung a grasping claw at Aidan, but Aidan lunged to the side and slammed Fury's keen edge hard upon his extended talon. The scales upon that dragon finger were not as stout as the wyrm's body armor, and a great gash was opened upon it. The Wyrm Lord shrieked in pain and wrenched back his arm.

"I am one of the Three Witnesses of Legend!" Aidan cried out. "You will not slay me!"

The Wyrm Lord looked at the dark blood oozing from his wounded talon. And then, for the first time since King Eliam closed the stone door imprisoning him beneath the lake of fire, there was fear in the eyes of the Wyrm Lord. But the king of all dragons would not quail for long. He turned and once again bent his gaze upon Aidan. His lips curled into a snarl, and his great jaws opened. And then the Wyrm Lord spoke. Aidan remembered the voice from his dreams and visions. It was the sound of words spoken from long ago, and each syllable scraped like great stones sliding off of a tomb. "You are already dead!"

The creature reared back and vomited forth a stream of liquid fire, but Aidan lunged out of the way. The flames enveloped the fallen horse, reducing it to cinders in mere seconds. Fire came at Aidan again. This time, he dove behind a ruined catapult and ran out as the fire consumed it. The Wyrm Lord tried twice more to burn Aidan, but somehow Aidan eluded the flames. The creature swiped at Aidan as he dove. Aidan sprawled onto the stone and lay in front of the great beast. He looked up and saw the ancient dragon's jaws open. The Wyrm Lord struck swiftly like a great cobra, but Aidan rolled to one knee, and with all his might brought Fury crashing down on the dragon's outstretched neck.

The scales on the great wyrm's neck, hardened and baked over centuries, were stronger than plate armor, and Fury shattered upon them. In shock, Aidan dropped what was left of Fury and fell backward to the road. The Wyrm Lord brought his massive talon down, pinning Aidan's legs, and swung his head toward the fallen warrior.

Aidan stared up at the creature and thought of the Scroll of Prophecy. He thought of his King. "I tried, King Eliam," he said. "I tried."

The creature opened his jaws and the great fangs drew closer to Aidan, but suddenly something slammed into the Wyrm Lord, lifting him from his feet and sending him crashing onto his back. And there, to Aidan's astonishment, grappling fiercely with the Wyrm Lord, was Falon.

And Falon's vengeance was terrible. She clawed at the wyrm with many sets of her limbs. The talons tore scales free and rent the dragon's flesh. She coiled her badly burned body around the Wyrm Lord's torso and began to constrict.

But the element of surprise lasted only a moment. The firstborn dragon spread his great wings and lifted himself and Falon from the ground. Then he let himself come crashing to the ground, the brunt of the impact on Falon's coils. Aidan heard the mortiwraith roar in pain, and part of her coils came free from the Wyrm Lord's body and dangled limply. Falon was losing.

Aidan watched in horror as Falon tore herself from the Wyrm Lord's grasp and slithered up the length of the dragon's neck. She grabbed the Wyrm Lord's jaws with five pairs of her talons and began to wrench the creature's mouth open. She let one segment of her serpentine body fall into the jaws of the dragon, and coiled the rest of her dying body around his neck and head.

The Wyrm Lord clawed and scratched. He had to get Falon out of his mouth, or he would choke to death. For a brief moment Falon's eyes met Aidan's, and Aidan understood: It was Falon's only way of ensuring victory over the dragon.

The firstborn dragon bit down with all the crushing power his jaws could manage. Falon shrieked and fell limp. No longer constricted, the Wyrm Lord threw the mortiwraith down and roared. Dark blood dripped from his mouth. Then, the triumphant dragon took flight, only to quickly fall to the ground screeching in agony and clawing at the sky. With one final shriek, the Wyrm Lord moved no more.

THE OFFER

A group of no less than twelve heavily armed Paragor Knights dragged Aidan through the wreckage en route to the castle. As Aidan was pulled into Alleble, his hope was shattered by what he saw: The thoroughfare of Alleble, once grand and sparkling, was now littered with the dead. The steady, peaceful rush of the fountains was destroyed by shrill cries from the wounded and the weeping of those who mourned. Several of the fountains ran red.

Fires burned out of control, engulfing blocks of Glimpse homes in flames. At least four of the Seven Sleepers still remained, and they rampaged unchecked, smashing into cottages, killing the families within for food or for sport. Alleble's once proud standing army had been reduced to pockets of resistance presently being surrounded by Paragor's forces. Smoke rose from the parapets of the Castle of Alleble, and Paragor's forces roamed freely upon its battlements.

"Lord Rucifel found where they were all hidden away," one of the knights whispered to another. "There are catacombs beneath the castle—crammed full of women and children!"

"Really?" said another. He whistled. "What is the master going to do with them all?"

The first knight laughed. "Those who know what is good for them will see things our way! The others are to be burned, I expect . . . or fed to the wolves!"

"Let that be a warning to you!" One of the knights smacked Aidan on the back of the head. "When you get your chance, join the victorious army!"

"He is already dressed for the part!" chided another. They laughed raucously. Aidan's head flopped to the side, and he saw the world of horrors.

As they passed the second fountain, Aidan's eyes met just for a moment with the dead eyes of a soldier of Alleble. He was draped awkwardly over the fountain pool wall, his pale face streaked with blood. Aidan blinked and looked away. It was Kindle. Aidan saw one more thing before the enemy dragged him into the Castle of Alleble. It was the last fountain, dry and empty.

They took Aidan to a cell beneath Guard's Keep. There was a heavy clank as a bolt slid free, and they shoved Aidan into the dark cell. He sprawled facedown, pushed himself up with his left hand, and then flopped onto his back. His right wrist was on fire, his body ached, and his thoughts were dark and dreary like the cell. He reached suddenly under his armor. The scrap of the Scroll of Prophecy was still there. It was the only hope Aidan had left.

⟨⟡⟩

The Paragor Knights had scoured the catacombs beneath the Castle of Alleble. But not carefully enough.

Kaliam and Lady Merewen crept stealthily through a chamber door, but froze when they heard a scraping sound. "Faethon?" Kaliam whispered.

"No," a voice came from the shadows. "It is Naysmithe. This way."

Kaliam and Lady Merewen followed the sound of his voice down a long, dimly lit corridor and eventually came face-to-face with the second Sentinel of the land. "Follow me," he said. And he led them through twists and turns of stone that they had not traveled before. They came at last to a place where the passage seemed to end. Naysmithe ran his hand along a seam in the stone. They heard a faint click, and then the wall swung inward as if on a hinge. Naysmithe shut the hidden door behind them and said, "Wait here."

Kaliam and Lady Merewen were left in the dark, but Naysmithe returned with a candle and led them farther inside. They found a small dusty room with a tower of square wooden shelves, each filled with piles of scrolls. There was an austere wooden desk adorned with only a quill pen and a dark bottle of ink. There was also a bench that drew the eye because upon it was the only thing in the room not covered in dust or cobwebs. There lay an intricate tapestry of Alleble's seal, the sun rising between the peaks of Pennath Ador. But it was clearly covering something . . . something longish with unusual humps at either end.

"You were looking for the mortiwraith?" Naysmithe asked, raising a dark eyebrow flecked with gray. "He is yet undiscovered."

"Good, yes!" said Kaliam. "We need him to help us. The Three Witnesses, Aidan, Antoinette, and Robby, are captured and—"

"And awaiting trial before Paragor," Naysmithe finished the sentence. "Yes, I know of Paragor's plans. It is all his servants talk about, carelessly, for they know not who might be listening." Naysmithe grinned.

"What is this place?" Lady Merewen asked.

"It is a sanctuary for my studies," Naysmithe replied. "And given recent events, it has also become a convenient place for me to wait."

"Well, the time of waiting is over, my friend," Kaliam said. "We must get Faethon and free the Witnesses. I believe that Mallik, Farix, and—"

"In vain!" Naysmithe interrupted. "You will not free the Three Witnesses. They will free you."

"What?" Kaliam exclaimed. "Aidan, Antoinette, and Robby are held in a cage beneath Guard's Keep—we must rescue them. Alleble has no hope without them!"

"Alleble's only hope is to let the Three Witnesses do what they must do."

"We cannot just wait and do nothing," Lady Merewen objected.

"That is precisely what we must do," Naysmithe replied enigmatically. "Turn and see what I have here. The last took me some time—I barely finished before Paragor's attack began."

Naysmithe turned, held up the candle, and lifted the tapestry. Kaliam and Lady Merewen gasped.

Aidan heard a groan from the shadows across the cell. Some flickering light filtered in through the cell door, and a band of gray came from the barred window high in the center of the cell wall. "Is someone there?" Aidan asked. He was not afraid.

"Aidan?" A pained whisper, but Aidan felt sure he knew the voice.

"Antoinette?" he called. He heard something slide, the grate of metal on stone, and then Antoinette walked into the gray light. Aidan ran to her and they embraced. "Oww!" Aidan yelped. "My wrist. I think it's broken."

"I'm sorry, Aidan!" Antoinette said, but then she made a noise something like a laugh. "It seems like every time we get together . . . you get hurt."

"So you caused this whole war, then?" Aidan said, and then he laughed too.

Antoinette smiled, but tears glimmered and ran down her cheek. "Aidan, what are we going to do?"

Aidan shook his head. "Where's Robby?"

"I . . . I don't know," she replied. "The last time I saw him . . . he was fighting by the armory and—"

"And that's where I got myself captured." Robby's voice came out of the shadows. He came into the light. His face was void of emotion. Aidan and Antoinette hugged him and then pulled away.

"So were you going to just sit there, hiding in the dark?" Aidan asked.

"What were you doing?" Antoinette asked.

"I was thinking," Robby replied, but he did not elaborate and would not make eye contact.

"Robby, are you all right?" Aidan asked.

"What, are you kidding?" Robby exclaimed. "No, I'm not all right, and neither are you. Look around. We're stuck in a cell in the city we were supposed to defend. So many died, Aidan. And . . . I don't know where Trenna is."

"Trenna Swiftfoot?" Antoinette asked.

Robby nodded. "She was one of the dragon riders," he said sadly. "But the Wyrm Lord knocked them all out, and . . . she is my friend, and I let her down."

"Robby, I don't know if Trenna survived," Antoinette said. "But you were fighting for Alleble! You were serving King Eliam, doing just what you were meant to do."

"What I was meant to do?" Robby stared at Antoinette incredulously. "You mean that *chosen one* stuff? So much for that—we're caught! How're we supposed to save the day down here?"

Aidan and Antoinette were speechless.

Robby stomped away and looked up at the window. "Any idea what time it is?" he asked.

"No," Aidan replied. "With that storm and the Wyrm Lord's breath, I don't even know what day it is—much less the time . . . why?"

"He told me we will stand trial in the morning," Robby replied.

"Stand trial?" said Antoinette.

"Who told you?" Aidan asked.

Robby ran his fingers through his hair. "Paragor."

"You talked to Paragor?" Aidan exclaimed.

Robby nodded. "I followed one of the Sleepers into the armory, but it was a setup. Paragor was in there waiting. That's how I got caught."

Aidan had a feeling there was more to the story than Robby was sharing. "What did you mean by us standing trial?"

"Paragor said we're each going to stand before him—in front of everyone—and then we have to make a decision."

"The Scroll of Prophecy!" Antoinette whispered.

Aidan reached under his breastplate and retrieved the ancient segment of the parchment. "This is a piece of it," Aidan said. "The end of it, but I can't remember it all. Something like . . . 'When the Witnesses decide, ancient deeds will be undone . . .'"

"'Former deeds will be undone,'" Antoinette corrected. "'The Seven Swords may be unveiled. Worlds once divided become one.'"

Aidan looked at Robby. "You know what we have to decide, don't you?"

Antoinette answered first. "I do," she said. "Kearn told me. He said we either have to give up our allegiance to King Eliam and serve Paragor or—"

"Or he'll kill us," Robby whispered. The cell became as silent as a tomb, and the three friends stared at the window.

"Stop pushing!" Mallik groaned as Nock squeezed by him through the trapdoor into the loft of the bell tower. "There is no more room! You will give us all away!"

"If I do not," Nock whispered harshly, "then you certainly will! Lower that voice, hammer-meister."

"What do you see?" Sir Rogan asked.

"There is a gathering upon the balcony," Nock said. "But it is still too dark to see what they are doing."

"What about on the ground?" Farix asked.

"Many soldiers—thousands," Mallik said. "They surround the fountain and . . . oh, by the King's grace, no."

"What?" demanded Farix, but Mallik and Nock were silent. "I cannot bear this," Farix said, and he yanked Nock down and forced his way into the trapdoor opening.

When he saw what was happening, Farix said, "No . . . not again."

"Aidan, I don't know if I can do this."

Aidan stared at his friend and pity tore at his heart. Robby stood there trembling, pleading like a lost child. "I know it's hard, Robby," Aidan said. "But King Eliam called us, he gave us a mission, and promised us we'd never be alone. We can't turn our ba—"

"Where is he now?" Robby asked, his voice rising, becoming more agitated. "We need him right now. King Eliam, where—are—you?!" Robby smashed his fist against the wall, and his head fell despondently.

Antoinette drew near and put a hand on his shoulder. But Robby shrugged it off and yelled, "He's going to kill us! You know that? He'll make an example of us and slaughter us like cattle. And for what, Aidan? Pride that we stood our ground?"

"It's more than that," Aidan whispered. "The Scroll says—"

"You're willing to die for a piece of parchment?" Robby shrieked.

"No," Aidan replied, and now he grew angry. "But I am willing to die for the one who spoke the words in it! King Eliam has a plan through this . . . a plan for good."

"What good can come of us dying?" Robby demanded. "This is death, Aidan. This is real. Any minute now, they're gonna come for us, and we're all going to die."

"So be it!" Aidan shouted. He charged up to Robby. "If I'm going to die, I for one want to die justly with the praises of the true King on my lips!"

Aidan continued to hold Robby with his eyes for a moment. Then he turned and walked away.

"But, Aidan . . ." Robby's voice was thin and scared, but quiet. "If he kills us, it's over."

"No," whispered Antoinette. And this time when she put her hand on Robby's shoulder, he did not shrug it off. "No, it will not be over. We will go to the Sacred Realm Beyond the Sun. And there . . ." She paused, tears welling in her eyes. Robby turned to look at her. "There we will be welcomed by all the faithful servants of Alleble who have gone before us."

"Trenna?" Robby whispered.

Antoinette nodded. "And there we will finally have answers to all the questions that haunt our minds."

"You mean," Robby said, "you have questions too?"

Antoinette burst out laughing through her tears, and she hugged him. "Of course I do," she cried. "We all do." And then Aidan was there. And they held one another for a long moment.

But soon after, heavy footfalls approached. The cell door swung open. The doorway and the hall beyond were choked with soldiers. They rushed in, grabbed Robby, and roughly drew him from the chamber. The cell door slammed shut, and they heard Robby's fearful voice. "Aidan . . ."

Aidan cried out, "Never alone, Robby!" And then a guard shoved Aidan hard into the shadows of the cell.

"This is madness," said Kaliam, looking up both sides of the torch-lit hall. "We will be caught."

"Do you see anyone in this corridor?" Naysmithe asked.

"No," Kaliam replied.

"And you will not for some time," Naysmithe said, waving them to follow. "Paragor and his lot have gone to the balcony."

"The balcony?" Lady Merewen asked. She turned to Kaliam, and his eyes widened with sudden recognition. But Lady Merewen was still confused. "If Paragor is going to the balcony, then . . . where are we going?"

"To the Library of Light," Naysmithe replied with a mischievous gleam in his eye.

"But The Stones of White Fire," Kaliam said. "We can pass, but Lady Merewen will not be able to."

"She will today," Naysmithe replied, and ambled ahead of them at great speed.

"But why are we going to the Library of Light?" she called after him.

His voice drifted back like the echo of a memory. "We go to witness the dawn."

Aidan and Antoinette waited in darkness and in silence for what seemed like an eternity until, at last, they heard again the sounds of marching feet. They stared into each other's eyes even as the guards took hold of Antoinette. She did not utter a word, but a gleam in her eyes and the peaceful expression on her face spoke volumes to Aidan.

The cell door slammed shut, and Aidan stood alone in the center of the room. *"Believin' in something is a special thing, my boy."* Grampin's voice came back to Aidan. *"It can be risky 'cause if ye believe in something, ye stand up for it . . . ye fight for it . . ."* He smiled, remembering his wheelchair-bound grandfather helping him to understand. It all seemed so long ago. Finding the Scrolls in the basement, being welcomed to Alleble by Gwenne, the adventure in Mithegard and beyond. So much had changed.

Aidan reached beneath his breastplate and once again removed the small segment of the Scroll of Prophecy. He looked at the old words, transcribed by Zabediel but spoken by the one true King. Aidan smiled and spoke then to King Eliam. He spoke aloud, saying things he had always wanted to say to his King. And though he never heard the familiar voice in reply, Aidan knew he was not alone in that cell.

"It is time," came a voice at the cell door. Aidan turned as if from a dream and saw the soldiers standing there.

"Come on, then!" demanded a guard. "Get moving!"

"Here now," said another, pointing at Aidan. "He has on our armor still! I will be bound if some Alleb spy will stand before the master in the garb of Paragory!" The guard disappeared for a few minutes and returned with a bundle of clothes and a pile of tarnished armor. "Put these on . . . spy!"

It wasn't easy with his injured wrist, but Aidan changed. The tunic and breeches were stained and tattered and stank in the worst way. The armor was tarnished, gouged, and crusted with dried blood. Even so, Aidan thought it was an improvement. He turned his back to the guards and tucked the scrap of parchment beneath his new breastplate.

They bound his hands and led him from the cell along endless passages and winding stairs until they came to a familiar door above Guard's Keep. The knights opened the door and waited. Aidan stepped through and found himself on the balcony beneath the still churning clouds. Rows of Paragor Knights stood there, but they parted, making way for Aidan.

They led Aidan forward between the soldiers, between torches that waved in the wind. Then they forced him to kneel.

Before Aidan, at the balcony wall, stood a tall warrior. His back was turned, but from the billowing burgundy cape and proud stance, Aidan knew who it was. He turned in that moment and spoke to a guard. "Unbind his hands. He is no danger to us now." The knights cut his bonds, and Aidan absently rubbed his throbbing wrist.

Paragor's long gray hair was drawn back, and a black circlet—like a thin crown—rested above his strong brow and penetrating hazel eyes. He stared as if measuring Aidan. And when he spoke, Aidan heard a very different voice than he had heard on the hill when Falon had brought them to assail Paragor.

"You have fought valiantly, Sir Aidan," he said, his voice noble and kingly—above all else to be trusted. It was the voice Aidan remembered from a vision long ago, but still there was an allure—a draw that compelled Aidan to listen. "I do not think on you as an enemy, for though your goals and ambitions were in contrast to my own, I cannot fault your passion, your resolve, or your skill at arms. You were a worthy adversary, and now . . . you shall be a worthy ally."

Aidan went to speak, but Paragor held up a hand and Aidan's mouth snapped shut.

"Though many would counsel me otherwise, Sir Aidan, I will make you the same offer I made your companions." Aidan turned slowly and saw two knights facedown not far from where he knelt. Blood pooled beneath them and they lay unnaturally still. Aidan knew them, and many things ran through his mind as he looked upon them. He choked back tears, but he felt a great swelling of pride most of all. Antoinette, Robby—they had done it. They had made the right decision.

Looming proudly over the bodies was a dark knight brandishing his twin blades, Lord Rucifel. He wore a dark helmet in the shape of a dragon's head, and from the darkness of that mask eyes flashed red.

"In spite of my generosity," Paragor continued, "they chose the weaker path." Aidan looked questioningly back to the warrior before him.

"They have lost," he said, clasping his hands before his chest. "But their loss is your gain. You will have all that was to be theirs and so much more."

The warrior seemed to grow. His presence intensified. And when he spread apart his hands, Aidan saw visions of grand towers, high thrones, and vaults of gold. It was all there for the asking, Aidan knew.

"Look about you," he continued. "All that you have defended is lost. There is nothing left."

Aidan turned and saw desolation. Everywhere were fallen towers, rent walls, charred debris, and broken bodies. The sky was black, but roiling with dark clouds and smoke from a thousand fires.

"Stand . . . come closer," Paragor said. "There is so much more to see."

Aidan slowly stepped to the balcony wall, and following Paragor's gesture, he looked down into the fountain below. Aidan wept.

For in the fountain, immersed up to their waists in ugly black oil, were more than a hundred Glimpse men, women, and children. "They are traitors of my kingdom," Paragor declared. "But at your command, I will make them free."

Aidan stared into the fountain at the pale, trembling forms, and he began to despair. But then he saw a face he recognized among those in the fountain. It was King Ravelle, the Glimpse of his father.

But next to him was a swordmaiden with large brown eyes that glinted blue. Aidan smiled, seeing the Glimpse of his mother and knowing at last that she believed. They looked up at Aidan, and there was no fear in their eyes. They nodded to Aidan's unspoken question.

Paragor drew Aidan away from the balcony wall and said, "You see? By the Scroll of Prophecy, the very words of Eliam, I have won the throne! All is mine to command. All is mine to offer.

"All you must do," said Paragor, and his voice became a gravelly whisper, "is deny the one who abandoned you. Deny King Eliam here before all these who witness."

Aidan looked over at the bodies of his friends. A profound wave of peace washed over him, and he looked steadily into Paragor's eyes. They glinted red and were greedy with expectation.

At last, Aidan spoke calmly. "I will never deny my King!"

The dark knight came forward with his two swords, but his master held up a hand. "I'll do it myself," Paragor said. His hazel eyes flared red as he drew a long, dark sword. Aidan reached into his armor just as Paragor drove the blade through Aidan's breastplate.

THE KING'S ARMY

Aidan's body slumped forward and fell at Paragor's feet. Immediately, Paragor knew something had not gone as planned. The clouds overhead stopped churning. There was not even a breath of air. It was eerily quiet.

But Paragor ignored the feeling of dread that crept up his spine. This was his moment of triumph! He had done all the Scroll of Prophecy commanded. He had captured the Three Witnesses and enticed them with offers of unfathomable wealth and power. When they refused, he had killed them—and in so doing, he had eliminated the last threat to his assuming the white marble seat he had long coveted.

"I am king now!" Paragor proclaimed. "King of Alleble and King of all The Realm!" He expected a roar from his armies, but none came. His words seemed to have been swallowed up, and there came a feeling over all of them—a feeling of impending doom. And the Paragor Knights looked about the city and even into the skies.

Then, the slightest breeze stirred on the balcony, and Paragor looked down and saw something shift in Aidan's hand. Lord Rucifel came near and asked, "What is that?"

The moment the sword pierced his heart, Aidan awoke as if coming up from a splash of cool water. Warm, glad sunlight shone down upon him, and before him stretched an ocean of rolling green hills. Birds chirped and sang in the distance, and bright butterflies danced above carpets of tiny white flowers.

"Well-done, servant of Alleble."

Aidan turned, and he beheld King Eliam in all his splendor. It did not burn Aidan's eyes, for he was changed. But Aidan felt compelled to kneel. The King came forward and lifted Aidan back to his feet. Then he embraced Aidan, and said again, "Well-done!"

Aidan wept, for he knew in that embrace many things that he had not known before. At last he understood why The Realm divided. At last he understood why King Eliam allowed Paragor to take his life. And at last Aidan understood why King Eliam at the beginning had not simply forced all his subjects to obey—why he had given the Wyrm Lord and then Paragor the power of choice from which so many evils had come. It was love.

"Thank you, my King," Aidan said when they parted. King Eliam smiled, and Aidan knew he would never cry again.

"Walk with me," said the King, and he led Aidan over hills and through patches of flowers to a great green knoll where three tall trees flourished. White petals fell from them like snow, and Aidan saw two figures. One stood at the base of the tree on the left; the other on the right. As Aidan and the King drew near, Aidan saw that it was Robby and Antoinette. And yet, as he stared, he saw that they were different—no, that wasn't quite the right word. Complete. In the gaze of each of his friends, he found two images. In Robby, he saw also Kearn! In Antoinette, he saw also Gwenne! And as they embraced Aidan, he realized that his memories were now mingled with those of Aelic's. "All things are made new," said the King.

When the trio parted, the King showed Aidan what lay at the base of the middle tree. It was a bundle of white armor with an emblem engraved upon the breastplate: a single vertical sword with two swords crossed behind it.

"It is the crest of a new kingdom," said the King, pointing to the horizon. Aidan looked, and there on a far mountain stood a brilliant white castle. And as Aidan continued to stare, the first legions of an immense army crested a distant hill. As they neared, Aidan saw faces that he recognized—faces he had missed but had not seen for a long time.

"Gird yourself, Sir Aidan," said the King. "There is yet one battle left."

Paragor bent down and pulled a small scrap of parchment from Aidan's hand. He slowly unrolled it and stared down at the writing. "Thisss!" he exclaimed, and his voice came out in a strangled hiss. "Thisss cannot be!" And he withdrew a large scroll from his belt and unrolled it. Then he compared the two pieces.

"What does it say?" Rucifel asked.

But Paragor never answered, for at that very moment a gale of wind surged down from the mountains and washed over the castle like a tidal wave. It slammed into those on the balcony and even the strongest knights faltered in its gusts.

Down in the fountain, the wind washed over captors and captives alike. Torches blew out and soldiers fell. When the wind had passed, King Ravelle turned and cried, "Look!"

In the center of the fountain, where the long-dry murynstil spouts protruded at the top of an ornate marble column, a trickle of water appeared. It bubbled up out of the spouts and flowed down the column until it met the black, waist-high oil. The moment the clear water touched that foul murk, the oil began to retreat! Water began to stream out of the top of the fountain, and soon it displaced the oil such that the acrid black liquid began to overflow the fountain walls.

"M'lord!!" Sanicrest yelled up to the balcony. The ruler of Inferness, who had been in charge of managing the prisoners in the fountain, stared at the water. It had nearly filled the fountain, and the last of the oil spilled over the edge onto the road at the feet of the enemy soldiers. But Paragor did not yet turn.

"M'lord!" Sanicrest called again. "Something goes amiss with the fountain!"

Up on the balcony, Paragor turned at last. He saw the prisoners in the fountain—no longer trembling, no longer afraid. And he yelled, "Let them burn then!" Paragor grabbed a torch and heaved it over the balcony wall. It plummeted from the sky and dropped into the center of the fountain. But there was no oil left there to ignite. The torch went out with a pathetic sputter.

Enraged, Paragor ordered his archers to kindle and fire flaming arrows. The first flaming arrows had been fired in haste, and whether it was by that or by some other design, they missed their mark and struck the road surrounding the fountain. *WHOOSH!!!* The oil on the road ignited and engulfed the enemy knights in a writhing ring of fire.

The pieces of the Scroll of Prophecy fell from Paragor's hands, and he turned away from the fountain. Suddenly, he stared at the fallen Three Witnesses. Their bodies remained motionless, but the blood that had pooled beneath them began to seep into the stone of the balcony.

Then there came from the east, shining between the castle's parapets, the first rays of dawn!

"The sun!" Kaliam cried, staring from the window of the highest room in the tower called the Library of Light. "The sun rises between the peaks of Pennath Ador!"

"Stand aside," said Naysmithe. "I have one last act to complete before I am done!" Kaliam moved quickly to Lady Merewen.

Naysmithe threw the tarp away and revealed five gleaming swords. He grabbed the first, a broadsword with a wide silver hilt and the longest blade Kaliam had ever seen. Naysmithe took the sword to the window, and behold! When the pink rays of sun shone upon the sword, letters in ancient runes appeared as if newly engraved upon the hilt and blade in white fire. "First *Charrend*, the Blade That Cleaves Darkness!" Naysmithe yelled. Kaliam and Lady Merewen gasped as Naysmithe lightly tossed the sword out the window!

But before the sword could begin to fall, a hand reached down, snatched it out of the air, and both were gone. "Was that . . . ?" Lady Merewen asked.

Naysmithe smiled and proclaimed, "Our King has returned!" Then he went to work tossing the other blades out the window, and as quickly as each left his hand it was grabbed by its owner. "For Sir Robby, *Wyrmfel*, the Dragon's Bite! For Lady Antoinette, *Thorinsgaet*, the Stormbringer. For Sir Aidan, *Adoric*, the Glory Seeker. And last, forged anew, is *Furyn*, the captain's blade called Fury!" When that last sword was snatched out of the air, there came a loud voice: "At last! My errant, earth-vexing blade! Ha-ha!"

Naysmithe turned to Kaliam and said, "Your sword is one of the Seven Swords from the prophecy, Sentinel." Kaliam unsheathed his broadsword and held it in the sun's light. Letters appeared, and Naysmithe seemed to read them. "*Wayebrynn!*" he pronounced it.

"The Pathcutter!" Kaliam took back the sword and his hands tingled as he gripped it.

"That leaves only one sword," Naysmithe announced. Lady Merewen looked at him questioningly.

Naysmithe took from his own sheath a marvelous sword with a thin silver crossguard and a long fluted blade. "This is the Seventh Sword," he said, offering it to Lady Merewen. "*Calvarian*, the Sword of Redemption. Many spans of years did it serve the Kingdom of Alleble in my hand, but my days of fighting are long over. Use it well, m'lady! And bear it long!"

Lady Merewen held the sword in awe.

"Now," Naysmithe said with an eyebrow cocked. "There is a final battle to be won!"

Paragor watched a lone dragon rider streak high above the castle. He watched the rider hold a sword aloft such that its blade pierced the storm clouds. As the warrior flew, the clouds began to glisten with the rays of the morning sun. And then the roiling thunderheads parted as if being unzipped from one end to the far horizon. Paragor knew then who it was that wielded such a blade, and fear clawed at him.

"The bodies!" Lord Rucifel shouted. "They are gone!"

Paragor looked down, but the Three Witnesses were no longer there. Paragor looked up again and he saw four more dragon riders begin to swoop down. And these were followed by innumerable others. Paragor turned and looked to the streets of Alleble. He held up his hand and closed his eyes. Suddenly, the four remaining Sleepers burst forth from either side of the road.

Paragor turned to Lord Rucifel. "Take up arms, my servants!" Paragor yelled. "Fight once more for final victory!" The moment the knights were gone, a dragon landed on the balcony. From its saddle leaped a hale warrior dressed in white armor, and from his sheath he drew a long broadsword. "Paragor," he said, "the time of your judgment is at hand."

⟨⬩⟩

As Rucifel and his warriors flowed into the streets of Alleble, the first fountain, which had for so long remained dry, now gushed forth in unmatched splendor, its high arching plumes of water glistening in the dawn sun. Rucifel hissed, for he saw that no one in the fountain had perished—only those on the outside. The prisoners had begun to break out of their bonds, so Rucifel drew his twin blades and rushed forward with his knights.

Four dragons landed between them and the fountains. "Hold, thou wretched lot of canker-blossoms!" Captain Valithor bellowed as he leaped off his dragon. Aidan, Antoinette, and Robby dismounted and drew their weapons.

"I watched you die!" Rucifel exclaimed. "I watched you all die!"

"Death is not the end," Robby said. "Not for us . . . and not for you."

Rucifel snarled, brandished his swords, and said, "You are no son of mine!"

"No," Robby replied coldly. "And I never was."

Rucifel shrieked and raced toward them. His knights, more than a hundred strong, charged too. Rucifel whirled and thrust both his blades at Captain Valithor's side, but Fury blocked them both. Rucifel stabbed low and slashed high, but was again easily blocked. He took both swords in a rage and slammed them like hammers, as if he would crush Valithor between them. But the captain brought Fury up between the two swords, snapped his wrist, and batted away the attack. Then he lifted Fury up beneath Rucifel's chin and flicked off his dark helmet.

"Now, you wayward, black-hearted rapscallion, I can see your face!" Captain Valithor yelled. "And in your eyes, I see your fear!"

Rucifel smacked Fury away and lunged for Captain Valithor. His left-hand blade stabbed for the captain's throat. The right-hand blade trailed behind it, raised high as if to crash down upon Valithor's snowy-white head.

But Captain Valithor was far too fast. He ducked the attack and, at the same time, slammed Fury into Rucifel. Paragor's lieutenant groaned as he fell to the road and breathed his last.

Aidan, Antoinette, and Robby found that their new swords were imbued with the power granted to the Three Witnesses—only many times more intense. In a very short time, the road between the fountain and the castle was clear of living enemies.

"This way, my valiant knights!" Captain Valithor yelled. "There are legions yet to conquer!"

Nock, Mallik, Farix, and Sir Rogan had seen all that transpired from the bell tower. And when they saw the Witnesses return, they burst from their place of hiding onto the field of battle.

Enemy soldiers swarmed at them by the thousands, but the four soldiers from Alleble did not care. They knew they were not alone. Dragon riders streaked out of the eastern sky and came to light among the fountains. Nock saw a particular Glimpse knight dismount, and he stared. He began to walk, then run, toward this familiar knight.

"Bolt!" he cried. "My brother!" And at long last, the twin archers embraced.

"I am glad to see you again!" said Bolt.

"Since the day you fell in Mithegard, I have missed you," said Nock.

"And for me it was only the beginning," said Bolt. "For now I have seen the Sacred Realm—I shall tell you of it before I go!"

"Before you go?" Nock echoed.

"No time now," Bolt said as he drew a white arrow from his quiver. "Now let us again let our bows sing for the glory of Alleble and King Eliam the Everlasting!"

Bolt let fly his first arrow.

Mallik roared as he brought low a brigade of enemy knights with his mighty hammer. "Hail, hammer-meister!" came a voice at Mallik's side. He turned and saw a Glimpse in white armor, with great bouncing locks of dark hair and the broadest smile he had ever seen.

"Tal!" Mallik cried. And he saw that running beside his old friend was another familiar face: Matthias. And together, they charged on.

Farix and Sir Rogan too saw old friends as the dragon riders in white armor continued to fill the road. Standing upon the side of one of the fountains, wielding his staff to deadly effect, was Eleazar, the ambassador who fell in Mithegard. Then, there were Tobias with his seasoned walking stick and Sir Gabriel with his two long fighting knives.

Finally, three other Glimpse warriors appeared from a narrow side street near the armory. They were haggard, gouged and scratched with many wounds, and tired beyond exhaustion, but nevertheless, they swept into the fray like a sickle through tall grass.

Warriant's spears flew into the ranks of enemies. Thrivenbard also felled his share of Paragor Knights. And everyone within a hundred yards of the second fountain heard Sir Valden when he and his axes joined the battle.

Slowly, the white tide overcame the dark. Captain Valithor and the Three Witnesses dispatched the remaining four Sleepers, and then all turned to the balcony.

Paragor whirled his flaming mace and swung it high for the King's head. But King Eliam moved to the side as if Paragor's attack had been in slow motion. Paragor's return strike brought the mace to crush the King's side, but when the King dodged, the mace's head stuck momentarily in the balcony wall. King Eliam brought his sword around hard against the flail weapon's chain. The links broke apart, leaving Paragor with a useless handle.

Paragor growled and drew a long, dark blade from his sheath.

The meeting of *Cer Muryn* and *Charrend* was fierce. Paragor's sword, black as night, slashed through the air and met with the King's blade. And indeed it seemed to those who watched from below as if night and day dueled upon the balcony. But it soon became clear that day was the stronger.

"This was to be my hour of triumph!" Paragor shrieked, and he locked swords with the King.

"You looked upon the First Scroll the morning you betrayed me," King Eliam said. "And tell me . . . what did you see?"

"Arrrggh!" Paragor lifted a foot to the King's chest and pushed. Their swords separated, and Paragor fell backward, but quickly leaped to his feet.

"Did you think my promises were false?" the King asked. "Or did you think by unleashing my ancient enemies upon The Realm, that you could by force break my word?"

Paragor tried to call for the wolvins, but he could find no echo of their presence. He lashed out with his dark sword, but the King smashed it away. Paragor backed up until he hit the balcony wall.

"But the Scroll of Prophecy!" Paragor screamed. "Your own words!"

"If you were pure of heart," said the King as he drew within a sword length of his former Sentinel, "you would have understood my words! And you would have understood that by fulfilling the prophecy you only brought doom upon yourself!"

"You have always kept the power for yourself!" Paragor exclaimed.

"That," said the King as he sheathed his sword, "is because I alone know how to use it!"

Paragor gripped his sword with both hands and raised the blade above his head for a mighty, killing stroke. But with a wave of King Eliam's hand, Paragor's sword came free from his hands and toppled over the balcony.

Paragor fell to his knees. The King looked down into his eyes. "You depart now, Paragor," said the King. "And I grieve for what you might have been if you had chosen otherwise. And how many have followed you?" Tears appeared on King Eliam's face. "Willingly followed you on the path to destruction? Depart now into the pit, and there, you also will grieve . . . for what might have been!"

Suddenly, Paragor wrenched and contorted. Blue electrical current began to spider its way across his body. It swirled around him and brightened. Paragor screamed. Then, having never once sat upon the white marble throne, Paragor The Betrayer disappeared from The Realm forever. And all those who followed Paragor in life now followed him into everlasting destruction.

ALL THINGS NEW

King Eliam came to the edge of the balcony and the full light of morning shone down upon him. The prisoners in the catacombs had been set free. The crowd below filled the road on both sides of the fountain. They cheered and roared and wept and laughed. But King Eliam silenced them all by lifting his hands.

"Behold, servants of Alleble!" he cried out. "At last, the debt of innocent blood has been repaid! Now The Schism will be repaired, and with it . . . many hearts as well!"

Aidan and Antoinette stood by King Ravelle and Lady Ariana. They looked up, and the bright orb of the sun began to tremble. The ground shook, and the color of the sky began to change, oscillating between pink and blue, night and day. Robby stood by Trenna and they looked out through the fallen front walls, and it was as if the whole Realm began to turn slowly around Alleble. They watched the plains pass and forests appear. Then mountains and a wide river. The sea came next and snow-covered glaciers.

All turned to see, but they were not afraid. The ground shook, and shadows wheeled around every Glimpse and every person. The turning of The Realm continued, and the watching crowd gasped, because the sights began to change. Images faded in and out. Modern houses, telephone poles, and street lamps appeared in the forests. Mountains faded and skyscrapers rose up. Bridges spanned the great rivers, and boats churned upon the seas.

Aidan watched as something began to happen to the Glimpses around him. Their pale skin began to change. Glimpse and human twin merged and became whole. And the sea of ivory faces turned to a kaleidoscope of color—every color Aidan had ever seen on earth. All turned and looked up at their King. And he looked upon them and smiled.

But his work was not yet complete. Aidan looked outside the city walls, and he was amazed, for the modern houses, the bridges, the buildings—all began rapidly to age. Paint peeled, iron rusted, and stone began to crumble. Soon the forests and jungles reclaimed their land. The mountains could again be seen with nothing in the way to block the view. Upon the oceans there were now no tankers or battleships—just whitecaps and flocks of seabirds. Slowly, The Realm stopped spinning, and as it came to a stop, all saw the dark mountains of Paragory collapse upon themselves. A large forest grew up where the Grimwalk had been, and the plains of Alleble became lush and green.

"It is done!" announced the King. "The faithful who have fallen in defense of me and my kingdom walk now on the grass in the Sacred Realm. The last blot of evil has been sent to its final abode. Look now, servants of Alleble! Look upon The Realm as it was in the beginning . . . only now it is made new with the best of both worlds!"

Several days had passed when King Eliam summoned all members of the Elder Guard, past and present, as well as prominent warriors from every nation, to the garden. He stood before the three-tiered fountain where the paths meet. To his right were Kaliam, Lady Merewen, Mallik, Nock, and Bolt. To his left stood Aidan, Antoinette, Robby, Trenna, Captain Valithor, King Ravelle, and Lady Ariana. The others filled the clearing and lined the paths within view.

"The time has come," said the King, "for me to go to the Sacred Realm to rule over those who have been faithful to me and to Alleble. I will take with me all those who have fallen for me and my kingdom, and wait patiently for the arrival of those who will come later."

The crowd was silent, but birds sang in the trees of the courtyard. "To Kaliam and Lady Merewen, I give the rule of Alleble and The Realm," King Eliam went on. "To Mallik, govern the Blue Mountains, land of your kin. Yewland will prosper under the reign of King Nock. May your judgments be as swift and true as your aim! And all the other lands will be led by their sovereigns, but not in isolation! For I will watch over you all. You will never be alone!"

And they answered their King as one, "Never alone!"

Over the next week, many good-byes were said. But on the morning that King Eliam and the fallen were to return to the Sacred Realm Beyond the Sun, many met for a meal in Guard's Keep, and all farewells took on special prominence.

Elspeth and her workers hustled around the room, filling plates with piles of scones, mountains of fried potatoes, and deep bowls of her famous stew. Everywhere Elspeth went, she put down her trays and hugged someone!

"When you have things back in order in Yewland," Bolt said to his brother, "visit the forest that now grows where the Grimwalk once was. I think you will find a very special tree growing there."

Nock looked at Bolt strangely. "What have you done?" he asked.

"Me?" Bolt protested. "Nay! It was Sir Aidan's doing! But still, go when you can."

"It is nearly time, my darling," Queen Illaria said when she came up behind Bolt. He turned and smiled at her, but then looked back at Nock. "I will miss you, brother!" he said.

And they embraced until Mallik came over and separated them. "Did you think you could just leave again without saying good-bye to me?" Mallik grabbed Bolt and crushed him in a bear hug.

Aidan spoke to Kaliam and Lady Merewen nearby. "It still looks funny to see you with my color of skin!" said Aidan.

"It still looks funny to see myself with your color of skin!" Kaliam said, and they laughed.

"The strangest part," Lady Merewen said, "is having the memories of my twin, mingled with my own. The Mirror Realm was no easy place to live."

"It wasn't so bad," Aidan said, smiling amiably.

"You are a valiant knight," Lady Merewen said at last, and she kissed him on the cheek.

They shared embraces, and Aidan said, "Rule well, Your Majesties."

But the hardest farewell for Aidan was with his parents. Aidan stood with his father and mother and they held one another for a long time. "We're proud of you, son," Mr. Thomas said.

"Very proud," his mom echoed. "Now that I know everything you went through—I . . . I'm sorry for doubting you."

"It's okay, Mom!" Aidan said. "You came around! And now you two get to rule Mithegard together!"

"The lad has a point!" said Grampin, who was now also his Glimpse twin Captain Valithor. "Not bad for a tardy-gaited puttock!"

Aidan grinned. It was so strange to see both Grampin and Captain Valithor in his grandfather's gaze . . . strange and wonderful.

The meal ended, and King Eliam signaled it was time to depart.

Aidan hugged his mother and father one more time—as did Grampin. And then, together, they left Guard's Keep.

Antoinette sat on a white dragon steed next to Aidan's on the great balcony over Guard's Keep. As soon as he was in the saddle, she leaned over and asked, "Ready?"

Aidan didn't answer. He looked out past the thousands of other dragon riders preparing for the journey to the Sacred Realm. He looked over the flourishing Seven Fountains of Alleble, out beyond the walls, and into The Realm. The memories came flooding in. "Do you remember when we slid out of that mountain tunnel and landed in the—?"

"Yes, Sir Aidan. I remember it well," she replied. "Do you remember zooming down the cable in Yewland and falling into the—?"

"Yes!" Aidan laughed. Aidan remembered every detail of all his journeys, both as Aidan and as Aelic.

At last, they maneuvered their dragon steeds to the edge of the ramp. King Eliam and his proud mount were to Aidan's left. Robby and Trenna were giggling to his right. The mighty King of Alleble was about to snap the reins when he felt Aidan's stare.

"King Eliam?" Aidan asked

"Yes, lad?"

"Are there adventures in the Sacred Realm?"

King Eliam's deep blue eyes twinkled, and he looked on Aidan kindly. He saw that Antoinette, Robby, Trenna, and many of the other knights waited to hear his answer. His snowy white mustache curled into a playful smile, and he said, "Beyond your wildest dreams."

Adventures are
funny things.
They always begin with
the unexpected,
but they always end
with the promise
of adventures
yet to come.

Acknowledgments

To my lady, Mary Lu . . . no fairer maiden can be found in all this realm. To think an errant knight like me might be so blessed as to win your favor and share twelve incredible years of adventure with you. If I had it to do all over again, I'd leave a Hawthorne branch at your doorstep! 1C13.

To Lady Kayla, my dramatic swordmaiden: I see stories (maybe novels) in your future. To Sir Tommy, tender warrior for the one true King: You are called to be a hero. To Sir Bryce, champion for good: To you it has been given to defend the weak. To Lady Rachel, great-heart, I name you: Light will shine wherever you go. I am blessed to have my children be my greatest cheerleaders. Your daddy loves you always.

To the Dovel family: Thank you for your endless generosity and for continuing to support my writing. I couldn't ask for a better set of in-laws.

To Bill and Lisa Russell: You guys SO rock! Thank you for being unpaid editors and publicists for the trilogy!

To Dave and Heather Peters, Doug and Chris Smith, Todd Wahlne, Danny Sutton, Chris and Alaina Haerbig, Dan and Courtney Cwiek, Steve and Janet Berbes, Chris and Dawn Harvey, Don and Valerie Counts, Mat and Serrina Davis, and Warren Cramutola: Whether it be cruising the Caribbean, playing dozens of hands of 500, laughing and growing in the Community Group, or jamming in the basement, you have all brought adventure into my life.

To the brilliant students of Folly Quarter Middle School: Thank you for never failing to inspire me! Your creativity and curiosity are powerful forces. I am privileged to be in the classroom with you. Pip Pip Cheerio! To the administration, faculty, and support staff at FQMS: Thank you for all the encouragement. Balancing two careers hasn't been easy. Your talent, flexibility, and understanding have really helped. To the Sixth Grade Teaching Team. It's a blessing to work among friends. {Deer!}

Special thanks to the managers and staff at my local bookstores: His Way Christian Books, Little Professor Bookstore, Barnes & Nobles, and Greetings & Readings . . . thanks for welcoming a new author.

To Michelle Black: Thank you for showing up at all the signings, helping set up and break down, making homemade scrolls and props, and letting me borrow your righteous battle gear! P.S. I hope to see a novel from you on the shelves one day soon. Wink, wink, nudge, nudge . . . say no more!

To the staff of Eldersburg Public Library: Thank you for letting me "live" in your little private study room. About a third of The Final Storm was penned there! P.S. I'll be back when the next story arrives in my head!

Special thanks to Gregg Wooding, my agent and friend, for stepping with me into uncharted territories! Who knows where this path will lead us?

To Dee Ann Grand, Beverly Phillips, June Ford, Patti Evans, Katie Broaddus, Michelle Saunders, Brian Mitchell, and everyone at Tommy Nelson: Thank you for letting me be a part of this mission. I am still in awe when I consider how so many have poured their lives into The Door Within Trilogy!

To Brian, Jeff, Leslie, and Mom & Dad: For many memories such as Cross Country in a little white car, Fireworks in Atlanta, Dallas Dates, and frequent visits to Waffle Houses and Dairy Queens—thank you for this adventure of life we've been on together.

Thanks to Bookcrossers in the States and Elsewhere: Qantaqa

(Germany), akg (UK)Cyzaki, (UK)tehuti (UK), Shelbycat (UK), Tiggsybabes (UK), Elina (Germany or Finland), Morgaine77 (Switzerland), raeliz64 (UK), Carlissa-Florida, Wistroll-Wisconsin, moraelyn-California, wolfprincess-Ohio, pkboo-Florida, cheeseball-Florida!

Special thanks to people all over the world who are spreading the word about The Door Within Trilogy: Barb Radmore, Travis Seiter, Cathy and Michelle Burkhard, Allen Shortt, Catriona Moore, Sue Dowling, Vicki Crawford, and so many who have done so without telling me!

SFFworld.com: Rob Hedford, Garry Wassman, Tempo, KatG, and others! Authors who have given sage advice . . . and empathy: JA Konrath, Alison Croggins, Leathel Grody, Gary Wassman.